M000190366

PATTON'S FIRST VICTORY

PATTON'S FIRST VICTORY

How General George Patton Turned the Tide in
North Africa and Defeated the Afrika Korps at El Guettar

LEO BARRON

STACKPOLE
BOOKS

Guilford, Connecticut

Published by Stackpole Books
An imprint of Globe Pequot
Trade Division of The Rowman & Littlefield Publishing Group, Inc.
4501 Forbes Boulevard, Suite 200, Lanham, Maryland 20706

Distributed by NATIONAL BOOK NETWORK
800-462-6420

Copyright © 2018 Leo Barron

All rights reserved. No part of this book may be reproduced in any form or by any electronic or
mechanical means, including information storage and retrieval systems, without written permission
from the publisher, except by a reviewer who may quote passages in a review.

British Library Cataloguing in Publication Information available

Library of Congress Cataloging-in-Publication Data

Names: Barron, Leo, author.
Title: Patton's first victory : how General George Patton turned the tide in
  North Africa and defeated the Afrika Korps at El Guettar / Leo Barron.
Other titles: How General George Patton turned the tide in North Africa and
  defeated the Afrika Korps at El Guettar
Description: Guilford, Connecticut : Stackpole Books, [2018] | Includes
  bibliographical references and index.
Identifiers: LCCN 2017010958 (print) | LCCN 2017019161 (ebook) | ISBN
  9780811766074 (e-book) | ISBN 9780811718325 (hardback)
Subjects: LCSH: World War, 1939–1945—Campaigns—Tunisia. | Patton, George S.
  (George Smith), 1885–1945—Military leadership.
Classification: LCC D766.99.T8 (ebook) | LCC D766.99.T8 B36 2018 (print) |
  DDC 940.54/2311—dc23
LC record available at https://lccn.loc.gov/2017010958

∞™ The paper used in this publication meets the minimum requirements of American National
Standard for Information Sciences—Permanence of Paper for Printed Library Materials, ANSI/
NISO Z39.48-1992.

Printed in the United States of America

Contents

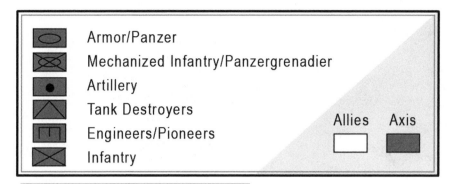

Armor/Panzer	
Mechanized Infantry/Panzergrenadier	
Artillery	
Tank Destroyers	
Engineers/Pioneers	
Infantry	

Allies   Axis

Smallest to Largest Unit

● ● ● Unit Size: Platoon
   I   Unit Size: Company
  I I   Unit Size: Battalion
  III   Unit Size: Regiment
  XX   Unit Size: Division
  XXX   Unit Size: Corps.
 XXXX   Unit Size: Army

HOW TO READ A UNIT SYMBOL

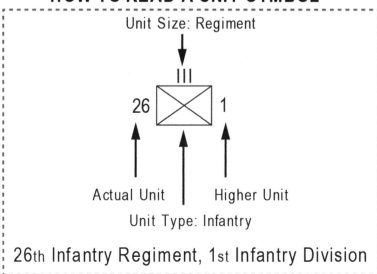

Unit Size: Regiment

III

26 ⬚ 1

Actual Unit   Higher Unit

Unit Type: Infantry

26th Infantry Regiment, 1st Infantry Division

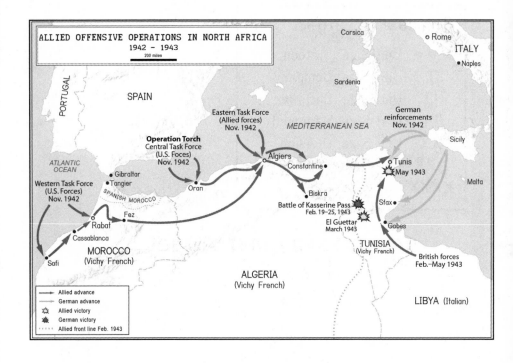

ALLIED OFFENSIVE OPERATIONS IN NORTH AFRICA
1942 – 1943
200 miles

PORTUGAL

SPAIN

ATLANTIC
OCEAN

Western Task Force
(U.S. Forces)
Nov. 1942

Gibraltar
Tangier

SPANISH MOROCCO

Rabat
Fez

Cassablanca

Safi

MOROCCO
(Vichy French)

Operation Torch
Central Task Force
(U.S. Foces)
Nov. 1942

Oran

Eastern Task Force
(Allied forces)
Nov. 1942

Algiers

Constantine

Biskra

ALGERIA
(Vichy French)

MEDITERRANEAN SEA

Battle of Kasserine Pass
Feb. 19–25, 1943

El Guettar
March 1943

TUNISIA
(Vichy French)

Corsica

Sardenia

German
reinforcements
Nov. 1942

Tunis
May 1943

Sfax

Gabes

British forces
Feb.–May 1943

Rome

ITALY

Naples

Sicily

Malta

LIBYA (Italian)

Allied advance
German advance
Allied victory
German victory
Allied front line Feb. 1943

VIII

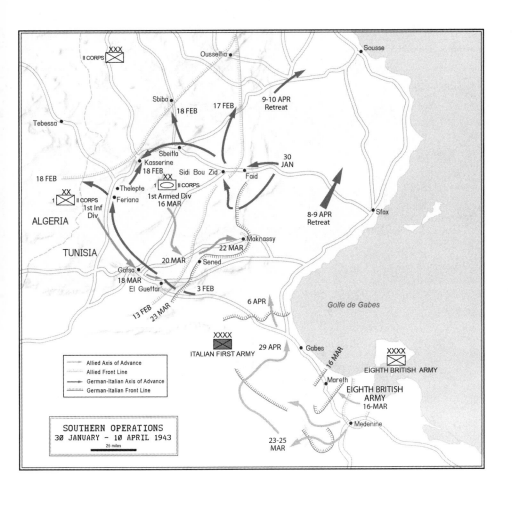

II CORPS

Ousseltia

Sousse

Sbiba
18 FEB

17 FEB

9-10 APR
Retreat

Tebessa

Sbeïtla
Kasserine
18 FEB

Sidi Bou Zid

30
JAN

Faïd

18 FEB

II CORPS
1st Armd Div
16 MAR

II CORPS

8-9 APR
Retreat

Sfax

1   II CORPS
1st Inf
Div

ALGERIA

Thelepte
Feriana

TUNISIA

Maknassy
22 MAR

20 MAR

Sened

Gafsa
18 MAR
El Guettar

6 APR

Golfe de Gabes

13 FEB   23 MAR

3 FEB

ITALIAN FIRST ARMY

29 APR   • Gabes

EIGHTH BRITISH ARMY

16 MAR

Mareth

EIGHTH BRITISH
ARMY
16-MAR

Medenine

23-25
MAR

Allied Axis of Advance
Allied Front Line
German-Italian Axis of Advance
German-Italian Front Line

SOUTHERN OPERATIONS
30 JANUARY – 10 APRIL 1943
25 miles

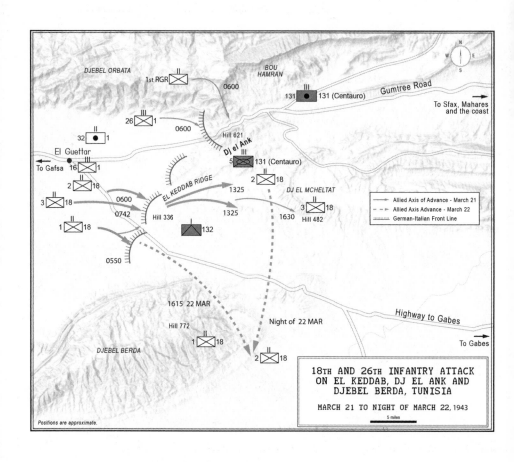

DJEBEL ORBATA

BOU HAMRAN

1st RGR ⊠ II

0600

131 ● III 131 (Centauro)

Gumtree Road

To Sfax, Mahares and the coast

26 ⊠ III 1

0600

32 ● II 1

Hill 621

Dj el Ank

El Guettar

To Gafsa

16 ⊠ III 1

5 ⊠ III 131 (Centauro)

2 ⊠ II 18

2 ⊠ II 18

3 ⊠ II 18

0600

EL KEDDAB RIDGE

1325

DJ EL MCHELTAT

3 ⊠ II 18

0742

1325

1630 Hill 482

1 ⊠ II 18

Hill 336

132

Allied Axis of Advance - March 21
Allied Axis Advance - March 22
German-Italian Front Line

0550

1615 22 MAR

Night of 22 MAR

Highway to Gabes

To Gabes

Hill 772

1 ⊠ II 18

DJEBEL BERDA

2 ⊠ II 18

18TH AND 26TH INFANTRY ATTACK ON EL KEDDAB, DJ EL ANK AND DJEBEL BERDA, TUNISIA

MARCH 21 TO NIGHT OF MARCH 22, 1943

5 miles

Positions are approximate.

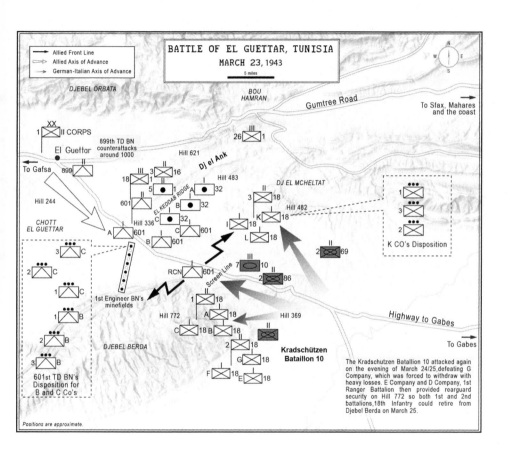

BATTLE OF EL GUETTAR, TUNISIA
MARCH 23, 1943

5 miles

→ Allied Front Line
⇨ Allied Axis of Advance
→ German-Italian Axis of Advance

DJEBEL ORBATA

BOU HAMRAN

Gumtree Road

To Sfax, Mahares and the coast

1 ⊠ II CORPS

26 ⊠ 1

El Guettar

899th TD BN counterattacks around 1000

Hill 621

To Gafsa   899

Dj el Ank

Hill 483

DJ EL MCHELTAT

18 ⊠ 1   ⊠ 16   3

5 ● 1   A ● 32

3 ⊠ 18

Hill 244

601   B ● 32

Hill 482

K ⊠ 18

1 ●●●
3 ●●●

CHOTT EL GUETTAR

Hill 336 C ● 32

C ⊠ 601

I ⊠ 18

2 ●●●

A ⊠ 601

B ⊠ 601

L ⊠ 18

K CO's Disposition

3 ●●● C

2 ▨ 69

2 ●●● C

1st Engineer BN's minefields

RCN ⊠ 601

Screen Line   7 ⬭ 10

2 ▨ 86

1 ●●● C

1 ⊠ 18

Hill 772

A ⊠ 18

Hill 369

Highway to Gabes

1 ●●● B

C ⊠ 18   B ⊠ 18

▨

2 ●●● B

DJEBEL BERDA

2 ⊠ 18

To Gabes

3 ●●● B

G ⊠ 18

Kradschützen Bataillon 10

601st TD BN's Disposition for B and C Co's

F ⊠ 18   E ⊠ 18

The Kradschutzen Batallion 10 attacked again on the evening of March 24/25,defeating G Company, which was forced to withdraw with heavy losses. E Company and D Company, 1st Ranger Battalion then provided rearguard security on Hill 772 so both 1st and 2nd battalions,18th Infantry could retire from Djebel Berda on March 25.

Positions are approximate.

XI

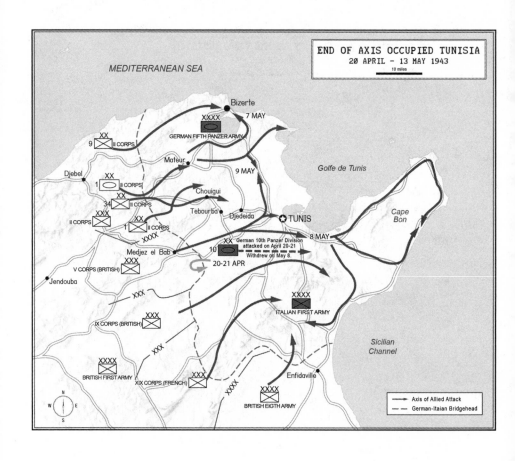

END OF AXIS OCCUPIED TUNISIA
20 APRIL - 13 MAY 1943
10 miles

MEDITERRANEAN SEA

Bizerte
7 MAY
GERMAN FIFTH PANZER ARMY

9 │II CORPS│

Djebel

Mateur
9 MAY

Golfe de Tunis

1 │II CORPS│

Chouigui

34 │II CORPS│

Tebourba
Djedeida

Cape
Bon

II CORPS

1 │II CORPS│

☆ TUNIS

8 MAY

German 10th Panzer Division
attacked on April 20-21
Withdrew on May 8.

Medjez el Bab

10

V CORPS (BRITISH)

20-21 APR

Jendouba

ITALIAN FIRST ARMY

IX CORPS (BRITISH)

Sicilian
Channel

BRITISH FIRST ARMY

XIX CORPS (FRENCH)

Enfidaville

N
W   E
S

BRITISH EIGTH ARMY

→ Axis of Allied Attack
--- German-Itaian Bridgehead

XII

Preface

Purple Heart Boxes versus Panzers

Before us in the valley was an entire panzer division.
—Captain Sam Carter, D Company,
1st Battalion, 18th Infantry[1]

0500 to 0625 Hours, Tuesday, March 23, 1943
El Guettar, Tunisia
C Company, 601st Tank Destroyer Battalion

Panzers—the valley below was crawling with them. Lumbering along at twenty kilometers an hour, they were an unstoppable army of metal elephants roaming across the savannah. Even worse, several were Mk IV G variants—the newest addition to Hitler's arsenal. Mounting a long-barreled 7.5cm gun, it could penetrate the frontal armor on the American M4A2 Sherman tank at a range of a thousand meters. In contrast, the standard M4A2 Sherman, with its stubby 75mm gun, had to close within 100 meters to penetrate the front glacis of the Mk IV.[2] Fortunately for the Americans, no Shermans were there waiting for the panzers to destroy them. Unfortunately, there were no other tanks in the immediate vicinity. All the hapless GIs had were the M3 tank destroyers of the 601st Tank Destroyer Battalion.

Despite the name, the soldiers quickly learned that the M3 was lousy at tank destroying. Though it had a mounted 75mm gun, it was a relic from World War I, unlike the more modern German tank guns. In fact, the original design was French and from 1897, predating tanks altogether.

Worse, the M3 was a deathtrap. The soldiers named it "the Purple Heart Box" because of its lack of armor. With an open top and ¼-inch metal skin, it was vulnerable to artillery fire, heavy machine guns, and spit wads.[3]

Alas, the M3 Gun Motor Carriage (GMC) was all the Americans had on the hills around El Guettar. Bill R. Harper from Mount Pleasant, Texas, was a driver in one of the Purple Heart Boxes. He had been in the army since 1939, enlisting at the age of nineteen because he could not find any other work. Asked about the advantages of the M3, Harper remarked, chuckling, "There wasn't too many good points about it."[4]

Captain Herbert E. Sundstrom was Harper's commander. He had nothing positive to say about the M3 Halftrack Tank Destroyer. "Everyone knew this was a joke," wrote Sundstrom. "Realistically we recognized that the army had to get something quick and this was the stop-gap. It certainly beat the towed guns we originally had. The gun was less than 1,000 velocity [sic] and it had limited traverse. Armor plate might deflect machine-gun fire but nothing bigger."[5]

Unfortunately, Harper's lackluster M3 was all the Americans had to square off against the panzers. The young Texan knew they were in for a fight as the panzer procession crept up the valley as he gripped the steering wheel on his half-track, waiting for the order to move to a new position. He rehearsed the fire commands in his mind, hoping that his muscle memory would assist his driving. If the 75mm peashooter was not in the right position, he would have to jam the stick shift into reverse and drive the box backwards.

Backing up the M3 was not like backing up a car, though. Harper described the hazards of navigating a half-track in a postwar interview: "Because those tracks are pushing you forward," Harper said, "if you try to turn too fast you'll throw a track."[6]

The Lone Star soldier probably wondered how he ended up driving a steel coffin like the M3. When Harper enlisted in 1939, he signed up to be a cannon cocker in D Battery, 5th Field Artillery. Then the panzers ripped through France. Then Yugoslavia. Then Greece. Then North Africa. And finally Russia. Realizing that horse cavalry and good intentions were not enough to lick the Nazis, the U.S. Army shifted its focus to killing tanks.

General George C. Marshall, the Chief of Staff of the Army, knew the United States was far behind the Wehrmacht and immediately ordered the establishment of tank and tank destroyer battalions.

D Battery was one of the units slated for reflagging, becoming C Company, 1st Provisional Antitank Battalion, on August 19, 1941. Several months later, on December 15, 1941, the Battalion officially became the 601st Tank Destroyer Battalion. Its first post was Fort Devens, Massachusetts, and its first commander was Maj. (later Lt. Col.) Herschel D. Baker.

Like Harper, Baker was a red leg—an artillery soldier. First Lieutenant Edward L. Josowitz, an officer in the 601st, described Baker as "a two hundred and twenty pound, rolly-polly [*sic*], cherubic looking, foghorn-voiced ball of fire. The Old Man was a battle wise veteran of World War I, a showman, something of a martinet with his officers but proud-as-hell of his outfit and 100% for his men."[7]

On the morning of March 23, 1943, Baker had thirty-one tank destroyers armed with the French 75s and six more tank destroyers armed only with 37mm guns, making them even less effective than the M3s. Since his mission was primarily a reconnaissance in force, he placed his B and C Companies in front of the forward-deployed artillery. A Company was closer to the main highway, poised to advance down Highway 15 and up the El Guettar Valley to the town of Gabes. In front of his three companies were reconnaissance platoons from the Reconnaissance Company. No one expected the Germans to mount a major attack with tanks that morning. As a result, the artillery was only a few kilometers behind 3rd Battalion of the 18th Infantry, an excellent fire support position if the Allied infantry were attacking. The Germans had their own plans, and they rumbled out of their assembly area early that morning with the intention of spoiling the 1st Infantry Division's offensive.

"The entire situation had changed for the tank destroyer battalion," Baker later wrote. "Whereas we had expected to repel small tank thrusts, we had taken our positions primarily with the idea of defending the artillery against infantry infiltration." Panzers, though, were not on the morning menu. Baker had realized what was rolling down the highway only when his forward screen intercepted a German motorcycle team conducting its own reconnaissance. Shots rang out. One German motor-cyclist slumped over dead, but 1st Platoon, Reconnaissance Company, captured one alive. It did not take long for the captured soldier to talk, and he revealed that the 10th Panzer Division was on its way.[8]

The tanks of the 10th Panzer Division moved in formation, as if they were part of a grand parade. Leading the way were more than fifty panzers from Panzer Regiment 7. Escorting them were the soldiers of 2nd Battalion from Panzergrenadier Regiment 69 and the soldiers of 2nd Battalion from Panzergrenadier Regiment 86. For command and con-trol, the regimental headquarters section of Panzergrenadier Regiment 86 accompanied them. Protecting the moving column from air attack was Company 9 of Panzergrenadier Regiment 86, with 2cm flak guns mounted on flatbed trucks and towing 8.8cm guns from the 3rd and 4th Flak Battalions. Engineer support for the assault force was the Panzer Pioneer Battalion 49. Providing a forward reconnaissance screen was the 10th Panzer Division's *Kradschützen* Battalion 10 (Motorcycle Troop Battalion). Finally, the *Kampfgruppe* (combat team) had one assault gun battery from Panzer Artillery Regiment 90. In total, the force numbered more than 6,000 men. What it lacked in manpower it made up in fire-power.[9] It was facing several elements of a green American division and a battalion of outgunned tank destroyers.

After surveying the terrain the previous day, Maj. Gen. Terry de la Mesa Allen Sr., commander of 1st Infantry Division, positioned his forces on the high ground that flanked the El Guettar-Gabes highway. In the north, hugging the forward slope of the El Keddab Ridge, was Colonel Baker's 601st Tank Destroyer Battalion. Providing additional support was 3rd Battalion of the 18th Infantry Regiment, the 32nd and 5th Field Artillery Battalions. On the opposite side of the valley, dug in along the forward slope of the Djebel Berda Hills, were the 1st and 2nd battalions of the 18th Infantry Regiment. Behind the 32nd Field Artil-lery was 3rd Battalion, 16th Infantry. In total, Allen had four infantry battalions, two artillery battalions, and one tank destroyer battalion in the immediate vicinity.

They were arrayed against two German panzergrenadier battalions, a regiment of panzers, a pioneer battalion, a motorcycle battalion, a company of assault guns, and a slew of flak guns. The Germans had designed their antiaircraft guns to be dual purpose, and therefore they were deadly in the direct fire role. The Germans had a significant edge in firepower.[10]

More importantly, the Germans had confidence. They had never lost to the Americans. Five weeks earlier at Kasserine Pass, the veterans of the 10th Panzer Division had defeated the Americans and sent them running westward like whipped dogs.

Joachim Kannicht was a logistics officer in the 21st Panzer Division who had fought with the 10th Panzer Division at Kasserine. "As far as I remember," said Kannicht, "they [U.S. soldiers] were inexperienced." Kannicht added, "But at that time we just felt we were vastly superior to them in every respect."[11]

Senior *Wehrmacht* officers shared the same opinion of the American army. Generalleutnant Alfred Gause was the Chief of Staff for the German-Italian Army Group Africa. According to Gause, the junior American commanders had a lot to learn in the art of war. "The subordinate commanders were noted for their adherence to prearranged plans and for their lack of flexibility," wrote Gause. "The Americans often did not take advantage of favorable moments, which, if the troops had shown personal initiative, could have been used as a springboard for successful local attacks and their development."[12]

Though the American army's overwhelming material superiority impressed Gause, the élan of the American fighting soldier did not. "However, in spite of this wealth of material," wrote Gause, "the American soldier fought very unwillingly. There were several cases in 1942, when separate groups of American soldiers prematurely laid down their arms, showing no desire to break through and emerge from an encirclement."[13]

Yet, on the morning of March 23, 1943, the inexperienced soldiers from the 18th Infantry Regiment and 601st Tank Destroyer Battalion had little choice but to fight or die. The panzers were coming. Shortly after 0500 hours, the battle began.

Thomas E. Morrison was a soldier from Able Company, 601st Tank Destroyer Battalion. The young man from Eastlake, Ohio, had been up all night, digging foxholes. After eating corned beef from a can, he finally went to sleep, unaware of the approaching enemy.

Suddenly, it was bedlam. "Somebody come over and kicked me and said, 'Hey, tanks are coming,' and about that time, bam, one of them shot through there," explained Morrison. "So, I jumped up and jumped on the back of the half-track and we started shooting back, and so, it was real foggy out there, and on top of that the Germans were throwing down smoke grenades, and the tanks kept moving out."

Morrison was not confident of his chances of survival inside his half-track. He recalled, "The armored division boys called us 'The Paper Armored Bastards.'"[14]

Major Harry H. Critz, the executive officer for the 32nd Field Artillery Battalion, recalled, "There were plenty of targets those days, such as when we were hit by this armored division, they were deployed in a valley and there was no vegetation. You could see every man move."[15]

On the opposite side of the valley was Sam Carter, the Dog Company Commander for 1st Battalion. Fortunately for 1st Battalion, the men in his unit were wide awake because they had been preparing for a dawn assault. "There were red, white and blue tracers being fired from the noise in the valley to the north across the valley," wrote Carter. "Soon these colors were joined by green, purple, yellow and orange tracers. Soon after this the larger guns began firing. . . . It was very dark at this time and nothing could be seen except the source of this large volume of fire slowly moving westwards."

For thirty minutes, the battle looked like a Fourth of July show with the multicolored tracers illuminating the early morning sky. As dawn broke, the men squinted to see what was coming. At first, the morning rays blinded them, but as their eyes grew accustomed to the light, they beheld an awesome but terrifying sight. "Before us in the valley was an entire panzer division," Carter later shared.[16]

The appearance of the 10th Panzer Division meant a fight to the finish for the men of the 1st Infantry Division and the 601st Tank Destroyer Battalion. The stakes were more than just control of single highway in a valley in Tunisia. The American army needed a victory against the *Wehrmacht*; after Kasserine, the officers and soldiers of the British army wondered if their American allies had the right stuff. That morning, many of the GIs defending the hills around El Guettar probably asked themselves the same thing. In the next twenty-four hours, they would have their answer.

Introduction

The Opponents

"We took about fifty German prisoners that time and they were whin-ing as if we didn't have the right to attack by night. Acted as if they thought we should fight by their rules. The German is arrogant in victory and servile in defeat."
                    —Major General Terry de la Mesa Allen,
                        speaking about his experience fighting
                    German soldiers during the World War I[1]

United States
1st Infantry Division

In 1943, the U.S. Army was far from the modern, professional force of today. It had more in common with the army of 1861 than it did with the army of 2017. In fact, like the Union army that marched on Bull Run in 1861, the army that faced the German war machine in the desert of North Africa was an army of eager volunteers and naive draftees led by inexperienced officers still learning how to lead large units.

The biggest personalities associated with the war were coming into their own as the scope of the war shifted and grew. Lieutenant General George S. Patton was the commander of II Corps in March 1943 and would lead Seventh Army later that summer. Yet Patton had been a divi-sion commander for only a few months when war broke out on Decem-ber 7, 1941. General Dwight D. Eisenhower—the Supreme Commander Allied Expeditionary Force of the North African Theater of Operations in February 1943—was only a colonel in March 1941. His ascension through five ranks had taken less than two years. Men who had led companies in 1940 were now leading battalions and regiments in 1943.

In 1939, the U.S. Army had 189,839 soldiers. By 1943, the number ballooned to 6,994,472—a 3,700 percent increase in size.[2] The army of 1943 was an army experiencing growing pangs associated with the throes of puberty. It had potential, but it was an unwieldy and gangly teenager.

In 1939, the army had only five infantry divisions and one cavalry division inside the continental United States. By 1945, the American army had sixty-seven infantry divisions, sixteen armored divisions, five airborne divisions, and two cavalry divisions. Entire divisions sprang up from nothing, as if spontaneously generated from temporary camps throughout the country. Most of the divisions existed only on paper in 1941 when the Japanese bombed Pearl Harbor, and most were far from combat ready when the Allies landed in North Africa in November 1942. As a result, the burden of combat in those first few battles fell on the divisions that existed prior to the outbreak of hostilities.[3]

One such unit was the 1st Infantry Division—The Big Red One. Its history began on May 2, 1917, when Gen. Hugh Scott, the Army Chief of Staff, ordered Gen. John J. Pershing to form the 1st (Expeditionary) Division for an immediate deployment to France. Pershing chose four infantry regiments and one artillery regiment to form its nucleus. Three of the original infantry regiments (the 16th, 18th, and 26th Infantry Regiments) were still part of the division when it deployed to North Africa in 1942.[4]

The Big Red One underwent its first major combat operation at Cantigny, France, in late April and May 1918, where it won a resounding victory against the German army. This was the U.S. Army's first victory against the Central Powers. After the 1st Division's baptism by fire, it saw further action in July at the battle of Soissons, where it emerged victorious once again, sustaining a horrific 7,200 casualties.[5]

The bloodletting continued into the fall. That September, General Pershing launched the St. Mihiel offensive, the U.S. First Army's first independent operation. It, too, was a tremendous triumph. The reeling and wounded German army withdrew further east toward its border.

Leading the assault was the Big Red One. After St. Mihiel, Pershing ordered the 1st Division off the front line to receive replacements. For several weeks, the soldiers rested and recuperated while other units marched into the cauldron that later became known as the Meuse-Argonne offensive.

By October 1918, the Big Red One returned to the maelstrom. For eleven days, it crawled and scraped through the Meuse-Argonne region. Success was measured in meters, and after incurring 7,000 casualties, the American Expeditionary Force pulled the battered 1st out of the trenches. It had pushed the front line only seven kilometers at a cost of 1,000 men per kilometer.[6]

The battle-tested but weary division spent three more weeks receiving replacements. Most of the veterans from Cantigny were gone as a result of battle wounds or death. By the beginning of November, the Central Powers and the German army's resolve were disintegrating. When the Big Red One leapt out of the trenches near Sedan for one last time, resistance was negligible. The 1st's units raced to the French-German border. In an embarrassing incident, the Big Red One captured Sedan, denying the French army the emotional prize of seizing the town that was the symbol of their defeat in the Franco-Prussian War. It mattered little to the soldiers on the ground, who saw it as just another name on the map. When statisticians tallied the final numbers after the cessation of hostilities, the 1st Division sustained more than 21,618 casualties, to include 4,111 dead.[7]

After the war, the Big Red One performed occupation duty in Germany and returned home in the fall of 1919. When demobilization occurred, the 1st Division remained intact while the army deactivated other divisions. In fact, throughout the 1920s and 1930s, the Big Red One continued to train. Maintaining combat readiness was a challenge due to a parsimonious Congress that did not want to fund a large, standing army.[8]

On September 1, 1939, Germany invaded Poland. On September 3, Great Britain and France declared war on Germany. Once again, Europe was a battleground. President Franklin D. Roosevelt appointed Gen. George C. Marshall as Army Chief of Staff on that same September day in 1939 as German panzers roared over the Polish frontier. It would be one of his best decisions.

Marshall had served as the G-3 for the 1st Division during World War I, and he was an organizational genius. He grasped that the American Expeditionary Force's divisional square structure of World War I would not work in the coming conflict. He proposed the triangular structure: Instead of four infantry regiments, a standard division would have only three infantry regiments. It was a leaner but more deployable unit. Moreover, it was easier to manage in battle. The 1st Division was one of the first units to undergo the transformation. As a result, it lost the 28th Infantry Regiment but retained the 16th, 18th, and 26th Infantry Regiments.[9]

In May 1940, Germany invaded France. Six weeks later, France was out of the war. The War Department concluded that the U.S. Army might have to fight its way onto the European continent, and so several units, including some from the 1st Division, were selected for amphibious invasion training in conjunction with the U.S. Navy for the next year. In November 1941, the entire Big Red One participated in the Carolina Maneuvers.

On December 7, 1941, Japan bombed Pearl Harbor. Several days later, Hitler declared war on the United States. Within just a few short months, units prepared to ship out to either the Pacific or the European theaters. Prime Minister Winston Churchill and President Roosevelt assessed Germany to be the greater threat; therefore, the United States concentrated its war-fighting effort to defeat that Axis power. The 1st Infantry Division was one of the first divisions to head to Europe, departing on August 2, 1942, from New York with the initial destination of Glasgow, Scotland.[10]

Besides the new name, the division had a new commander: Maj. Gen. Terry de la Mesa Allen. "Terrible" Terry assumed command of the division on June 19, 1942, the day he pinned on his second star. Marshall had seen Allen, then deputy commander of the 36th Infantry Division, perform during the Carolina Maneuvers. The scrappy cavalryman impressed the Army Chief of Staff, who rewarded him with a division command.[11]

A. J. Liebling, a reporter for the *New Yorker* magazine, accompanied Allen to North Africa and wrote several articles about the general. Liebling described him as a "medium-sized soldier with a thick neck, sloping shoulders, and the slightly rolling gait of a man who has spent a great deal of time on horseback. He has the kind of dented nose that is usually associated with prizefighters and his breathing is audible as he talks, like the breathing of old boxers as they spar. . . . He has a long skull, a heavy jaw, high cheekbones, and deep-sunk brown eyes; his hair is black flecked with gray, and one lock generally stands up on the top of his head."[12]

Allen was a member of the West Point Class of 1912, except he did not graduate, flunking out in 1911, much to the chagrin to his father, Sam, a career army officer. Despite the failure, following his father's example, he earned a commission as a second lieutenant of cavalry shortly after his graduation from Catholic University the following year.

His first assignment was with the 14th Cavalry in Texas, where his first combat experience was against Mexican cattle rustlers. It was a brief skirmish, and he lost his horse. In 1916, he participated in the Punitive Expedition that went after the Mexican bandit Pancho Villa. Though Allen did not find himself in as many scrapes as his contemporary George S. Patton Jr., he did learn valuable leadership lessons from the operation.[13]

When the United States entered World War I in 1917, the young, pugnacious Allen wanted to fight. His first combat command was with 3rd Battalion, 358th Regiment, 90th Division, and he was made major. Allen led his command into combat for first time on September 3, 1918.

Later that month, the fearless Allen sustained several injuries during the St. Mihiel offensive. His most serious wound was the result of a gunshot wound to the jaw. Terrible Terry refused to remain bedridden and checked himself out of the field hospital until, on September 15, the regimental surgeon ordered him to remain there. In October, Allen rejoined his unit, leading it into the cauldron of the Meuse-Argonne.[14]

On October 26, 1918, Allen's battalion seized the town of Aincre-ville. A seemingly unimportant town, the victory had a major influence on Allen's career. Because of the enemy's defenses, the young major devised a plan to seize the village under the cover of darkness. While nighttime operations are now common in the twenty-first century, they were not the norm in the early twentieth. Commanders felt that command and control was nearly impossible under nighttime conditions. Fratricide, therefore, was a real possibility. However, Allen concluded that the concealment afforded by the night sky would allow his soldiers to approach the objective unobserved. He risked fratricide for the sake of surprise, and his gamble paid off.

"I had one goddam company commander who was a pessimist," Allen explained two decades later to A. J. Liebling. "'This is suicide' he said. I pulled out my revolver and shot him in the behind. 'There. You're out,' I said. 'You're wounded.' He was glad to get out of it, and I sent a second lieutenant up to take the company and he did fine. We took the position with loss of twenty killed, and if we'd done it by day we would have lost three hundred. . . . We took about fifty German prisoners that time and they were whining as if we didn't have the right to attack by night. Acted as if they thought we should fight by their rules. The German is arrogant in victory and servile in defeat."

The victory at Aincreville taught Allen that surprise saved lives when he was the attacker and that nighttime assaults provided the necessary concealment for the attacker to achieve the element of surprise. In North Africa, Sicily, and northwest Europe, Allen conducted several successful nighttime assaults. In his after action report on the Tunisian campaign, he wrote, "Night operations proved of extreme value for attaining surprise and, occasionally, as the only means of getting our troops across open country without severe losses. Night operations should be emphasized in training." In World War II, as most of his contemporaries conducted their operations during daylight hours, Allen conducted attacks at night. He was a pioneer.[15]

On November 11, 1918, World War I ended. For his extraordinary bravery in battle, Allen earned the Silver Star. He remained in Europe to perform occupation duty in Germany with his battalion. Unlike many other officers who lost their rank because of downsizing, Allen was demoted but then was promoted back to the rank of major in September 1920. In 1921, he returned to the United States.

Throughout much of the 1920s, Allen was in Texas serving as a cavalryman. Several years after returning to the states, Allen attended the Command and General Staff School at Fort Leavenworth, Kansas. Once again, academics dogged him. He graduated 221st in the class, while his contemporary, Dwight D. Eisenhower, graduated first.

Allen's lack of seriousness was one reason for his poor showing. Recounting his first tactical problem at the course with Liebling, he said, "It was all full of silly questions like 'What are the enemy's intentions?'" His written response was, "The enemy didn't tell me." Yet, the combative cavalryman solved the tactical problem without divining the enemy's goals. His instructors were less than moved by his overall performance. One of them described him "as the most indifferent student ever enrolled there."[16]

The 1930s were better for the scrappy officer. Allen attended the Infantry Advanced Officer's Course at Fort Benning, Georgia, from 1931 to 1932. There, he impressed the army's future boss, then Lt. Col. George C. Marshall, who was the assistant director of the school at the time. On Allen's evaluation report, the future chief of staff wrote, "By training, experience, and temperament, highly qualified as a leader . . . qualified as of now as commanding officer of a regiment and in wartime a division."[17]

In October 1940, Marshall selected him for promotion to brigadier general. Ironically, Terry was the first from his West Point class to reach the rank of general. His promotion was not without grumbling from those in the upper echelons of the army. Allen had jumped over 900 officers to reach the coveted rank. Many were not pleased with Marshall's selection and asked the chief of staff to rescind the promotion. Marshall refused.[18]

When the Army Chief of Staff appointed him as the commander of the 1st Infantry Division, Allen was ecstatic. He wrote a personal note to Marshall, thanking him for the promotion to major general and command of the division. Marshall wrote back, "I received your note of appreciation of your appointment to command the First Division. You were assigned because I thought you would make an excellent job of it, particularly in view of its probable assignment."[19] Allen had earned Marshall's trust but had to prove that it was well founded. The Army Chief of Staff knew that the division commander would have that chance later that fall in North Africa.

Allen may have captivated Marshall, but his contemporaries were less than enthused by his leadership style. General Omar Bradley, who eventually ended up as Allen's commander at the end of the Tunisian campaign, wrote, "They [Allen and his assistant division commander, Brig. Gen. Theodore Roosevelt Jr.] looked upon discipline as an unwelcome crutch to be used by less able and personable commanders. Terry's own career as an army rebel had long ago disproved the maxim that discipline makes the soldiers. Having broken the mold himself, he saw no need to apply it to his troops."[20]

After Patton assumed command of II Corps in March 1943, Allen traveled to the corps headquarters in Tebessa, Algeria, to hear the brief from his new corps commander on an upcoming operation. According to Col. Stanhope Mason, Allen's chief of staff at the time, Patton berated the Big Red One. Mason paraphrased the speech in a postwar account, writing, "He [Patton] then proceeded to say that the soldiers (all in the 1st Division in this case) were undisciplined, looked more like a mob than a smart soldierly unit, and were too cowardly to fight. But, he continued, if they would just try to show some guts in this forthcoming operation maybe it would not be too fouled up."[21]

Allen did not agree with Patton's assessment, but as his subordinate, he had little recourse but to take the verbal abuse while in a public forum, as was military custom. Mason, who went on to become a major general in his own right, described Allen as "volatile but considerate, believing in his unit, dedicated to accomplishing his assigned military objectives at least cost of lives, anxious to get every possible break for his own men, no personal image builder, and fully believing that teamwork was the key to winning."[22]

Many of enlisted soldiers shared Colonel Mason's opinion of General Allen. Andrew J. Jacobson was a soldier in Headquarters and Headquarters Company, 16th Infantry Regiment, and participated in all of the Big Red One's World War II campaigns. Of Allen and Roosevelt, he said, "They were a soldier's general. . . . They were up there with us all the time. They didn't hang back and tell us what to do. They would show us what to do."[23]

Similarly, Roy S. Ehrhardt, a corporal in the 18th Infantry Regiment, had fond memories of Allen and Roosevelt. "They were individual people," said Ehrhardt. "I never met men like them. They enjoyed combat. They just got a kick out of it." When asked if they exposed themselves to combat, the seasoned veteran Ehrhardt laughed and remarked, "Teddy Roosevelt had a walking stick, and he had a helluva time going up a hill . . . [but] he'd go right along with the rest of us."[24]

At first glance, Roosevelt and Allen seemed an ill-suited pair. Allen, the son of a career army officer, spent his childhood roughhousing with the children of enlisted soldiers. Roosevelt was the scion of American aristocracy, growing up in the Gilded Age in a famous family. Yet their upbringings did not define their relationship.

Theodore Jr. was a minor legend in his own right. The son of a president, he was born on September 13, 1887. After the United States entered World War I, he was determined to serve in wartime like his father. He became a battalion commander in the 26th Infantry Regiment, part of the newly formed 1st Division. He eventually saw combat in places like Cantigny and Soissons, where a German machine gunner shot him in the leg, wounding him severely. After several months of convalescence, he returned to 1st Division to serve as the commander of the 26th Infantry Regiment and ending the war as a lieutenant colonel. For his bravery at Cantigny and Soissons, the army later awarded Roosevelt the Distinguished Service Cross.[25]

Between the wars, Roosevelt enjoyed some success as a politician. The citizens of New York elected him to the State Assembly in 1920. He ran for governor in 1924 but lost to Alfred E. Smith. In September 1929, President Herbert Hoover appointed him the governor of Puerto Rico, and in 1932, Hoover moved him to the Philippines, where he became the governor-general of the colony. He returned home to New York in 1935. Throughout the 1920s and 1930s, Roosevelt maintained his reserve commission in the army and attended the various U.S. Army schools required for promotion and advancement.[26]

With war on the horizon in 1941, Roosevelt was not one to sit on the sidelines. He wanted to be in the ring like his father had. Returning to active duty at the rank of colonel, he assumed command of his old regiment, the 26th Infantry, in April 1941. That December, General Marshall recommended him for promotion to brigadier general. In a letter to Roosevelt, the Chief of Staff wrote, "I proposed your promotion on the recommendation of your commanders, particularly General [Leslie J.] McNair. I have been absolutely cold-blooded in this business, but when your name was brought up in high recommendation for the leadership you displayed, it was a great pleasure to me to confirm my opinion of the old days in France."[27]

In 1942, Roosevelt became the assistant division commander of the 1st Infantry Division. In the same congratulatory letter that George Marshall penned to Terry Allen about his assumption of command to the 1st Infantry Division, he added a note about Roosevelt. "Theodore Roosevelt and you are very much of the same type as to enthusiasm, initiative and a restless desire to get into things," he wrote. "I am a little fearful that two people so much of the same type will probably not get along too well, in other words, that he will probably get in your hair. I hope this doesn't develop, for he has had a long history with the First Division, is an A No. 1 fighting man with rare courage, and what is rarer, unlimited fortitude." As it turned out, Marshall's fears were unjustified. In fact, the opposite was true.[28]

As Marshall had observed, Theodore Roosevelt Jr. had much in common with his new boss. Like Allen, Roosevelt enjoyed being up front in the thick of combat. He also shared Allen's foibles. As Bradley wrote, "Had he [Allen] been assigned a rock-jawed disciplinarian as assistant division commander, Terry could probably have gotten away forever on the personal leadership he showed his troops. But Roosevelt was too much like Terry Allen. A brave, gamy, undersized man who trudged about the front with a walking stick, Roosevelt helped hold the division together by personal charm."[29]

Managing the division was the G-3 Operations Officer Lt. Col. Frederick W. Gibb. Born on July 24, 1908, in New York City, Gibb was another West Pointer, commissioned as a second lieutenant of infantry in

1933. His first assignment was with the 20th Infantry Regiment in Fort Frances E. Warren, Wyoming. Like most officers during the interwar years, Gibb's progression through the ranks was glacial. He did not pin captain's bars until September 9, 1940, but with war on the horizon, rank came quickly. Less than two years later, he was a major, and on November 10, 1942, the army promoted him to lieutenant colonel.

When the Japanese bombed Pearl Harbor, Gibb was serving as the operations officer for the 16th Infantry Regiment, and by Operation Torch in November 1942, he was in command of 3rd Battalion, 16th Infantry Regiment. Shortly after the landings, Allen recognized his talents, making him the division's operations officer.[30]

Allen's command was not the same division that went to France in the previous war. It had three infantry regiments instead of four. However, the regiments had more firepower than their predecessors had. In 1942, each regiment had three infantry battalions, and each battalion had 884 enlisted men and thirty-two officers on paper. The regiment had six 75mm and two 105mm self-propelled howitzers mounted on M3 half-tracks, eighteen 81mm mortars, twenty-four 37mm towed antitank guns, twenty-seven 60mm mortars, ten .50-caliber machine guns, twenty-four .30-caliber heavy machine guns, and eighteen .30-caliber light machine guns.[31]

The division had four battalions of artillery for fire support. Three of these battalions had twelve 105mm towed howitzers each. Typically, each battalion provided indirect fire coverage for one of the infantry regimental combat teams in a direct-support role. The fourth battalion had twelve 155mm towed howitzers. These were the older M1918A3 Howitzers. These fell under the control of the division and provided general support where needed during battle.[32]

In addition to the artillery battalions and infantry regiments, the division had one reconnaissance troop, one engineer battalion, one medical battalion, one quartermaster battalion, and several other service companies. The division had an overall strength of more than 700 officers and nearly 15,000 enlisted soldiers. It was a powerful but lean fighting organization designed for deployment for Europe or the Pacific theaters.[33]

U.S. Army doctrine placed an emphasis on the creation of regimental combat teams when the division went into battle, especially during offensive operations. A regimental combat team centered around one infantry regiment with an additional battalion of artillery in direct support. Depending on the mission, an engineer company, reconnaissance detachments, and other support units would join the team.[34]

The regimental combat team that saw the heaviest fighting during the battle of El Guettar was the 18th Infantry Regiment. "The Vanguards," as it was known, entered federal service shortly after the bombardment of Fort Sumter on May 3, 1861, making it far older than the 1st Infantry Division. During the Civil War, the 18th served in the western theater, participating in battles such as Murfreesboro in 1862–1863, Chickamauga, and Chattanooga in 1863. After the Civil War, the 18th headed west to the frontier, earning several campaign ribbons for service in the Indian wars. During the Spanish-American War, it took the city of Manila and remained in the Philippines to quell the insurrection that followed. In 1917, it became part of the 1st Division, leaving for France with the division later that year. While in France, it earned the French *Croix de Guerre* for service in the Aisne-Marne campaign and another *Croix de Guerre* for the Meuse-Argonne campaign. Between the wars, the regiment remained part of 1st Division. Prior to the U.S. entry into World War II, it was headquartered at Fort Devens, Massachusetts. Emblazoned across the regiment's insignia was the motto *In Omnia Paratus*, Latin for "prepared for all things." The Germans would test that motto in North Africa.[35]

The commander of the 18th Infantry was Col. Frank Greer, born on September 24, 1895, in Washington, D.C. The author Robert W. Baumer described Greer as "a large, bald-headed man with a no-nonsense personality."[36] Like his commanders, Greer was a veteran of World War I. He left the service after the Armistice, but civilian life did not suit him. He returned to the army; attended the Infantry School, Basic Course, at Fort Benning, Georgia; and graduated in 1921. Like many officers, he bounced around the country, serving in different jobs. Several years later, he returned to Washington, D.C., where he became the adjutant of the Military District of Washington. During that time, he earned his law degree from George Washington University in 1926. In 1934, Capt. Frank Greer graduated from Command and General Staff

School at Fort Leavenworth and two years later graduated from the Army War College at Fort McNair. Shortly after Pearl Harbor, Greer became the regimental executive officer for the 18th Infantry, assuming command on July 1, 1942, while the regiment trained at Indiantown Gap, Pennsylvania.[37]

Greer's three infantry battalion commanders were all veterans by El Guettar. The 1st Battalion was under the command of Lt. Col. Robert H. York from Alabama. Born on April 23, 1913, he was commissioned as an infantry lieutenant in 1938 from West Point. On February 18, 1943, he was promoted to lieutenant colonel after serving as the battalion's executive officer. He had climbed through five ranks in less than six years and was only twenty-nine years old.[38]

York's subordinates, peers, and superiors were universal in their acclaim for the officer. Tenio Roncalio was a platoon leader in his battalion and wrote, "Bob York was a soft spoken commander in combat. He liked to keep in touch with his company commanders and his platoon leader. . . . He was more than a commander. He knew how to counsel his troops. He knew how to assist in maintaining the moral [*sic*] and the physical excellence and the devotion to the job at hand."[39]

Stanhope Mason, the division chief of staff, agreed with Roncalio's assessment. He wrote, "Essentially York was a very stable individual, not inclined to panic under the most adverse conditions and always exhibiting a calm, cheerful outlook on whatever situation existed. This being a natural trait of his character he projected a staunchness and sense of stability which, in turn, was transmitted to everyone around him."[40]

The 2nd Battalion was under the command of Lt. Col. Ben Sternberg, born on February 28, 1914, in Florida. Unlike York and many of the other officers in the 18th Infantry, Sternberg started his army career as a grunt. He first joined the Florida National Guard and then enlisted as a private in Company G, 22nd Infantry Regiment, on July 2, 1933. A year later, he enrolled at West Point and was commissioned as a second lieutenant in the infantry on June 14, 1938. Prior to battalion command, he had served as Colonel Greer's Regimental S-3.[41] Finally, 3rd Battalion's commander was Lt. Col. Courtney P. Brown. He was born on November 2, 1904, and was from Monroe Township, New Jersey.[42]

The 32nd Field Artillery Battalion supported the 18th Infantry Regiment's three infantry battalions. The 32nd was not an old unit. Organized on August 5, 1918, at Camp Meade, Maryland, the unit saw World War I end before it could deploy overseas to France. For much of the 1920s and early 1930s, it was part of 3rd Division. It did not become part of 1st Division until October 1, 1940, when it was activated at Fort Ethan Allen, Vermont.[43]

The commander of the 32nd Field Artillery Battalion was Lt. Col. Percy W. Thompson. Like Greer and Allen, the forty-four-year-old Thompson was not a West Point graduate. He graduated with a bachelor of science from Purdue University in 1925 and subsequently attended the Field Artillery School, Basic Course. He went to the Battery Officer's Course in 1932 and a year later went to the Infantry School and the Company Officers' Course at Fort Benning. His three batteries of artillery provided direct support for Greer's regiment during the battle.[44]

Germany
10th Panzer Division

The 10th Panzer was one of the first panzer divisions in the German army. Formed on April 1, 1939, in the then recently conquered regions of Bohemia and Moravia, the young division was less than six months old when it participated in the invasion of Poland. Nine months later, it led the invasion of France, crossing the Meuse River near Sedan. From there, it zipped across the undefended French countryside and reached the English Channel in less than two weeks. The 10th defeated British and French units hunkered down in Calais, France, and swung south to finish off the French army. The whirlwind campaign lasted six weeks, and the 10th Panzer Division emerged as one of the premier units in the German army.

It did not rest on its laurels for long. A year later, the 10th Panzer was in Russia as part of Operation Barbarossa. It almost reached Moscow, but on December 5, 1941, the Russians counterattacked. Despite the onslaught that shattered scores of German units, the 10th Panzer Division survived and fought through the winter and spring of 1942.

By that summer, it was a shadow of its former self. The German High Command ordered it to return to France for rest and refit. There it remained until the following November, when it received orders to ship out for North Africa.[45]

The commander of the 10th Panzer Division was *Generalmajor* Friedrich Freiherr von Broich. Born on New Year's Day 1896 in Strasbourg (when it was still part of Germany), von Broich entered the army on July 2, 1914, as a cavalry cadet in the 9th Uhlans (2nd Pomeranian) Regiment. The army commissioned him a *Leutnant* on December 24, 1914, while serving on the front lines in Russia. During World War I, he earned two Iron Crosses for bravery while rising through the squadron's ranks. After the war, his rank was downgraded to *Oberleutnant* (first lieutenant) as the army shrunk to accommodate Treaty of Versailles restrictions. Although his future in the military looked bleak, von Broich remained in the Reichswehr and served with the 6th (Preuss) Cavalry Regiment near the town of Demmin, Germany, on the Baltic coast. On October 1, 1928, he was promoted to the rank of *Hauptmann* (captain) and assumed command of the 2nd Squadron, 8th (Preuss) Cavalry Regiment.

Von Broich's career progression continued its steady ascent over the next decade. He became an aide for the Reichswehr's 1st Cavalry Division in 1933 and was subsequently promoted to the rank of major on his birthday, January 1, 1935. Shortly afterward, the army transferred him to Berlin, where he was appointed to serve in the cavalry inspectorate for the next three years.

When war broke out on September 1, 1939, von Broich was the commander of the 34th Reconnaissance Battalion. Itching to go to war, he sought another command and was rewarded when the army offered him the 21st Cavalry Regiment. He commanded the regiment throughout the campaign in France. In recognition of his performance, the army promoted him to colonel on September 1, 1940. He then took over the 22nd Cavalry Regiment and led it into Russia in 1941. Von Broich's career survived the Russian counteroffensive of 1941, and he later assumed command of the 24th Rifle Brigade, which became the 24th Panzergrenadier Brigade in July 1942. He held that post until October

1942, when he was transferred again to serve in North Africa. His first Tunisian command was an ad hoc unit named Brigade von Broich. On February 15, 1943, he took over the 10th Panzer Division after receiving a promotion to major general.[46]

His ascension to division command was not without incident. The previous commander, *Generalleutnant* (Lieutenant General) Wolfgang Fischer, had died in a tragic accident on February 1. Fischer was conducting a terrain reconnaissance when his car drove through an unmarked Italian minefield and detonated one of the mines, destroying the car and killing him. His men buried the fallen officer on February 3 northeast of Tunis. Fortunately for the 10th Panzer Division, von Broich was an excellent replacement. He proved his worth when his division cut through several American units at Kasserine Pass later that same month.[47]

Leading the 10th Panzer Division's attack at El Guettar was Panzer Regiment 7. Unlike the 18th Infantry, it was a young unit. But, like the 18th Infantry, it was older than its parent organization, the 10th Panzer. Organized on October 1, 1936, in Ohrdruf, Germany, Panzer Regiment 7 first saw combat in the Polish campaign in September 1939. Two months later, it joined its new unit.[48]

The regiment had a mixture of tanks, sprinkled amongst its two battalions. Typically, each battalion had one company of Mk IVs. At full strength, this company would have ten Mk IVs and five Mk IIs. The other three companies had seventeen Mk IIIs and five Mk IIs each. The battalion headquarters company provided an additional five Mk IIs and one Mk III. The regimental headquarters had another Mk III and five more Mk IIs for a total of twenty Mk IVs, 105 Mk IIIs, and fifty-five Mk IIs in the regiment.[49]

Unfortunately for the 10th Panzer Division, some of the panzers it was supposed to have were forming reefs for the fish at the bottom of the Mediterranean. A convoy scheduled to arrive on December 3, 1942, lost two Mk IIs, sixteen Mk IIIs, and twelve precious Mk IVs when the ship carrying them sank because of Allied bombers and submarines. This meant that the regiment had less than its allotted Mk IVs when it entered combat later that month.[50]

At El Guettar, the commander of Panzer Regiment 7 was *Oberst* (Colonel) Rudolf Gerhardt. Born on March 26, 1896, in Greiz, Thuringia, Gerhardt entered the German army as an enlisted man in August 1914. His unit was the 96th Thuringian Infantry Regiment, which shipped out to fight the Russians in southern Poland. He quickly proved to be a capable soldier, and by November he was an *Unteroffizier* (sergeant). That December, he earned his first Iron Cross. Recognizing his potential, Gerhardt's superiors granted him a battlefield commission in March 1915. As a *Leutnant*, Gerhardt saw some of the worst fighting in World War I at Verdun and the Somme in 1916. By the end of the war, he had been wounded four times and earned an Iron Cross First Class.

After the war, Gerhardt left the military. In 1934, he rejoined the army as a *Hauptmann* and was a company commander in Panzer Regiment 1. Two years later, his company became the nucleus for Panzer Regiment 7. By the beginning of 1939, now Major Gerhardt was a battalion commander for Panzer Battalion 66. He led the unit that September into Poland, where he was wounded a fifth time. In May 1940, he took command of a battalion in Panzer Regiment 7 and participated in the mad dash to the English Channel that ultimately led to the fall of France in June. He remained with the regiment when it invaded Russia in June 1941 and became the temporary regimental commander in November 1941. Promotions came quickly. In January 1942, the army promoted him to *Oberstleutnant* (lieutenant colonel). By April 20, he was an *Oberst* and the official commander of the regiment. That same month, the army transferred Panzer Regiment 7 and the rest of the division for refit to southern France, where it remained until it left for Africa in late 1942.[51]

The 10th Panzer Division had two panzergrenadier regiments. Formed on April 1, 1940, both Panzergrenadier Regiments 86 and 69 were originally named Schützen (Rifle) Regiments 86 and 69, respectively, and were part of Schützen Brigade 10 of the 10th Panzer Division. Both became panzergrenadier regiments on July 5, 1942. The commander of the Panzergrenadier Regiment 86 was *Oberst* Hans Reimann, and the commander of the Panzergrenadier Regiment 69 was

Oberst Rudolf Lang. Although Lang was not at El Guettar, his 2nd Battalion played a pivotal role in the battle.[52]

———

Both divisions were on a collision course in March 1943. The 1st Infantry Division was part of an army trying to rehabilitate itself after the disaster at Kasserine Pass. Its future adversary, the 10th Panzer Division, was a well-oiled machine but, thanks to Allied bombing, a machine running out of parts. On March 23, 1943, the two combatants squared off to see who was master of Tunisia.

CHAPTER ONE

Prelude

"In the lead car Patton stood like a charioteer. He was scowling into the wind and his jaw strained against the web strap of a two-starred steel helmet."
—Major General Omar Bradley, describing
Patton's arrival at II Corps Headquarters[1]

Friday, March 5, 1943
Casablanca, French Morocco, and then to Algiers, Algeria, and Thence to Constantine, Algeria
Major General George S. Patton was ready. The previous night, he had received a phone call from his boss, General Eisenhower. Patton was out when the call came, so he did not speak with him directly. Ike's only message was for him to be ready for "extended field service" and to leave for Algiers the next morning. Naturally, Patton was intrigued.

"I phoned Beedle Smith [Lt. Gen. Walter Bedell Smith], Ike's Chief of Staff, and asked what it was about," recalled the general. Ike's chief of staff informed Patton that he was replacing Maj. Gen. Lloyd Fredendall, the soon-to-be-former commander of II Corps.

The next morning, as instructed, Patton bid his staff farewell. It was 1000 hours when he left his office for the aerodrome. Waiting for him outside were military police who lined the street as an honor guard. For pomp and ceremony, an army band played martial tunes as his column of cars sped off. Accompanying him on the trip were several staff officers, including Brig. Gen. Hugh J. Gaffey, who would serve as his acting chief of staff; Col. Kent Lambert, who would be the G-3; and Col. Oscar Koch, who was his current G-2. Their plane took off quickly and soon touched down at Maison Blanche Airfield outside of Algiers. Both Eisenhower and Smith waited for them on the tarmac. The Supreme Commander Allied Expeditionary Force of the North African Theater of Operations did not waste time with small talk. War was a ruthless business, and the Allied bosses needed a scapegoat. Fredendall was the perfect candidate.

— ◆ —

Fredendall's fall from grace had been swift. Shortly after Pearl Harbor, Marshall selected him to be one of the first corps commanders to lead men into combat against the Germans. Initially, he seemed like a good choice. As commander of the Central Task Force for Operation Torch, he landed his forces on November 8, 1942, and defeated the Vichy French units at Arzew and Oran, Algeria, within a few days. There, he waited while other Allied forces pushed east into Tunisia.

Then–Lieutenant General Eisenhower argued for a coup de main using small task forces to seize the Tunisian ports of Tunis and Bizerte before the Axis could establish a defensible lodgment. By the end of November 1942, Allied units had secured a foothold in Tunisia, but it was not enough. The German and Italian forces had interior lines of communication, and, thanks to the short distance between Italy and Tunisia, Field Marshal Albert Kesselring, the commander of *Oberbefehlshaber Süd* (German Army Command South), built up his forces quicker than the British and Americans. The Allies attempted to seize the ports two more times at the end of November and December, but both attempts floundered after bruising German counterattacks. Coupled with the winter rain that turned roads into quagmires and ever-increasing German combat power amassing along the Tunisian coast, Eisenhower called off the offensive shortly after Christmas 1942. Ike decided to husband his resources for another go when the rainy season ended in two months.[2]

Like much of western North Africa, geography divides Tunisia into two regions: the fertile coast and the arid interior. Dominating the interior is the Atlas Mountains. This range acts as a twisting spine dividing the northern half of the country along a southwest-to-northeast axis. The Tunisian portion of the Atlas Mountains is the Dorsal. Millions of years ago, tectonic plates split the range into the Eastern Dorsal and Western Dorsal. Several mountain passes crisscross the Dorsals, and both sides considered these passes key terrain during World War II.

By January 1943, the British First Army under Lt. Gen. Kenneth Anderson occupied the northern flank of the Eastern Dorsal as it made its way toward the Mediterranean. To the south and headquartered near Tebessa was General Fredendall with his newly constituted II Corps. Eisenhower instructed Fredendall to "provide a strategic flank guard for our main forces in the north." In addition, Ike wanted II Corps "to hold the mountain passes with light infantry detachments and to concentrate the assembled 1st Armored Division in the rear of the infantry outposts, ready to attack in force any hostile column that might attempt to move through the mountains toward our line of communications." If the II Corps commander believed an opportunity presented itself, he had permission to strike eastward and cut the Axis line of communication to Rommel's army withdrawing from Libya.[3]

With a clear task and purpose, Fredendall went to work building his corps for the upcoming spring offensive. During this time, the Allied command regularly divvied up American units amongst the various contingents depending on the mission. For example, Allen's Big Red One did not conduct a single operation in January or February 1942 as a complete division. Fredendall's opponent, the Fifth Panzer Army, did not share the same issues. On the contrary, while Fredendall hunkered down for a protracted defense, its commander, *Generaloberst* Hans-Jürgen von Arnim, prepared his army to go on the offensive.

At the end of January, Fifth Panzer Army struck the French XIX Corps near Faïd Pass, which was north of II Corps' area of operations. Earlier that month, Eisenhower had identified the underequipped French forces as a weak point in the Allied lines. Von Arnim discovered the same shortcoming and exploited it. On January 30, the 21st Panzer Division penetrated French lines at Faïd. Anderson ordered Fredendall to dispatch the 1st Armored Division to counterattack and restore the lines. The Germans were waiting for the inexperienced American tankers who rushed headlong into German antitank kill-sacs. The result was a stinging rebuke, and the Americans failed to recapture Faïd.

Several days after the battle, now-General Eisenhower (Ike received a promotion to four stars on February 11) visited II Corps headquarters outside of Tebessa. When he arrived, he was startled to see combat engineers digging into the side of a ravine. It looked like someone was building the Hoover Dam in the middle of the desert. Eisenhower remarked, "It was the only time, during the war, that I ever saw a divisional or higher headquarters so concerned over its own safety that it dug itself underground shelters."[4]

His trip did not improve when he visited front-line troops on February 14. He noticed a lack of defensive preparations near the pass at Sidi Bou Zid, which was only several kilometers west of enemy forces at Faïd Pass. Three hours after he left the area, the Germans attacked Sidi Bou Zid and overran the American units defending it. Once again, it was the Fifth Panzer Army. Leading the way were the 10th Panzer and 21st Panzer divisions. The name of their plan was Operation *Frühlingwind* (Spring Wind). The Fifth Panzer Army's mission was "to weaken the Americans by destroying some of his elements and thereby confuse and delay his advance."

In this regard, the two panzer divisions were successful, overrunning several units and isolating two infantry battalion task forces, one of which was under the command of Lt. Col. John K. Waters, Patton's son-in-law. When the tanks of Combat Command C, 1st Armored Division, counterattacked to rescue the surrounded Americans on February 15, it was a repeat of Faïd Pass. The Germans slaughtered the rescuers and eventually captured the remnants of Waters's command, including the man himself. For the Allies, the loss of Sidi Bou Zid meant that the remaining positions in the Eastern Dorsal were untenable. General Anderson authorized a withdrawal of all remaining forces to the Western Dorsal.[5]

Field Marshal Erwin Rommel's *Deutsch-Italienische Panzerarmee* (German-Italian Panzer Army) reached Tunisia after a long odyssey through western Egypt and Libya. Fortunately for Rommel, Montgomery's 8th Army was not nipping at his heels thanks to Axis obstacle efforts that disrupted the British advance. This meant that the Germans had a chance to assume the offensive in Tunisia and possessed numerical superiority at the point of attack. On February 18, Rommel, nicknamed the Desert Fox, proposed a daring plan to Kesselring to strike Fredendall's II Corps. The ultimate objective was capturing the American supply dumps at Tebessa. After their poor performance at Sidi Bou Zid, Rommel sensed that the American II Corps was a staggering, punch-drunk boxer. He wanted to knock it out of Tunisia.[6]

However, von Arnim felt that the Desert Fox's plan was too timid. He argued for an even more ambitious mission when he met with Kesselring on the morning of February 19. He wanted the reunited German and Italian forces to penetrate American lines northeast of Tebessa and then envelop the Allied forces by swinging north toward Le Kef (modern-day El Kef, Tunisia) and further onward to the coastal port of Bône (modern-day Annaba, Algeria). This would trap the entire British First Army. Kesselring had his reservations but concurred that von Arnim's proposal had "many advantages and a prospect of success." Operation *Sturmflut* (Storm Surge) was a go.[7]

Rommel now had his orders: attack through Kasserine Pass and penetrate "in the deep flank and rear of the British forces standing opposite the northern Tunisian front." This time, the Axis brought a meaty *Kampfgruppe* (battle group) from *Deutschse Afrikakorps* (German Africa Corps) (*D.A.K.*) to augment the 10th and 21st Panzer Divisions. The main effort centered on Kasserine Pass, where *Kampfgruppe D.A.K.*, with additional support from the 10th Panzer Division, was to breach the American lines. Fredendall could spare only two infantry battalions from two different divisions (1st Battalion, 26th Infantry, and 3rd Battalion, 39th Infantry) and a regiment of combat engineers to stop them. The engineers were not infantry and therefore had not trained to fight as infantry. The result was another disaster.[8]

On February 19, the Axis resumed their offensive. North of Kasserine, the 21st Panzer Division ran into a hodgepodge force of British and American units (including elements of the 18th Infantry Regiment) defending the town of Sbiba, Tunisia. Despite their muddled command and control while trying to manage units from three separate divisions, the Allies held the panzers in check. At Kasserine, the panzers and pan-zergrenadiers of *Kampfgruppe D.A.K.* were initially bogged down at the mouth of the pass, even though they faced only a few battalions.

Rommel committed the 10th Panzer Division to break the logjam. On February 20, von Broich's men entered the fray. This time, the Germans succeeded, and the Americans broke. Many soldiers from the two battalions of the 26th and 39th Infantries became prisoners of war as the German forces enveloped them. The survivors withdrew to the northwest.[9]

Meanwhile, the 10th Panzer Division continued its advance north toward Thala, where a scratch force from the British 26th Armoured Brigade blocked its attack. On February 22, the Allies stabilized the situation at Thala and elsewhere. To the south, *Kampfgruppe D.A.K.* tried to push through the U.S. Army's Combat Command B, 1st Armored Division, defending the Bou Chebka Pass and the road to Haïdra, Tunisia. Its advance ran out of steam thanks to the stubborn defenses of 2nd Battalion, 13th Armored Regiment, and other units. Despite the drubbing, the Allies blocked the German offensive along all three of its axes.[10]

During the afternoon of February 22, Kesselring visited the Fifth Panzer Army command post. After hearing about the repulses at Thala and Haïdra and the miscarried attack at Sbiba, he called off the operation and ordered all units to assume defensive postures. Yet he had other reasons to end the offensive. The First Italian Army reported earlier that day that Montgomery's Eighth Army had reached the outskirts of the Mareth Line. The Axis no longer enjoyed numerical superiority in the Tunisian theater. On the evening of February 22, the Axis commenced withdrawal operations. Von Broich's command, together with *Kampfgruppe D.A.K.*, were to "fall back at dusk to the old pass positions northwest of Kasserine, mining roads and trails." Over the next few days, the Axis forces pulled out of the Western Dorsal, withdrawing even from Kasserine Pass. Rommel never again attempted an operational-level offensive operation against II Corps. For Fredendall, the danger had passed, but the repercussions were forthcoming.[11]

On February 22, Eisenhower sent Maj. Gen. Ernest N. Harmon to assist Fredendall in regaining control of the situation. Harmon had been in Morocco training his 2nd Armored Division for the upcoming Sicily campaign when he received Eisenhower's summons to rescue the beleaguered II Corps. When Harmon arrived at Fredendall's headquarters, the dazed and confused II Corps commander ceded control of his command to a bewildered Harmon, who thought he was there to assist—not take command of the corps. Despite the strange and confusing situation, Harmon took control and brought order to the chaos. Afterward, Harmon alleged that Fredendall was drunk and in bed.

Harmon reported to Morocco on March 1 and told Eisenhower what he thought of the harried corps commander. "He's no damned good," he remarked. "You ought to get rid of him."[12]

The next day, Harmon spoke with Patton. He told Patton privately that Fredendall was "a physical and moral coward." Patton wrote in his diary, "Fredendall never went to the front at all and tried to make Harmon the goat." Patton concluded, "Harmon won the battle."[13]

Major General Omar Bradley, who would later serve as Patton's II Corps' deputy commander, went on a fact-finding mission for Eisenhower after the Kasserine fiasco. After his short mission, he reached the same conclusion as Harmon when it came to Fredendall. Bradley discovered a breakdown in trust among the senior officers in II Corps. "Although I tried to sidestep the issue of command, it became apparent in my first week on the front that Fredendall had lost the confidence of his division commanders," said Bradley. "While Kasserine could not be blamed solely upon him, he was deeply enough implicated in the eyes of his subordinate commanders to destroy his future effectiveness with them."

When Eisenhower asked Bradley about II Corps' command climate when they were at Tebessa together, Bradley responded, "It's pretty bad."[14]

Word of Fredendall's abysmal performance spread. Shortly before assuming command of the new 18th Army Group, General Alexander toured his new area of operations, which included Fredendall's II Corps. He was less than impressed with the frazzled commander. When Alexander met with his American boss, Eisenhower, he allegedly said of Fredendall, "I'm sure you must have better men than that."[15]

Perhaps Alexander's comment was the straw that broke the camel's back. Lloyd Fredendall had to go. Someone had to replace him. Eisenhower's first choice was Lt. Gen. Mark W. Clark, who was preparing the

U.S. Fifth Army for the Italian campaign. Clark refused the offer, arguing it would be a demotion for him, as he was already an army commander. Eisenhower then offered Patton the job. Patton had learned that the Germans had "destroyed" his son-in-law's battalion at Sidi Bou Zid and knew that the War Department had listed him as missing in action. Perhaps he saw the command as a chance for revenge, but initially Patton reserved judgment on Fredendall. He wanted to see for himself just how bad the situation was.[16] Eisenhower's reason for the change in command was more mundane, according to Patton. "[Eisenhower] told me I was to replace Fredendall on ground[s] that it was presumably a tank show and I knew more about tanks," wrote Patton.[17]

The Supreme Commander did not blame Fredendall totally for Kasserine. "I had no intention of recommending Fredendall for reduction or of placing the blame for the initial defeats in the Kasserine battles on his shoulders, and so informed him," Ike wrote. "Several others, including myself, shared responsibility for our week of reverses."[18]

On the evening of March 5, the new II Corps commander left for Constantine, Algeria, where he met with Gen. Harold Alexander, the commander of the newly constituted 18th Army Group. The brash American's opinion of Alexander was positive. His new British boss informed him that II Corps would receive its own sector and that, instead of reporting to the British First Army, Patton's command would answer directly to Alexander's 18th Army Group as an independent command. In less than ten days, "Old Blood and Guts" (Patton's nickname among his troops) would take his new command into combat.[19]

Saturday, March 6, to Friday, March 12, 1943
Djebel Kouif, Algeria (Northeast of Tebessa)
Headquarters, II Corps
At 1000 hours, Patton arrived at his new headquarters. Fredendall was at the mess hall eating breakfast, but Bradley was there to greet him. To onlookers, it was a memorable spectacle. "With sirens shrieking Patton's arrival, a procession of armored scout cars and half-tracks wheeled into the dingy square opposite the schoolhouse headquarters of II Corps at Djebel Kouif," wrote Bradley. He described the incoming

corps commander: "In the lead car Patton stood like a charioteer. He was scowling into the wind and his jaw strained against the web strap of a two-starred steel helmet."[20]

When Fredendall returned, his meeting with Patton was brief but cordial. Patton even wrote, "He [Fredendall] was nice and conducted himself well—very well." Fredendall left without fanfare early the next morning. II Corps was Patton's show. However, the new corps commander felt the II Corps staff was not war-winning material. "His staff in general is poor. Discipline and dress is poor," wrote Patton in his daily journal.

This observation extended to some of the divisions, too. On March 8, he inspected the 34th Infantry Division. Although the 34th Infantry "fought well," Patton was less than enthusiastic about other aspects of their appearance and behavior. He wrote, "The discipline and dress and condition of weapons is very bad—terrible."

However, other units were in better shape. When Patton inspected the 1st Infantry Division on March 10 with his new boss, General Alexander, the Big Red One did not disappoint. Describing Allen and Roosevelt, Patton wrote, "They made a good impression on me and on General Alexander."[21]

To restore order and discipline, Patton immediately instituted a strict uniform policy. All soldiers—at all times—had to wear their helmets with the chinstrap fastened. It did not matter if you were on the front lines or serving in the rear. Everyone wore helmets. To fix another deficiency, "Old Blood and Guts," ordered all II Corps soldiers to wear their regulation necktie and leggings. Even soldiers digging a foxhole were expected to sport a professional appearance with his necktie tied. To enforce this policy, an unkempt uniform violation resulted in a fine of $25 for enlisted and $50 for officers. "When you hit their pocketbooks, you get a quick response," remarked Patton.[22]

The new regulations were unpopular with the men in the 1st Infantry Division. "While we were re-equipping we got into a tangle with our good friend, General Georgie Patton, because Patton couldn't go ahead and fight a war if he weren't in proper uniform," explained Allston Goff, a battery commander in the 32nd Field Artillery. "So we had to go ahead and take off all our British battle dress uniforms, with which we'd been equipped. . . . This British battle dress was far superior to ours because the pockets were big and loose, so even while you were sitting in your jeep you could take out or put in things in your pocket."[23]

Allen N. Towne was a medic attached to the 18th Infantry Regiment. He recalled hearing about General Patton's draconian dress policy. "General George S. Patton was the new II Corps commander, and he made sure we all knew it," wrote Towne. "We still had woolen uniforms, and it was hot in the desert. Now, Patton insisted we had to wear leggings, full helmets and ties all the time. Any soldier who disobeyed his dress order would be fined $25." Towne then explained why the punishment did not deter the rank and file. "We all had some money but it was sort of valueless because we did not have any place to spend it." He noted, "The division must not have enforced the order because I never did hear of anyone paying a fine."[24]

Unlike his troops, Roosevelt was more upbeat about the change. In a letter to his wife, he wrote, "Big news—Fredendall goes [and] a man I like comes in [and] that means all the difference in the world."[25]

As part of the whirlwind of upheaval spinning throughout the command, Patton changed some of the corps staff. He replaced Col. Robert A. Hewitt, the G-3, with Col. Kent Lambert, who had served as Patton's G-3 for Operation Torch. In addition, Brigadier General Gaffey became the corps chief of staff, replacing Col. John A. Dabney. Colonels Benjamin A. Dickson and Robert W. Wilson, who were the G-2 and G-4, respectively, kept their staff positions. In the case of Dickson, Patton's own G-2, Colonel Koch had recommended Dickson remain. Patton trusted Koch, so the general accepted his advice. General Bradley, who had served as Eisenhower's fact finder, became the corps deputy commander.[26]

Roosevelt was thrilled with Bradley's ascension to deputy corps commander. "Also another cake eater has gone [and] a very fine fellow, Omar Bradley takes his place. All this will mean a lot to our effort here."[27]

In addition to his battlefield circulation and his new uniform policy, as he assumed command, Patton learned the extent of the losses suffered at Kasserine. Between January 1 and March 17, the corps sustained 5,275 casualties. The majority of the casualties occurred in a four-week period, starting on January 30 and ending on February 25. More than 2,500 casualties were soldiers and officers labeled as missing in action by the army. In the following weeks and months, the Red Cross reported them as prisoners of war. Another 2,500 casualties were wounded. Nearly 300 were dead. Fortunately, the army replacement system had filled the personnel gaps.[28]

Manpower was not the only casualty at Kasserine. II Corps lost 183 tanks, 104 halftracks, 208 artillery tubes, 512 jeeps, and huge stocks of ammunition and fuel. Much to the corps commander's relief, the army supply system had replaced most of these losses. Despite the thrashing sustained at Kasserine, the II Corps' depot at Tebessa was stocked and ready to support a large-scale offensive on Patton's arrival.[29]

And Patton was going to lead an offensive. Even before Fredendall's dismissal, his staff worked toward an operation to support the new 18th Army Group's effort to shrink the Tunisian lodgment. The name of the plan was Operation Wop. The original scheme required II Corps to recapture Gafsa, establish a base of supply for Montgomery's recently arrived Eighth Army, and then, on order, push east to Maknassy "to threaten Rommel's Line of Communication."[30]

Patton's first formal mission brief with the entire staff and all the division commanders was on the night of March 8. Thanks to Eisenhower's recommendation for promotion, he was Lieutenant General Patton. Despite the leadership changes, the objective for Operation Wop had not changed. The 1st Infantry Division's mission was to "attack and capture GAFSA by well coordinated attack." After the seizure of Gafsa, the Big Red One needed to defend it. II Corps expected the division to "be prepared to support action of 1st Armored Division on Corps order." To accomplish this mission, II Corps allocated several units to Allen's command, including 1st Ranger Battalion, 601st Tank Destroyer Battalion, several batteries of artillery from 17th Field Artillery Brigade, and numerous combat support units. Allen's axis of advance would take him from Bou Chebka to Feriana and then onto Gafsa. Air support for the 1st Infantry Division would fly from Thelepte and Kasserine Airfields.[31]

The Corps G-3 issued Field Order #3 on March 11 at 1100 hours. It had no major changes. Both 1st Armored and 1st Infantry Divisions would lead the show. The 9th Infantry and 34th Infantry Divisions would provide security to the northeast. To prevent fratricide, Colonel Lambert, Patton's G-3, required Allen to inform II Corps and XII Air Support Command ninety minutes prior to his division's execution of H-hour.[32]

Later that day, Colonel Gibb issued Field Order #16 for the 1st Infantry Division. In it, he outlined the mission for each of the regimental combat teams. Greer would be without his 1st Battalion, which had the mission to "secure the LD [line of departure] prior to daylight D-day." York's battalion would answer directly to the division. The rest of the 18th Infantry had the mission to "protect the northeast flank of the division." Meanwhile, the 16th Infantry would "clear GAFSA of enemy, be prepared to repulse counterattack from south and southwest." The majority of the 26th Infantry would serve as the division reserve. The 1st Ranger Battalion had a be-prepared mission "to move on division order D-day to vicinity EL GUETTAR, push active reconnaissance northeast and south." In addition, the Rangers had a follow-on mission to "secure important terrain features east of EL GUETTAR from which Combat Team 26 can attack."[33]

The enemy was also moving but in the opposite direction. At the end of February, Fifth Panzer Army attacked British V Corps in the north. Its meager gains did not justify the losses it suffered. In the south, Rommel had one more go at Montgomery's Eighth Army when he launched Operation Capri. Thanks to British Ultra intercepts, Monty knew it was coming, and on March 6, Rommel's last offensive operation in North Africa was stillborn. From this point on, the Axis forces were reacting to Allied attacks.

In II Corps' sector, the Axis forces continued their withdrawal from the Western Dorsals. On March 2, they abandoned Sidi Bou Zid. For the next two weeks, enemy defensive activity continued in the Eastern Dorsals, but Allied patrols closed in on Gafsa. To keep the Americans honest, the Axis shelled the recently recaptured Sidi Bou Zid almost daily while massing aircraft at their bases near the front lines. Meanwhile, Allied reconnaissance reported Italian forces operating and digging in around Gafsa.[34]

Friday, March 12, was a time for Patton to reflect. Although he had heard many opinions about Fredendall, he kept an open mind and drew his own conclusions. A week after arriving, Fredendall's foibles were too numerous for him to ignore. "Fredendall just existed," wrote the new II Corps commander. "He did not command and with few exceptions his staff was worthless due to youth and lack of leadership." Later, he wrote, "I cannot see what Lloyd did to justify his existence. I have never seen so little order or discipline." He hoped that the rot was not permanent.

Friday, March 12, to Saturday, March 13, 1943
Bou Chebka, Tunisia
Staging Area for 18th Infantry Regiment, 1st Infantry Division

On March 12, Patton had a pleasant lunch with Allen. Afterward, Allen took Patton on a tour to see his troops. This was the first time the Big Red One was together for an operation, and Allen wanted to show his new boss that they were up to the task. One unit they visited was the 18th Infantry, now bivouacked at Bou Chebka, Tunisia. Colonel Greer's 18th Infantry made an impression on Patton. "The 18th has done well and is quite cocky," he wrote. He liked troops who showed confidence. Greer's boys would not disappoint him. Patton left the command post at 1710 hours. Allen departed forty minutes later.[35]

By March 13, plans changed. Greer had all of his battalions back under his command for the upcoming operation. His overall mission was the same—secure the northeast flank of the division. His staff issued the regimental order for the upcoming operation titled Regimental Field Order #14. (The division's orders were numbered differently.) In it, 2nd Battalion replaced 1st Battalion and would "secure LD [Line of Departure] prior to daylight D-day." Greer then added another task. He wanted Sternberg's command to "seize high ground vicinity of [Hill] 340; capture GAFSA GARE, and protect the combat team from South." Brown's 3rd Battalion were asked to "seize LALLA; and block EL GUETTAR Road. Protect left flank of Combat Team." And York's 1st Battalion, the reserve, also had the mission to "block" the road to Maknassy northeast of Gafsa.[36]

The regiment's S2, Capt, Henry B. Middleworth, estimated what his regiment could face in Gafsa. In his intelligence annex, he assessed that the Italian 7th Bersaglieri Regiment had two infantry battalions defending the town. Supporting the 7th Bersaglieri was one battalion of artillery, the 18th Carabinieri Battalion (military police), and approximately two companies of tanks from the Centauro Division. North of Lalla, he reported that the Italians had positioned two batteries of artillery. In addition, the Italians had established defenses northwest of Gafsa to block the Bou Chebka–Gafsa road. Behind Gafsa, he believed the Italians had positioned one more infantry battalion near El Guettar and more infantry and artillery in the mountains near Dj el Ank and Bou Hamran. According to Middleworth, the Italians were withdrawing this force southeast toward El Guettar. To disrupt any Allied pursuit, they were "leaving behind many booby traps and mine fields [*sic*]."

Allied analysts expected that the Axis could reinforce Gafsa or Maknassy with 3,000 *Fallschirmjägers* (German airborne troops) from the Ramcke Brigade. If they flew from the port of Gabes, then they could arrive in four hours. If they traveled by truck from the same place, then the travel time would be anywhere from seven to twelve hours. More worrisome were the panzers from the 15th Panzer Division. The Corps G-2 estimated that the Germans could send up to seventy panzers with an escort of 5,000 panzergrenadiers, and they would reach the battle zone in twelve hours. For air support, the Luftwaffe could fly seventy sorties on the first day of operations, and that number would steadily decline with fifty on the second day and even fewer thereafter.

At the end of the intelligence annex for Field Order #14, Middleworth concluded that the Axis would "probably hold GAFSA lightly and attempt a withdrawal to the southeast to take up a strong defensive position on the high ground DJEBEL ORBATA—DJEBEL ANK to defend the GAFSA-GABES road." He felt that the pressure from the British Eighth Army on the Mareth Line would not allow the Germans to shift forces elsewhere. Hence, the Axis would likely shorten their lines to more defensible positions behind the Italian First Army. Middleworth finished his assessment with a potential warning: "However, if Rommel decides to quit the MARETH LINE and withdraw to TUNIS—BIZERTI Bridgehead he will undoubtedly counterattack from MAKNASSY and EL GUETTAR and attempt to drive out our troops who have occupied GAFSA."

Middleworth was mistaken. The Germans did not have to quit the Mareth Line before counterattacking. Unbeknownst to the 18th Infantry's S2, von Arnim had the 10th Panzer Division in reserve. If he felt that the threat justified its deployment, he would commit it to save the Italian First Army.[37]

Despite the planning and preparation, no one could control the weather. On March 13, the late winter rains intervened. "Got signal to postpone two [days]," Patton wrote in his diary. "I fear Rommel will take the initiative. But I will not become defensive." Patton's boss, General Alexander, concurred with the decision to delay the attack.[38] Unbeknownst to Patton, Rommel had left on March 9. Von Arnim had assumed command of Army Group Africa. Other than minor reconnaissance activity, nothing occurred in the Gafsa sector during that period.

D-Day was now March 17. Even though the date had shifted to the right, many of the unit commanders initiated their respective movements prior to March 15. The Big Red One completed its movement to Bou Chebka and was in position on March 14.[39]

On March 15, Allied scouts indicated German reconnaissance east of Gafsa. The analysts determined they were from the 580th Reconnaissance Unit. The intelligence analysts poured through their files and discovered that the 580th Reconnaissance Battalion belonged to the 21st Panzer Division. According to their records, the battalion had one company of armored cars, an antitank company, an antiaircraft weapons company, and two companies of light artillery. A Captain Voss was the commander.[40]

The waiting was interminable. "I have had a horrible day," a despondent Patton penned. "Everything that there has been time to do has been done. . . . Now it is up to the others and I have not got too much confidence in any of them." The corps commander opined, "I wish I was triplets and could personally command two divisions and the corps. Bradley, Gaffey, and Lambert are a great comfort." All Patton could do now was pray, and he did pray that night. "Oh God help me and see to it that I do my duty but I must have your help," he beseeched the Lord.[41]

While Patton prayed, Dickson's intelligence collectors provided more data. At 1925 hours, Arab sources reported that around fifty Italian soldiers were operating near El Guettar. The Corps II G-2 disseminated this information at midnight to the various divisions, including the Big Red One.

Meanwhile, American units were staging closer to their respective objectives. At 2145 hours on the night of March 15, the 18th Infantry left Bou Chebka on trucks and rolled south to Feriana.[42]

At midnight, the division issued its final order before the operation. Field Order #18 had one significant change. Originally, II Corps wanted Allen's command to capture Gafsa and then wait for further orders before a possible advance to the east. Now, Patton wanted the Big Red One to seize both Gafsa and El Guettar. Allen passed the El Guettar mission to Greer's 18th Infantry.[43]

The next day, March 16, units began their final movements to their assault positions. Many of them left late at night after dinner. Patton was sanguine about the mission's overall success. "I feel well this morning," he wrote in his diary. "Actually, I am quite confident and not at all worried the way I should be." He then scribbled, "The hardest thing a general has to do is wait for the battle to start after all the orders are given."[44]

Patton visited Allen shortly after 1100 hours. He discovered that Terrible Terry's plan had no antitank support for the 18th Infantry as it approached the line of departure. He ordered Terry to fix it by attaching tank destroyers to the infantry. Allen obliged. The division commander then ordered Colonel Baker, the 601st commander, to allocate one tank destroyer company to provide antitank support for Greer's boys. Patton was worried that the 21st Panzer Division was near Gafsa. Although it was "supposition only," it was better to be safe than sorry.[45]

At 2030 hours, the 18th Infantry command post closed shop at Feriana. It would resume operations north of Gafsa early the next morning. Farther south, four mine detector crews from the 1st Engineer Battalion removed mines from the main road that linked Feriana and Gafsa. By morning, they had removed more than 2,000 mines. When the engineers were done, they provided security at the detrucking points as the infantry arrived. It was now up to the grunts.[46]

0130 to 1625 Hours, Wednesday, March 17, 1943
North of Gafsa, Tunisia
Command Post, 18th Infantry Regiment, 1st Infantry Division

At 0130 hours, Greer's command post resumed operations at its new location north of Gafsa. Within a few hours, the subordinate units began to update their status. The 3rd Battalion reported they were in position at 0630 hours, followed by 1st Battalion at 0700 hours. The 2nd Battalion was last to reach their assault position, as Sternberg signaled he was ready at 0850 hours. H-hour was 1000 hours.[47]

At 0945 hours, air support roared in to bomb the objective. Roosevelt watched the event as it unfolded. "I had a forward O.P. [observation post] where I could see the attack spread out before me like a panorama," wrote the general. "The planes came in a great, orderly flock, black dots in the sky. They swept over the objective and passed on followed by the thunderous rumble of their exploding bombs."[48]

The only major mishap of the morning was when two P-39 Aircobras mistakenly strafed several half-tracks in the assembly area. Fifteen minutes later, the soldiers of the 18th Infantry crossed the line of departure and advanced to their respective objectives around Gafsa. Within minutes of jumping off, Greer discovered the area directly north and east of Gafsa was free of enemy forces. Units were crossing their phase lines in minutes and hours instead of days. Shortly before lunch, General Roosevelt arrived at the command post to watch the show. He did not stay long, and he left to join Colonel Greer, who was observing the battle from an observation post closer to the fight.[49]

Roosevelt and Greer did not observe any fighting. This was because the Italians would not fight and die for Gafsa. At 1130 hours, regimental reconnaissance reported traveling twenty miles to the northeast along the Gafsa–Sidi Bou Zid road, finding no enemy forces. Another unit reconnoitered another road ten miles east toward Maknassey and found nothing.[50]

"One step was taken," Roosevelt recalled. "It turned out to be rather easy. The enemy ran. We came down to the attack in good weather—It was quite a show. It entailed a 45-mile approach over a plain that had to be made at night." To the son of the president, it was an adventure. "It was quite exciting as one never knew when one might run into the enemy cars or tanks."[51]

At noon, 3rd Battalion reported it was inside the town of Lalla. The 2nd Battalion was along its northern outskirts. Division ordered the 18th Infantry to "press attack—Develop El Guettar as soon as possible." The regimental command post relayed the message to Brown's 3rd Battalion. It read, "Recce in force to El Guettar—Continue present mission—prepare defense of town. [Send] motorize patrol [to] El Guettar." Back at the division command post, Colonel Gibb telephoned II Corps at 1255 hours to inform them of Greer's success in capturing Lalla. At 1620 hours, Greer's headquarters picked up, moved to Lalla, and reported it was open for business. The battle for Gafsa was over before it began.[52]

Like Roosevelt, Patton had found a good seat to watch the show. In some ways, it was underwhelming for him. "The great and famous battle of GAFSA has been fought and won," he wrote in his journal. "So far as I now know we did not have a single casualty."

Even though the doughboys did not need to fight for Gafsa, Allen's Big Red One still impressed Patton. "The show was well done by Terry Allen and the 1st Division," he wrote. "They jumped off at 1000 as per schedule but according to them [they] could have done so at 0700. . . . Allen did well and his communications and control were fine."[53]

Wednesday, March 17, to Thursday, March 18, 1943
El Guettar, Tunisia
1st Ranger Battalion, 1st Infantry Division
The evening of March 17, a reconnaissance patrol from 3rd Battalion, 18th Infantry, departed sometime around 2000 hours for El Guettar.

Several hours later, on the morning of March 18, the Rangers followed them with the mission to find the enemy. General Allen and his G-2, Col. Robert W. Porter, believed the Italians had more than 2,000 soldiers around El Guettar. The division intelligence officer also thought the Axis had forces east of the town, dug in and around the mountain strongholds of Dj el Ank and Dj Chemsi. Allen wanted the Rangers to "advance on EL GUETTAR, securing contact with the enemy in that area, develop his strength and dispositions, obtain identification."

"This mission is vital since we must develop the enemy and ascertain his strength, disposition, etc. in that area before being able to attack him," Allen wrote to Darby. The division commander had lost contact with the Axis forces. He needed to know where they were and what they were doing because that night he was blind.[54]

Lieutenant Colonel William O. Darby, the commander of the 1st Ranger Battalion, decided the best way to approach El Guettar was an assault from the mountains. He figured the enemy's defenses were oriented on the road, facing west. He would bypass them by hugging the ridge that bordered the north side of the town. Allen did not want them to wait until morning and ordered Darby's men to strike out at night.

"It was dark," wrote Darby, "but the Rangers like cover for our movements. In two hours we were approaching the town from the mountain side. Not a light showed in El Guettar that night. . . . Nevertheless, we had been told that the enemy troops numbered about two thousand; against that overwhelming force the Rangers' five hundred seemed puny."

For most of the morning and early afternoon, the radios and telephones remained silent at the division and regimental headquarters. Toward the east, a deceptive stillness was in the air. "Walking warily, our scouts slipped to the edge of town with other rifles and automatic weapons covering them, but no shots were fired," recalled Darby.

The ranger commander realized the birds had flown. He believed the Italians departed after they saw what was rolling down the road toward them, and he reckoned they had withdrawn east toward the hills and ridges that overlooked the valley. At 1625 hours, he reported the good news that the Americans now controlled El Guettar.[55]

1220 to 1630 Hours, Thursday, March 18, 1943
Lalla, Tunisia
1st Battalion, 18th Infantry Regiment, 1st Infantry Division

At 1220 hours, while the Rangers cleared Gafsa, Greer ordered York to push his 1st Battalion east toward the town of Lortress. From there, they could easily defend the Gafsa-Gabes road. York selected a spot inside a wadi, three miles west of El Guettar and just outside of Lortress. He anchored his southern flank on the highway, while his northern flank butted up against Hill 456 and Dj Seffaia Ridge.

Captain Sam Carter, York's weapons company commander, described the position. "Large rocks and boulders made a direct tank threat very improbable on this position," he wrote. "At our rear the ground inclined gently for 100 to 200 yards and then declined gently toward Gafsa. Our left flank was a sheer wall approximately 2500 feet high. The right flank was open and flat affording an excellent avenue for tank operations 1000 yards wide. South of this strip was a salt lake, Chott el Guettar, which was an impassable barrier for tanks and vehicles."

Carter explained why the main threat was panzers. "German tank units had been very active during the past five or six weeks in Southern Tunisia and were apt to strike in great strength most any time, any place, especially to regain an area that had just been taken from them," he wrote.

Thanks to York's terrain analysis, the wadi concealed much of the battalion from direct observation from anyone driving up the road from Gabes. For early warning, each company established an outpost inside one of the many gullies that crisscrossed in front of the wadi. York took control of all the company and battalion mortars so that he could maximize his indirect fire on a single target. Next, he ensured that all of his machine guns had interlocking fields of fire. For additional support, Greer attached a platoon of M10 tank destroyers from the 899th Tank Destroyer Battalion. York positioned this platoon in defilade and behind the front lines so that it could react to any panzer penetration. To block his southern flank between the road and the salt lake, the engineers emplaced a large minefield seeded with antitank mines.

To conceal themselves from artillery observers, York ordered his men to conduct most of their business at night. "The men did a good job of staying down out of sight, for units to our front and rear received occasional artillery fire but we received no artillery fire while on this position," recalled Carter.[56]

At 1630 hours, Greer issued Field Order #15. The regiment's mission was to "occupy, organize and defend GAFSA from the south and southeast against light arty fire." The 1st Battalion was the main effort. It had the task to defend against forces approaching along the Gafsa-Gabes highway from the southeast. The 3rd Battalion's mission was to block any enemy forces coming from the south. The 2nd Battalion was in reserve.[57]

Corps learned at 1817 hours on March 18 that the enemy positions in front of El Guettar were empty. The II Corps G-2, Col. Benjamin "Monk" Dickson, analyzed captured documents found in Gafsa. He assessed that the 502nd Antiaircraft Artillery Battalion and the *Reggimento Cavalleggeri di Lodi 15* (15th Lodi Cavalry Regiment) were the units around Gafsa when II Corps arrived.[58]

Later that evening, Allied intelligence sections knew more about the enemy forces occupying the hills beyond El Guettar. Colonel Dickson gathered that the Italians who had abandoned the town of Gafsa to the 1st Infantry Division belonged to the 131st Armored Division (Centauro). The division was under the command of Giorgio Carlo Calvi di Bèrgolo, who had been its commander at Kasserine. Allen now believed the Centauro Division was in the hills, overlooking the El Guettar Valley from the northeast and southeast. He was right.

Dickson assessed the division was in the hills, but he did not know which units were there. The 5th *Bersaglieri* (Motorized) Regiment, a unit of the Centauro, occupied positions along El Keddab Ridge and Dj el Ank in the north. The regiment had three battalions: the 14th, 22nd, and 24th *Bersaglieri* Battalions. In addition to its normal complement, the division attached the 11th Battalion from the 7th *Bersaglieri* to beef up the 5th's defensive position. For antitank support, the 132nd Antitank Regiment positioned one battery of antitank guns behind El Keddab. The division's 131st Field Artillery Regiment set up two firing positions for its 90mm howitzers in the valley northeast of the Dj el Ank as artillery support. Signals intelligence also indicated that the Centauro's 502nd Antiaircraft Artillery Battalion had withdrawn to the southeast of Gafsa and El Guettar.[59]

The next day, on March 19, II Corps G-2 informed Allen that the German 580th Reconnaissance Battalion was still in the area and east of El Guettar.[60] Corps analysts believed the bulk of the 21st Panzer Division was still on the coast near Sfax, Tunisia.[61]

The success of the last forty-eight hours stunned the Americans. The 1st Infantry Division spent most of March 19 consolidating and reorganizing around Gafsa and El Guettar. Pleasantly surprised, Alexander's staff at 18th Army Group ordered II Corps to maintain its control of Gafsa. In the north, Alexander wanted the 1st Armored Division "to secure and hold heights east of MAKNASSY and send light armored raiding party to airfield at MEZZOUNA, to destroy installations and return."

By this time, the British Eighth Army prepared to launch Operation Pugilist to penetrate the Mareth Line. Alexander expected success and planned for it accordingly. Once the Eighth Army advanced north of Maknassy after breaching the Mareth Line, the British First Army would assume control of the U.S. Army's 9th Infantry Division from II Corps. Alexander wanted Patton's three-division corps to "attack FONDOUK [Pichon-Fondouk Pass] from the west and southwest for the purpose of securing the heights in that vicinity."[62]

Friday, March 19, 1943
El Guettar, Tunisia
1st Ranger Battalion, 1st Infantry Division
Fortunately, General Allen had an excellent vantage point to see his new area of operations east of El Guettar. Shortly after the Rangers had cleared El Guettar, Colonel Darby ordered his battalion to occupy a piece of high ground, a kilometer east of the town, and establish an observation post there. On the map, it was Hill 276, but the Rangers called it "The Pimple." Captain Sam Carter, Commander of D Company, 1st Battalion, 18th Infantry, visited the post with his commander, Colonel York, and the other company commanders on March 19. He later wrote, "The observation was excellent. There we studied the approaches and routes of

advance to different parts of the enemy's position. Routes to the east were through the low hills at the foot of the mountains to the left or through the wadi south of the Gafsa-Sfax road."

Then Carter looked to the southeast. He did not like what he saw: "routes to the southeast were open, flat and void of cover and concealment of any kind," the company commander wrote. "There were not even any large rocks or small scrubby bushes. Just a sparse amount of grass six inches high covered the plain. . . . We left the OP and went back to our Command Post wishing all the time for any route except to the southeast."[63]

Colonel Darby later sent out patrols to find out the strength of the Italian units dug in around the hills. On their return, they reported the Italians had a regiment of infantry, up to two battalions of artillery, and some antitank and antiaircraft weapons scattered amongst the ridges. They did not see panzers. This was a relief to Darby, Greer, and Allen. Corps also reported several more enemy artillery pieces firing from the area south of Hill 336, along the southern edge of El Keddab. They might not know which units of the Centauro Division they faced, but they had a better idea of their strength. This information became far more valuable the next day, when General Patton ordered the Big Red One and the Rangers to take the high ground and the valley of El Guettar.[64]

CHAPTER TWO

Night Attack

"I feel that we will lick him so long as the Lord stays with me."
—LIEUTENANT GENERAL GEORGE S. PATTON,
WRITING ABOUT FIELD MARSHAL ERWIN ROMMEL[1]

1630 Hours, Saturday, March 20, 1943
Gafsa, Tunisia
Danger Forward, Headquarters, 1st Infantry Division
AT 1630 HOURS, THE DIVISION COMMAND POST RECEIVED AN ORDER
from II Corps "to attack east along the GABES Road and secure the
commanding positions east of EL GUETTAR." General Patton realized
that if he wanted to control El Guettar, he needed to control the heights
directly east of it. Fortuitously, General Allen had anticipated the order
and devised a simple plan beforehand.[2]

To accomplish the mission, the division commander and his operations officer, Colonel Gibb, selected three objectives. The northern
objective was the Dj el Ank. Allen described it as a "knife like ridge,
seven miles northeast of EL GUETTAR, which anchored the north
[*sic*] flank of the enemy's main defensive position." The center objective
was the Dj el Mcheltat, "a horse shoe shaped hill mass, eight miles east
of EL GUETTAR, which was the central [*sic*] back-bone of the enemy's
main defensive position." In the south, it was Djebel Berda, "a strongly
held mountainous hill mass, south of the GABES highway, nine miles

southeast of EL GUETTAR, on the south flank of the enemy's main defensive position."

The division commander's scheme involved two infantry regiments and the attached Ranger Battalion. To seize Dj el Ank, Allen tasked the 26th Infantry Regiment and the 1st Ranger Battalion. In the center and the south, Allen tasked the 18th Infantry Regiment to seize and hold Dj el Mcheltat and Djebel Berda. Colonel Greer allocated one battalion (3rd) for the center objective and two battalions (1st and 2nd) for the southern one. York and Sternberg's battalion had an intermediate objective to seize the small hill south of Hill 366, and after they secured it, they would continue on to Djebel Berda. To ensure complete surprise, Allen authorized a night assault.[3]

That night, the man who ordered the assault on the hills east of El Guettar scribbled in his diary, "I hope to get in tomorrow with the 1st Division. Both the 1st Infantry and the 1st Armored will attack. The 8th Army jumped off tonight. I think that if Rommel reacts, he will do it tomorrow."

Patton, who believed in Divine Providence, then added a final note for the day. "I feel that we will lick him so long as the Lord stays with me." Patton was both right and wrong. Rommel had left North Africa on March 9. The Germans would react but not until March 23.[4]

All Day, Saturday, March 20, 1943
Lortress, Tunisia
B Battery, 32nd Field Artillery Battalion, 1st Infantry Division
For the men on the gun line, March 20 was a reminder that war was a dangerous business, even far from the front lines. For several days, the Italian artillery south of El Keddab shelled them. On the morning of March 20, the Italians' gunners found the range and hit B Battery, 32nd Field Artillery Battalion, hard throughout the morning and afternoon. Captain Carter wrote, "As soon as they opened fire the morning of 20 March they were taken under fire by very accurate enemy artillery. Missions had to be cancelled, for the gun crews had to pull the lanyards and get into their foxholes on the double."[5]

B Battery relieved C Battery, 7th Field Artillery, the previous night so that the cannon cockers from the 7th could support the Ranger Battalion in the upcoming operation. Instead of doling out punishment, the red legs of Battery B were on the receiving end. First Lieutenant Francis E. Silva Jr., the executive officer for the unit, recalled what happened when they established their firing positions. "We went to 'register' with the 1# gun, having put our forward observer out ahead," wrote Silva. "But every time we fired that gun, we'd get four or five volleys of enemy artillery right in on the old 'C' Battery position."

Silva's gunners devised a simple solution. He continued, "So we attached a long rope to the lanyard of the #1 gun, the crew would get the gun laid, and then, starting north of the gun the crew ran like hell south towards a little Arab mosque down in there, and when they hit the end of the rope the gun would fire while they had a running start for shelter!"

To mitigate the effects of Italian counterbattery fire, Silva located three of the howitzers (tubes #2–4) north of the Gafsa-Gabes highway behind an oasis, while gun #1 was south of the road. For most of the morning, the Italians could not find the other three guns and spent most of their time harassing the team for gun #1. Then the weather intervened.

"Everything went all right at first," explained Silva. "I was careful to fire the guns one at a time so there'd be no big cloud of smoke gathering over us; But then [sic], on one fire mission, a freak breeze blew the smoke from #2 to #3 to #4, making it visible from way out."

The battery was exposed. The Italians quickly spotted the rest of howitzers. "It turned out there was an Italian observation post out on the escarpment to our left, and they got their guns to shift and then pounded the devil out of us! We got shellacked," wrote Silva.

The Italian gunners had set delayed fuzes so that they would not explode on impact. Instead, as the battery XO explained, "their incoming shells ricocheted off the hard shaly [sic] ground and scattered fragments all over, though they were just too long to our guns."

The deadly barrage resulted in six casualties. Silva later commented, "It was a hell of a time."[6]

2200 to 1000 Hours, Saturday to Sunday, March 20–21, 1943
Lortress to Djebel Orbata, Tunisia
1st Ranger Battalion, 1st Infantry Division
Elsewhere, planning for the upcoming operation continued. The most difficult task fell to the Rangers under the command of Lt. Col. William O. Darby. The West Point Class of 1933 graduate had served as aide-de-camp to Maj. Gen. Russell P. Hartle when Hartle was in command of all U.S. forces in Northern Ireland at the beginning of 1942. At the time, the exploits of the British Commandos dazzled the recently arrived U.S. Army brass. The Americans wanted to replicate the success of the specialized British units. The Army Chief of Staff, Gen. George C. Marshall, approved the request, and the Rangers were born. Then-Major Darby was their first commander.

The Ranger Battalion was not a typical infantry battalion. Instead of the standard three infantry companies, the Rangers had six line companies, and each company had only three officers and fifty-nine enlisted men, making them much smaller than their regular infantry counterparts. The first Ranger operation of World War II was the Dieppe Raid. Although the Rangers' contribution was small, it was a huge learning experience for them.

After Dieppe came North Africa. There, the hard training and meticulous planning bore fruit when Darby's Rangers knocked out coastal batteries at Arzew and *Batterie du Nord* as part of the coastal invasion of North Africa in November 1942. The Rangers repeated their success, raiding an Italian position two months later at Station de Sened, Tunisia, on February 11, 1943. They captured a dozen prisoners and killed more than fifty Italians. Their accomplishments impressed Allen, who decided to use Darby's men to spearhead the attack on March 21.[7]

Facing the rangers was an estimated one battalion of Italian infantry and several 77mm guns. The Italians' advantage was the terrain. Ralph Ingersoll was a correspondent who accompanied the Rangers on their mission and wrote a book about his experience titled *The Battle Is the Pay-Off*. He described the valley of he Gafsa-Sfax highway as a "funnel." Flanking the south side of the funnel was the Dj el Ank, and lining the north side was the Djebel Orbata.

Ingersoll wrote, "Standing in the funnel, the enemy looked at its steep sides rising 1800 feet, in some parts almost vertically, to [*sic*] sharp, jagged peaks. He [the Italian commander] said to himself: 'These sides are no problem, for only mountain goats could climb them. There's only the mouth of the funnel to defend.' So the enemy dug his positions and sited his guns and laid his mines and wire to make the entrance of the funnel impregnable."

The Italians left the mountains and, as a result, themselves undefended save for the few small observation posts "from which to look a long way off and give warning if the Americans were massing for an attack."[8]

The supposedly impenetrable mountains served as the Rangers' avenue of approach. Darby wanted to swing his command behind the Italian positions "by moving the battalion in a single file over the difficult terrain of Djebel Orbata during the hours of darkness preceding the attack." Then, Companies A, B, D, E, and F would attack abreast and roll down the slopes of the mountainside like an unstoppable avalanche. C Company was the reserve.[9]

The Rangers did not have enough organic combat power to accomplish the mission. Even though the battalion had six rifle companies, each company had only two platoons. Each platoon had only two assault sections. The battalion itself had no heavy mortars in its headquarters company. Each line company had only two 60mm M2 mortars. For suppression fire, the battalion had twelve .30 caliber M1919A4 machine guns consolidated in the battalion's headquarters company. In theory, the commander could allocate one M1919 machine gun to each assault section. It could strike fast and hard, but the Ranger company did not have the firepower for a protracted fight.[10]

To remedy this, General Allen attached mortars from D Company, 1st Engineer Battalion. In fact, by MTOE (Military Table of Organization and Equipment), D Company did not exist, but the engineer battalion commander, Lt. Col. Henry C. Rowland, needed more firepower and requested a change to his MTOE. With the permission of General Allen, Rowland then created a "D" Company for the battalion. This company had all of the battalion's heavy weapons, including the 37mm towed antitank guns. In addition, Rowland procured two 81mm mortars for the unit. In total, this new company had nine half-tracks, nine jeeps, nine antitank guns, two mortars, and several machine guns. For the mission with the Rangers, Rowland assigned the two 81mm mortar teams to Darby's battalion. Leading them was the D Company Commander, Capt. Gordon Pope. The mortar men called themselves "hell squads." According to Ingersoll, the name fit.[11]

Colonel Darby knew the trek would be tough for the mortar men. He asked Captain Pope before they left, "Do the engineers think they can keep up with the Rangers?" He did not record Pope's answer.[12]

At 2300 hours, the Rangers stepped off and began their ascent. It was a grueling trek. Gorges and gullies cut the route, so the Rangers used their toggle ropes to pull the men over the crevices and cracks that dotted the trail. The Ranger pace was too fast for the mortar men, and they began to fall behind. Lagging farther and farther back, the hell squads did not lose heart. They shuffled forward like persistent tortoises.

Ingersoll was with them. He later wrote, "Now I walked, watching the ground ahead, playing a game with the ground, trying to outwit it by finding spaces between the stones in which to place a footstep—or if there were no places, flat stones that would not tax my ankles. I could see now that it was going to be a question of how carefully I played that game for there was no reserve strength in my ankles, and if I put my weight on a foot that was not firmly on the ground my ankle would go and that would be the end of it."[13]

Soon, they were behind the Italian front lines. Everyone tensed. "The thought kept coming back to me that we were well behind the enemy lines now," wrote Ingersoll. "And we were coming close to a place where the slightest slip in the discipline of the march would count. The shuffling whisper of the hundreds of footfalls blended into a monotone." Occasionally, some careless grunt would accidentally kick a rock. "Then the heads in the column would raise in disapproval or to listen more carefully," recalled the reporter. "Each man in the column was feeling what I was beginning to feel, our nearness to the enemy."[14]

Up ahead, the Rangers kept going. Colonel Darby received a report around 0300 hours that Pope's men had fallen behind. Undeterred,

Darby found Pope and told him "to do the best he could." It was too late to turn around.

Still, Darby needed the mortars. "We've got to keep going fast now," the Ranger commander said to the engineer officer. "The attack begins at six. About eight we'll want your mortars, and will leave you out files, Pope, to show the infantry the way? [*sic*] They could get lost in here."

Pope said nothing.

Ingersoll was with them and wrote that Darby's "enthusiasm bubbled up again."

"You know what this means to them out there, don't you?" asked the colonel. "We've got to get this show under way on time. Their flanks will be wide open if we don't get this show under way on time. But I've got five companies past here and they are on up ahead."

Pope said nothing.

Together with two other Rangers, Darby then turned and faded into the darkness. Somewhere ahead was the rest of the battalion, and beyond them were the Italians.[15]

Around 0500 hours, the Rangers reached a sharp drop. Darby recalled, "The trail disappeared in a heavy shadow. There was a cliff ahead—the reason for the hesitation. Down the men went, one by one, passing their equipment from hand to hand. As each man got down he sped away in the darkness, leaving the men behind him with a choked-up feeling—they had to catch up so as to be with friends in the attack."

Darby watched as the last man in the column passed by him. He looked over at his executive officer, Maj. Herman Dammer, and several other officers and remarked, "Do you realize what we have done, men? Do you realize? We've got five whole columns through!" His elation and relief was palatable, but the approach march was only the beginning of the battle. Next, Darby's Rangers had to tackle an entire dug-in battalion of Italian infantry who had all their heavy weapons and artillery primed for a battle. Except, thanks to Darby's flanking movement, they were all facing in the wrong direction.[16]

The colonel grabbed his SCR 536 radio and reported, "Battalion ready to jump of[f] from position. 3rd Battalion, 26th Infantry behind us." His rear command post then relayed this message back to the division headquarters over a field phone. It was ten minutes after six when the division received the message. By that time, the attack had begun.[17]

Shortly after Darby alerted higher-ups, he heard the sounds of battle off to his right. It was probably from the 26th Infantry Regiment. It had started its attack at 0600 hours almost on the dot.[18] The colonel issued the order to initiate the assault.

"A bugle call . . . launched the attack. Under a heavy covering fire from the heights along the line of departure, the assault group swept down the slopes," wrote Street. "Surprise was complete! The enemy was caught totally off-guard. Many of his gun positions had not yet been manned and the few that were prepared were sited to fire down the road toward El Guettar."[19]

Farther back, Ingersoll and Pope waited with the mortars behind a hill. They heard the bugle blast. "Come on, let's go up there and see what's cooking," the reporter said to the company commander.

Pope motioned to one of his sergeants. "Give me two men for runners and wait here until I send for you. Keep the men together," he said to the noncommissioned officer.

The two clambered up the slope. By now, the sun was peaking over the horizon. BMCT, or Before Morning Civil Twilight, was at 0603 hours, which meant they had enough light to identify soldiers and vehicles. As they climbed, Ingersoll heard "rifle fire and then the heavy coughing of a machine gun, and finally a succession of explosions."

The reporter felt like he was "hurrying, out of breath, up the ramp of a football stadium with the sound of cheering from inside, knowing that the game had begun and that something exciting has happened but not knowing what it is and being excited and impatient." After several hurried minutes, he reached the top.

From his location, Ingersoll had a stunning view of the entire morning's proceedings. In the valley, he could see the fork in the road. From there, one highway led to Gabes, and the other, the one closest to him, squeezed its way through the "funnel" and east toward Sfax. Both highways had vehicles on them. Mesmerized, he watched the vehicles inch along the road to Gabes.

"The dots seemed to be moving, but very slowly," recalled Ingersoll. "They were in no formation that could be recognized but the front line of the field of them was a well-defined line."

Looking eastward, the reporter saw "a succession of little puffs of smoke." Wondering what they were, his gaze returned to the vehicles snaking westward. "The cannon in the vehicles were firing and those were shells bursting on enemy positions further out on the plain," wrote Ingersoll. "The little puffs of smoke were gray and hung above the ground for only a moment and then dissolved. . . . The sounds from them could not be heard above the noise of the rifles crackling around me."[20]

The Italians, along with their German allies, did not intend to lie down without a fight. They responded. Artillery began to zoom in and explode near Darby's command team, who had silhouetted themselves atop the ridge. The colonel spotted the source: a German 88mm gun down in the valley. He dispatched two squads to destroy the offending weapon. Ingersoll wondered if the two squads would reach the gun in time before it destroyed most of the battalion.

"And as I watched," began Ingersoll, "things began to happen on the hillside—sharp explosions, shattering sounds quite unlike the hollow BOO! [sic] noise mortars made. And with each explosion there was a scattering of rock, fan-shaped, and thin dirty smoke. Explosions followed one another and after each the smoke hung higher up along the slope of the hill. The last two of a succession of explosions were, one on the plateau just beyond where we lay, and the other on the side of the pinnacle, just under where the officers waited." The 88mm gunners bracketed the command team.

Ingersoll took no chances. He hit the dirt and lay behind a rock on his belly with another Ranger. They were so close together that their faces almost touched. Both wanted to hide behind the same rock. The nameless Ranger said to Ingersoll, "There are two squads down after that baby. It's an eighty-eight. It's over just behind the point—you know, the narrow place there."

Suddenly, the explosions ceased. The Ranger rose to his knees and said, "Yeh, they must have got it all right."[21]

Closer to Darby's location, an Italian machine gunner opened fire on the Rangers as they cascaded down the hill. Corporal Robert Bevan was a designated sharpshooter and carried a 1903 Springfield bolt-action rifle with a scope mounted on its receiver. Peering through the lens, he spotted the gun team more than 1,300 yards away. He adjusted his scope and loaded a round.

"I ranged in with tracers and then put two shots right into the position," said Bevan. "The machine gun was quiet for a couple of minutes and then somebody threw a dirty towel or something over the gun and the crew came out and sat down."[22]

Most of the Italians were unprepared for the Ranger onslaught. The Americans gunned down many of them as they ran to their positions. Many more became prisoners of war.[23]

Darby sensed the enemy was on the run and wanted to exploit the opportunity. He grabbed his radio and said, "Darby to C Company, Darby to C Company. We need a little bayonet work; we need a little bayonet work. Report to Lieutenant [Charles] Shunstrom."

By coincidence, Ingersoll had linked up with C Company, the Rangers' reserves. He was with Captain Pope when Darby's summons came over the radio. He heard another voice say, "C Company to Darby, C Company to Darby. Coming up, sir. Coming up. Over."

The response was immediate. Ingersoll described how "men scrambled to their feet, shaking the sleep out of their heads and some of them rubbing fists in their eyes like sleepy children." They grabbed their bayonets and clicked them onto the muzzles of their rifles while they formed a single line. Within minutes, the file snaked its way over the crest of the hill.

Ingersoll recalled that one soldier, not part of the bayonet charge, shouted to the group, "Bring 'em back alive, big boys."

"Bring 'em back alive, nuts!" replied one of the Rangers.

"You tell him, pal," added another.

After the last man left to join the charge, a group of soldiers remained. One of them said to another, "I bet they don't bring them bastards back alive. I bet they kill them bastards. They don't like not to kill them bastards. You wait and see, they won't bring no prisoners back."

Thirty minutes later, Ingersoll heard yelling and shouting, followed by a stream of tommy guns and the intermittent cackling of rifle fire. He decided to see for himself what was happening. From his new location, he could see a white flag pop out from the enemy position "notched into the side of the hill."[24]

From behind the reporter, a voice ordered, "Stay where you are, stay where you are, stop right there." Ingersoll turned around to see the radio operator. The voice was coming from his handset. The journalist recognized it immediately: Darby.

"Don't go in after them," Darby said. "C Company there, you there, don't go in after them. Make them come out to you." The men stopped. Ingersoll stared across the road to see what would happen next.

"There was a little wait," wrote the reporter. "The only movement beyond the road was the waving of the little white symbol of surrender. And then running, scrambling, trying to keep its footing and its balance with its little hands in the air, a tiny gray figure coming down towards where the doughboys waited. And then another and another."[25]

Soon, scores of Italians emerged with their hands above their head. The battle was almost over. It was after 0800 hours. Most of the Italians had surrendered, and all that remained was a nasty machine-gun nest and the last of the enemy reserves. However, the Rangers were pinned down and could not destroy the last enemy crew-served weapon. They had exhausted all their 60mm mortar ammunition, leaving them with only their rifles and light machine guns. This meant the Italian machine-gun team had more firepower. It was a stalemate.

As if by design, Captain Pope's tardy mortar squad arrived. They had fallen behind during the approach march, and they were tired and sore. But their guns were still operable, and they had plenty of 81mm mortar ammunition in their packs. Pope and Ingersoll directed the two gun teams to set up their tubes inside a hollow opposite the pesky enemy machine-gun team. From there, they were in defilade. To provide shell adjustments, the two officers located themselves on high ground to observe the impacts. Pope was closer and could see the target.

"The mortar was ready," recalled Ingersoll. "I heard [Pope] call out his estimate of the range and looked back over my shoulder to see one of the men by the mortar pick up a fat yellow bomb, brace one foot on the metal plate which supported the mortar and, with a quick darting motion, slam the bomb into the muzzle, fins first. Almost instantly there was a terrific bang, with a swishing noise in the echo."

The first round rocketed upward. For an instant, nothing happened. Then, Ingersoll saw the explosion. From where he was, he knew that Pope might not have seen the impact. So, it fell to the reporter to call out adjustments to the mortar crews.

"Seven o'clock and a hundred yards short," he shouted through cupped hands, as if he were a coach calling a play from the sidelines.

The crew hung another round. This was one closer, but it was not close enough. They tried a third time. Pope watched the round impact and decided the mortar crew had found the range. He ordered them to fire for effect.

"There was again the bang, the wait and the second bang," recalled Ingersoll. "There was a gusty crosswind blowing down the valley and the first of the bigger shells hit further away from the target. Its explosion was visibly greater. Whoever was in that machine gun nest now knew that the jig was up—that sooner or later we would score a direct hit."

Two more rounds detonated. "And then again, up came the white rag on the end of the rifle."

"Darby to Pope, Darby to Pope, nice work, nice work, over," Darby's voice cracked over the radio. Once again, a parade of prisoners appeared. Shell-shocked and defeated, they stumbled down the hill toward their new captors.

Around 1000 hours, the Ranger command post reported over the field phone to Danger Forward. "Have seen Colonel Darby," said the staff officer. "Everything cleared up except a few machine gun nests. 1st Battalion, 26th Infantry has reached their destination. 2nd Battalion has not yet arrived." Street and Darby both claimed they had collected over two hundred prisoners in less than few hours of fighting. Even better, the Rangers sustained only six casualties, none of them killed in action. Except for the paperwork, the battle for Dj el Ank was over. Along the Gafsa-Gabes highway, the battle was also nearing a climax.[26]

2200 to 0600 Hours, Saturday to Sunday, March 20–21, 1943
Lortress to El Keddab, Tunisia
1st Battalion, 18th Infantry Regiment, 1st Infantry Division
Like the Rangers, the soldiers of 1st Battalion started their planning late Saturday night. Colonel Greer received a summons to visit the division headquarters at 1740 hours. Twenty-five minutes later, all of his battalion commanders showed up at the regimental command post for a snap meeting. There, they learned that their regiment had a mission. All of them returned to their respective battalions around 2200 hours.[27]

When Colonel York returned to his command post, he gathered his company commanders and grabbed a wool blanket. The officers huddled under the blanket, like children reading books in the dark by flashlight. York briefed his plan of attack.

He explained to his subordinates the division's overall mission to control both major highways leading from El Guettar. In the north, the Rangers and the 26th Infantry would secure the Gafsa-Sfax highway while the 18th Infantry secured the highway from Gafsa-Gabes in the south.

Captain Sam Carter was one of the company commanders under the blanket. He later wrote, "The 2nd Battalion was to seize that part of the Oued El Keddab north of the Gafsa-Gabes road. The 1st Battalion was to seize that part of Oued el Keddab south of the Gafsa-Gabes road."

For transport, the men would take trucks from Lortress to El Guettar, and then they would debouch and walk the rest of the way. York was not thrilled with the prospect of loud trucks, rambling along under a moonlit sky, because "he feared the noise would draw a great deal of artillery fire on us but since other units were using motors anyway he finally decided we might as well use them." The men later thanked him because the trucks saved them from hiking an extra three miles.

The news about the vehicles was good. But Greer had selected York's command to tackle the southern avenue of approach, "the route most dreaded, the open plain with nothing between bullets and us," as Carter described it.

York outlined the plan. The order of march for the rifle companies was C, B, and then A. D, Carter's weapons company, would be last. C and

B companies each would have one attached platoon of heavy machine guns from D Company. The battalion's 81mm mortar platoon would transport their tubes on jeeps with the ammunition on the trailers. Since the men would be marching on foot, York dictated that the companies spread out to prevent an enemy artillery barrage from destroying entire units with a single volley.[28]

Later that evening, the trucks arrived, and the men climbed aboard. Carter wrote, "There was a light haze and a perfect halo around the moon. This gave enough light for the men to see how to move around, load and unload." In the distance, the D Company commander saw Djebel Berda to the southeast. Since he could see the mountain, he wondered if the Italians could see them as the trucks lined up as if they were starting a parade.

The convoy rolled out. "Our column moved slowly down the road," the weapons commander recalled, "turned south at El Guettar and then east again. The trucks stopped and we got off against a large dirt wall and formed up for the march across the desert."[29]

At 0310 hours, the staff at the regimental command post informed the battalions they had moved to their new location near El Guettar. Twenty minutes, a half-track ran over a mine. The subsequent explosion resulted in one casualty. It was the only significant incident prior to the assault.[30]

The soldiers in Colonel York's battalion continued their movement toward the knob south of the Gafsa-Gabes highway. "Our column suddenly reached the wire that marked the [enemy] minefield," wrote Carter. "Quietly and carefully we crossed the wire and the minefield. There before us was the objective."

The battalion was on the backside of Hill 336. Company C continued forward and headed northeast. At one point, an Italian sentry challenged C Company's lead element. Luckily, an Italian American soldier responded in Italian. It was enough to mislead him, and the sentry walked away. At 0530 hours, all battalions radioed that they were in position. The 18th Infantry command post called its division counterpart and told them that the lead patrols had reached the top of the hill south of 336 and "found nothing there."

At 0550 hours, the regiment added that it was ready for the assault.[31]

"Their [The Italians'] surprise at our approach from the rear was complete." remarked Carter. "It was becoming daylight rapidly and C Company did not want to be caught out in the flat. Their only cover was a small ditch and some grass that barely covered an individual."

Suddenly, an unidentified self-propelled gun opened fire along the battalion's eastern flank. The C Company commander, Capt. Herbert H. Scott-Smith, hesitated. He called Colonel York over the radio to ask for instructions. According to Carter, it was fifteen minutes before H-hour. Waiting for his commander's guidance, Scott-Smith realized the element of surprise was blown. So the C Company commander ordered his men to attack.

Carter later wrote, "This assault was so rapid and spontaneous that every man rose as one and moved to the top of the hill."

Farther back in the column, Colonel York heard staccato gunfire from Hill 336. It was now or never. He ordered the rest of the battalion to follow C Company's lead. B Company sprang up, ready to follow Scott-Smith's unit. However, C Company did not need the help. As Carter remarked, "The assault so caught the Italians off guard that the battle was over immediately."[32]

0600 to 1000 Hours, Sunday, March 21, 1943
El Guettar, Tunisia
Forward Command Post, 18th Infantry, 1st Infantry Division
At 0600 hours, 1st and 2nd Battalions attacked. The regimental staff huddled by the radios, waiting to hear more information. It was not long in coming. Five minutes after six o'clock, 2nd Battalion reported that Sternberg's men had reached their objective on the hill. At 0610 hours, York's battalion alerted the command that they were in contact with enemy forces. Almost simultaneously, Sternberg chimed in and told the command that his battalion was sweeping around the eastern flank of the enemy, but they were not in direct fire contact with them.

Greer committed Brown's 3rd Battalion into the fray. Reports were flooding into the command post. Fifteen minutes after six o'clock, someone radioed that they found an enemy artillery battery ten kilometers east of El Keddab. The command ordered the 32nd Field Artillery to fire a concentration on the suspected location. A few minutes later, York reported that his right flank was under artillery fire. In response, Greer ordered all of his artillery to conduct counterbattery on the offending Italian guns. The guns boomed.[33]

Rounds impacted on Hill 336 and on top of American troops. The 1st Battalion's artillery liaison officer barked into the radio that they were firing on friendly soldiers. His words fell on deaf ears. Another salvo detonated atop the summit. This process repeated itself several times. Colonel York finally grabbed the phone. Carter recalled, "The artillery said that they could see men on Hill 336." They could see the enemy, they claimed. The irate battalion commander assured them that the men were Americans.

"The artillery very reluctantly ceased their fire," remembered Carter. The time was 0727 hours.

Despite the terrible barrage, not a single soldier was injured or killed. "Fortunately the men of Company C were in holes and many ran behind the crest of the hill when they heard the artillery shells coming in," wrote the weapons company commander.

Greer's men had an impressive haul that morning. The regimental cage reported that night that they had processed more than 400 Italian prisoners of war. Most of them were from the Centauro Division.[34]

Not far from the regimental forward command post was the assistant division commander. As always, General Roosevelt was with the men, up front, and in the thick of things. In a letter to his wife, he wrote, "When the units were in place it was still dark. I went forward to the top of a hill where I had an O.P."

The battle began. He wrote, "By dawn the show was on. Machine guns spluttered, artillery rumbled. We caught the Italians unprepared. On the north we came down on them from the mountains . . . on the south we swept around their left flank. By ten the original objectives were taken and crowds of prisoners were being marched to the rear."

Interestingly, Roosevelt observed that when it came to the business of war and the treatment of prisoners, "our men will fight like the devil, but when the battle's over, it's over. They treat war like a football game. When the games [*sic*] over let's all get drunk together—They gave the prisoners candy and cigarettes and roared with laughter." Roosevelt probably wondered whether his men would share the same camaraderie with German prisoners.[35]

1010 to 1205 Hours, Sunday, March 21, 1943
Lortress, Tunisia
Forward Command Post, Danger Forward, 1st Infantry Division
At 1010 hours, Patton arrived at the division command post to observe the progress of the battle. He wrote about his visit in his diary that night. "Went to watch [the] attack of 1st Infantry Division. Had a good visit at Division OP but it was too far back so I went to [the] front and sat in [a] French farm [on?] hill."[36]

Colonel Gibb was probably happy to see him leave. He did not have time to entertain the corps commander and his chief of staff. He had a battle to manage. Fortunately, the battle was progressing according to plan, a rare occurrence. At 1014 hours, a staff officer from the 26th Infantry Regiment called him over the phone to tell him that the regiment's advance elements were east and north of the Rangers, who were consolidating on the Dj el Ank. Shortly before 1100 hours, Dextrous (the code name for 26th Infantry) called again to inform Gibb that they were "moving forward" and had established communication with their advance elements.

At 1205 hours, the good news continued. Dextrous reported they had rounded up fifty to sixty prisoners. As for their current locations, one Dextrous infantry company was on the Dj el Ank, while another company occupied the ground between Hill 621 and Hill 890. This meant that the narrow pass, Ingersoll's "funnel," was under complete American control. Even better, Dextrous claimed "no opposition." South of the 26th Infantry, along the Gafsa-Gabes highway, the offensive continued apace.[37]

Between 1100 and 1145 Hours, Sunday, March 21, 1943
Southern End of Hill 336, Tunisia
Command Post, D Company, 18th Infantry, 1st Infantry Division
After Patton's command group left the division command post, it drove east toward the front line. They found it at D Company's command post,

an old French farmhouse. With them was General Allen. Captain Carter vividly recalled the visit and wrote, "The D Company Commander [Carter] explained the attack and the situation to the front in few words, with the caution that they could be observed by the enemy and also, that as soon as the enemy had time to place their guns we could expect to receive artillery fire."

Sure enough, the Italian gunners spotted the gaggle of officers and opened fire. "Wheeeeee boom, boom, boom, boom," wrote Carter, impersonating the sound of the incoming artillery barrage. "A battery salvo hit the road to our immediate left rear. Since the Company Commander of D Company had just dug himself a hole on his OP behind a two-foot bank he made for same. Everyone else also made for the hole."

It was a dog pile, and Carter was near the bottom. Despite the suffocating atmosphere, the company commander survived the artillery assault. Patton reportedly uttered, "It's too damned hot. Let's get the hell out of here."

Carter smirked. "Never before has the Company Commander of D Company had so many 'stars' trying to get to the bottom of his hole," he later wrote.

Ironically, Patton did not describe the events the same way. In his diary, he penned, "Some soldiers told me the enemy were shelling [*sic*] it [the farmhouse] but I sat in. After a while I decided to visit 1st Armored Division and left [the OP]. A few minutes later a shell struck just where I had been sitting. It was a dud."[38] With the command teams gone, the shelling died down, much to Carter's satisfaction.

1130 to 1335 Hours, Sunday, March 21, 1943
El Keddab Ridge, Tunisia
Forward Command Post, 18th Infantry, 1st Infantry Division
While his division and corps commanders dodged incoming fire, Colonel Greer kept pushing his men forward. Much to his pleasant surprise, the morning's advance had been so rapid that he had to move his command post. At 1130 hours, a forward headquarters element took over operations from the one housed near El Guettar. Its new location was on the southwest base of Hill 336 (El Keddab Ridge). The regimental

commander wanted to keep the pressure on the enemy, and he issued a new fragmentary order to his three subordinate commanders who were with him at the new CP.

Greer's plan was clear-cut. He wanted York's battalion to occupy and defend Hill 336. Meanwhile, like a swinging door, with 1st Battalion serving as the hinge, Sternberg's battalion and Brown's battalion would sweep down from the north and push southeast. Sternberg would be on the left while Brown would be on the right, as Greer told them, "to secure the high ground six miles in front of Dj el Ank. 1st Battalion was in reserve—Time of attack was 1200 hours."[39]

Shortly after briefing his plan and surviving a harrowing enemy mortar barrage that damaged his jeep and left his radio operator wounded, Greer radioed his rear command post to share his strategy. Relaying the information, Colonel Gibb learned of Greer's plan at 1208 hours. He had no objections.

It did not take long for Greer's pursuit to achieve results. By 1325 hours, Sternberg's 2nd Battalion pushed up Hill 483 and along the rest of the Dj bou Rhedja while Brown's 3rd Battalion reported no opposition as it advanced toward the Dj el Mcheltat. Ten minutes later, General Allen arrived to observe the regiment's forward progress. His ears probably still were ringing from the near miss he survived at Carter's observation post. Unfortunately, the ringing was about to get worse thanks to the Luftwaffe.[40]

1350 to 1445 Hours, Sunday, March 21, 1943
El Keddab Ridge, Tunisia
C Battery, 32nd Field Artillery, 1st Infantry Division
Captain Allston S. Goff was the commander of C Battery, 32nd Field Artillery. That morning, his battery had supported the 18th Infantry Regiment's attack on El Guettar Pass. "There the 18th Infantry captured a lot of the Italian Centauro Division," wrote Goff. "They were absolutely demoralized. The Germans had just left them as rear guard to slow us up if we tried for Gabes and the sea."

Goff recalled one Italian soldier in particular. "One of the prisoners had a big wooden box," wrote the battery commander. "When I made him open it, it was filled with rolled-up woolen bellybands! The Italian soldiers were in cotton uniforms, and in the cold African desert nights [they] needed the bellybands to resist the cold."

After the 18th Infantry gutted the Italian defenses in the pass, the cannon cockers of C Battery established their gun line not far behind El Keddab Ridge. To adjust his fires, Goff ordered his observers to set up a forward observation post on Hill 336. "We had a good view down the valley, and in the distance saw all kinds of activity, most of it out of our gun range. Trucks, tanks, men etc.," recalled Goff. "We fired out there quite a bit, stirred up a hornet's nest I guess."[41]

Around 1350 hours, II Corps G-2 alerted the Big Red One that enemy air units were approaching. It was already too late. At first, they were tiny specks. But within seconds, they were over the valley. It was a lethal force—ten BF-109 fighters escorting twenty JU-87 Stukas. Their target was the 18th Infantry Regiment. For a Stuka pilot, cruising along at several thousand feet above sea level, a single infantryman was hard to spot, but artillery and vehicles were not. One of the first targets the enemy pilots identified was Goff's battery.[42]

"The German Stukas with their gull wings came past in a line, then peeled off one after another in these screaming dives and struck my battery from the rear," described Goff.

The JU-87 Stuka dive-bomber was the iconic symbol of Germany's blitzkrieg. In 1939, it led the way through Poland, smashing counterattacks and cities. In 1940, it tore asunder French defenses along the Meuse River. In 1941 and 1942, it continued its success, hunting Russian tanks rumbling across the steppes and British soldiers hiding under the sands of North Africa. By 1943, it was one of the older planes aloft, but it was still a deadly bird of prey for men on the ground.

With its telltale fixed landing gear designed for use on makeshift runways and inverted gull wings that made it appear like it was flapping, the Stuka lumbered along; its cruising speed never exceeded 390 kilometers per hour. It had a short range of 500 kilometers and a maximum bombload of 500 kilograms. Usually, it carried one large bomb under the fuselage and four smaller bombs under the wings. For strafing, it sported several MG 17 7.9mm machine guns, while for rear protection it mounted the MG 15 or MG 81 machine gun. Despite its low speed and limited range, the Stuka was a lethal and accurate weapons platform that was superb at killing men, wrecking tanks, and destroying artillery and even ships at sea. Added to this wicked combination was its terrifying siren called the Trumpet of Jericho. When it dove, the Stuka screamed, and for those cowering on the ground, it was a petrifying experience.[43]

Lieutenant Frank Silva's B Battery was also behind El Keddab Ridge when the Stukas struck. "I jumped into the ditch along side [*sic*] the road and in desperation was shooting my .45 pistol at those damned bombers," recalled the battery executive officer. "They came in so low that I know I hit them, but of course it had no effect."[44]

Goff's battery, though, was the main target. "I was up on the ridge observing, and when the Germans put one bomb right on the quadrant seat (the top of the breech) of our #3 gun, it blew a piece of the gunshield up to our OP," described the battery commander.

The concussion knocked over man and machine alike, while the fragment from the gun shield turned into a supersonic dagger. "That piece cut off Sergeant [Wadislaw F.] Wesgan's leg, right at the thigh. He was right beside me but there was no way to stop the bleeding. Nothing we could do," explained Goff. The young soldier from Worcester, Massachusetts, bled out and died shortly thereafter.

Goff had no time to grieve. The bomb had set off several fires in the area. If he did not act fast, the flames would cook off the artillery ammunition. They were discarded matchsticks, just waiting for someone to light them. "So I ran back down the ridge to where the gun's tires and tarred ammunition cartons were burning," he said.

When he reached the ridge, he discovered several more survivors. "The gun crew was still in the fox holes around the piece, wounded, and we had to get them out," recalled Goff. "From the rear of the gun position aid men would start forward, but then burning powder bags would go 'Poomf! Poomf!' and scare them back."

Goff knew he had to think fast, or the wounded would die from secondary explosions. He devised a simple solution. "I managed to scoop up and roll the shell cases in the sand and we got the fire out," he wrote. "Then the battery position men who had been hunkered down in their holes came up with medics and pulled the gun crew away from the wreckage."

The battery commander's courage came with a price. He burned his hands when he tried to roll the shells in the sand. It was a small price to pay. Despite the large strike force, the Stukas destroyed only one gun and one jeep and damaged the #4 gun. Thanks to Goff's quick thinking, that was it. The battalion suffered only twelve casualties that day. Most of them were from the bombing raid.[45]

However, the red legs were not the only ones who had attracted the Stukas' attention.

1350 to 1445 Hours, Sunday, March 21, 1943
El Keddab Ridge, Tunisia
A Company, 601st Tank Destroyer Battalion, 1st Infantry Division
First Lieutenant Lawrence R. Marcus was the commanding officer of 1st Platoon, A Company. The young officer from Dallas, Texas, had earned his commission through ROTC before the war, and the army recalled him to active duty in January 1942 after the bombing of Pearl Harbor. Now, he was in Tunisia, serving with the 1st Infantry Division.

Marcus had positioned his platoon along the southern edge of El Keddab Ridge. His company was in reserve. It was serving as an antitank counterpenetration force in case panzers appeared on the battlefield. It also provided security to the 32nd Field Artillery, which was less than a mile away from his position. Unfortunately, his tank destroyers, which mounted only one .50-caliber machine gun on each gun truck, were almost powerless against air attack.[46]

The morning had been a success. Up until that afternoon, Marcus's platoon had seen little action other than waves of Italian prisoners streaming back through the lines. Bill Harper, who served in C Company nearby, recalled the events of that morning. "The infantry took off in a line across the whole area. And the tanks were behind them, and tank destroyers were behind the tanks. . . . Then the artillery was set up in back of us."

Everyone had expected a long, bitter battle. Harper said, "They had estimated it would take three days to take them out, to take the hill, because [they] . . . had quite a few people up there."

Much to Harper's surprise, the big battle did not materialize. "We took the mountain in three hours," said Harper. "I've never seen so many white flags, I thought it had snowed, and it turned out that all the soldiers . . . were Italians and they weren't ready to fight. And here they see all this infantry, the tanks, the tank destroyers coming at them, and they were ready to quit. So that allowed us to get in position."[47]

For several hours, the men of the 601st rested and waited atop El Keddab Ridge. Then, the tank destroyer crews heard the wail of the air raid siren. Men scrambled back and forth. Some dove into slit trenches, while others got behind machine guns. Lieutenant Marcus chose to fight. He ran to his command half-track and jumped in the front seat, "where I had a .50 caliber machine gun, cocked it, [and] got it ready to shoot."

Within a few minutes, Marcus spotted them. "I saw these planes, about thirteen of them, coming over in formation . . . making a U-turn over the valley, coming from the east, making the turn to go back towards the east. And in the course of that, they were passing almost overhead."

Thomas Morrison was one of the soldiers burrowing under his helmet in one of the nearby slit trenches. "We were hit by German dive bombers as we sat in the open desert," Morrison shared in a postwar survey. "The only thing one can do is dig a deep foxhole, keep a tight asshole."[48]

Harper also recalled the bombing raid. "These Stukas would come in, dive bombing and turning their sirens on. . . . If they couldn't kill you with the armor [panzers], they'd scare you to death with their sirens, because it was kind of that weird combination."[49]

When Marcus spotted the aircraft, he opened fire with his half-track's M2 .50-caliber machine gun. The range was the problem for the lieutenant. His weapon had a maximum effective range around 1800 meters. The Stukas barreled toward him at 200 miles per hour, leaving little time to engage the target before they released their deadly cargo.

"So I fired several rounds, the machine gun jammed," Marcus confided. "[I] cleared the jam, fired it again. It jammed again. Fired it again."

One of his sergeants saw the repeated jams and rushed over to help his lieutenant clear the M2's feed tray. The platoon medic climbed aboard the half-track and plastered away with the other .30-caliber machine gun mounted on the back of the vehicle. Despite the fusillade, they were too late.

"Soon I saw a bomb coming down and [I] could tell from the angle that it was going to land on my right," said Marcus.

The lieutenant, the sergeant, and the medic had milliseconds to act. "I jumped outta [*sic*] the halftrack and before I hit the ground the bomb must've gone off, hitting the ground and going off," recalled the officer. "And the fragments went under the halftrack and hit me in three places." Shrapnel from the 500-pound bomb punctured his heart, his left arm, and his kidneys. The bombing raid resulted in the deaths of two soldiers: S/Sgt. Kenneth Lynch and PFC Henry H. Hunt.[50]

The bomb blast still ringing in his ears, Lieutenant Marcus was in shock. "The next thing I was aware of," recalled the officer, "I landed on my face and looked at my two hands and my fists were closed. And I tried to open my fists and I was able to open my right fist but I couldn't open my left fist."

His half-track was gone, but Marcus did not notice the bedlam around him. He could focus only on himself. "So with my right hand, I opened my fingers on my left hand and found I could retract my fingers. So I said, oh, my arm is still attached," the lieutenant quipped. Marcus survived the incident. Medics evacuated him to the United States for surgery and convalescent leave. He did not return to combat and received a medical discharge. His replacement was First Lt. Frederick C. Miner.[51]

Morrison was thrilled with the choice. He later commented that the new platoon leader "knew what he was doing."[52]

Despite the carnage and chaos, the damage to the division was actually minor. A fleet of Stukas and Messerschmitts had knocked out two artillery pieces, some jeeps, and a half-track. Considering the number of bombs dropped, it was a small price to pay.

The division staff believed the German army would not remain idle while the Americans consolidated their hold on El Guettar Pass.

1400 to 1940 Hours, Sunday, March 21, 1943
Lortress, Tunisia
Forward Command Post, Danger Forward, 1st Infantry Division
Division operations officer Colonel Gibb knew the American position was tenuous. Stukas had just pounded the 18th Infantry's positions.

He did not know if that portended a German panzer counterattack. At 1400 hours, he called II Corps headquarters over the field phone for reinforcements.

"What is the possibility of getting one company of the 899th Tank Destroyer Battalion?" he asked.

The officer on the other line did not have the authority to answer. "I will ask the Chief of Staff." A short pause followed. The staff officer inquired, "Did you see any tanks this operation?"

Gibb quickly replied, "Saw seven this A.M." He knew he had a better chance of receiving reinforcements if the panzer threat was real. He argued his case, "We are not strong enough on our open flank in case of a counterattack which looks probable." The corps staff officer spoke with him for a few more minutes, but they resolved nothing. Lieutenant Colonel Russell F. Akers, assistant G-3 on the corps staff, had to make the decision.

At 1426 hours, Akers rang Gibb over the phone. He wanted to know more information about the panzer sighting. Gibb replied, "Tanks were on the skyline at 0640 this A.M. We have eight miles of country, which is not tank proof. Tanks can come over the main road. The pressure at present is not too great."

Updating Akers on the air raid, he shared, "The Stukas were not shot down." Gibb's voice dripped with frustration.

"Do you plan to reorganize?" asked Akers.

"Yes," answered the division operations officer.

"When you are on your objective and reorganized let us know. Lay out your defensive position," Akers instructed his counterpart.

Gibb assured him, "Recon will be made on both flanks." He then said good-bye and hung up the phone. Matters were progressing, but Gibb knew the Germans were wily and cunning foes. He wondered when the panzers would appear on the horizon. And he wanted to be ready for when that happened.

Shortly after his conversation with Colonel Akers, Gibb received word that the 18th Infantry was still pushing and would reach their objectives by dusk. Several seconds after that report, the G-2 relayed the message that General Allen wanted the engineers to assist the 18th

Infantry. Gibb understood Allen's concerns. The Gafsa-Gabes highway bisected the 18th Infantry's area of operations. It was a likely avenue of approach for a German panzer thrust. The engineers needed to block that route with antitank mines to prevent a disaster.

Shortly before three o'clock, the Division G-3 contacted the 1st Engineer Battalion over the field phone. "What is the dope on the mines and wire?" he asked.

The engineer officer on the other end replied, "We have four thousand mines and three trucks of wire. All engineer personnel will help Combat Team 18." He then added, "We can get more mines and wire. At present, Companies A and B each have two thousand mines. We will get another 24-hours supply tonight."

This answer partly assuaged Gibb's concerns. He was not the only one thinking about the massive gap along the Gafsa-Gabes highway. An hour later, Dog Tag called on the phone. The 18th Infantry requested that the "minefield must be laid across our front. Need wire and mines. Two units of wire total."

At 1545 hours, General Allen called Gibb on the field phone. He had just left the 18th Infantry Regiment's command post. Thanks to his visit, he had a better appreciation of the tactical situation facing Greer's unit. He said to Gibb, "In order to provide AT defense to make up for what we won't get [this was in reference to the 899th Tank Destroyer Battalion], I want the two 75mm platoons from the 16th and 26th Infantry to go to the 18th Infantry."

Gibb jotted the message down. Allen continued. "32nd Field Artillery lost two guns," the general confirmed. To replace the losses, he ordered, "two guns are to be sent from the 7th Field Artillery Battalion to the 32nd Field Artillery Battalion. I want the ordnance officer to send two new guns to the 7th Field Artillery." For additional antitank support, Allen wanted the 601st to remain "flexible for use with Greer [18th Infantry]."

Eight minutes later, Allen called again and amended his original instructions. "The 899th Tank Destroyer Battalion should be dispersed for a defense to the north. The one company, if released to us, should be given to the 601st Tank Destroyer Battalion."

By 1630 hours, Gibb felt he had a better handle on the situation. He called Dog Tag to confirm their current disposition and inform them that help was on the way. "Tell Greer the engineers will do everything they can," Gibb informed the regiment's current operations officer. "He is getting a platoon of 75mm's from the 16th and 26th. He can have enough wire and mines for all he can lay. A battery of 155mm rifles is coming up. General Andrus will be out. Ammunition is under corps control but Eymer [the division G-4, Lt. Col. C. M. Eymer] will draw all he possibly can."

For the rest of the day and into the evening, Colonel Greer was on edge. At one point, he reported fifteen tanks attacking his 3rd Battalion. The clerk logged it at 1650 hours. The originator of the report was a patrol from A Company, 1st Battalion, 18th Infantry. According to Capt. Sam Carter, "This patrol had moved out about two and one-half miles to the east when they spotted about fifteen tanks and some infantry further east up the plain." The information even made its way up to the Corps G-2, who included it in his daily intelligence summary.

It was a false alarm. Colonel Porter, the Division G-2, confirmed that it was a false sighting at 1940 hours that night. His observers reported they saw nothing east of El Guettar Pass.

To mollify Greer, Gibb ordered the 601st Tank Destroyer Battalion to send out its Reconnaissance Company eight miles east of the 18th Infantry and establish a screen line. Its main mission was to provide early warning in case the Axis returned. Few believed the Germans were going to allow the Americans to consolidate their recent gains without a fight. For Allen, Gibb, and Greer, it was a question of *when* and not *if* the Germans would attack.[53]

Morning, Monday, March 22, 1943
Tunis, Tunisia
Headquarters, Army Group Africa
Field Marshal Albert Kesselring, the commander of *Oberbefehlshaber Süd* (or German Army Command South), pondered just such a counterattack. He expected a major operation to squeeze the Axis out of Tunisia that March. In the southeast, British general Bernard Montgomery's

Eighth Army had reached the Mareth Line and resumed the offensive against the 1st Italian Army under Gen. Giovanni Messe. Fortunately for the Axis powers, in the northwest, the British Lieutenant General Kenneth Anderson's First Army was dormant for the first few weeks of March. Kesselring later said, "We were greatly relieved when we saw no indication whatsoever of an offensive by British First Army."

Kesselring could not say the same in the southwest sector where the U.S. Army II Corps was operating. There, the Americans had started their push toward the sea. Almost immediately, the Italian Centauro Division yielded Gafsa and Tozeur to the advancing American and Free French forces by March 17. Kesselring was willing to give up Gafsa, but the loss of Tozeur without a fight was unforgivable. "I protested against giving up TOZEUR," wrote the theater commander. "The garrison there should have fought to the last man. It would have been worth our while to expend the garrison in view of the fact that it stood there, blocking the enemy's path like a fortress." At the time, the Italian First Army had their hands full with Montgomery's Operation Pugilist about to kick off, leaving the Centauro Division on its own.

Generaloberst Hans-Jürgen von Arnim, the commander of *Heeresgruppe Afrika* (Army Group Africa) and Kesselring's subordinate, was not as confident in his army group's ability to parry the Allied blows. By late March 1943, he was playing a shell game with his forces. This time, the Allies found the right shell. Within days, the Centauro Division yielded not only Gafsa but also El Guettar. Reports indicated the Americans were threatening Maknassy to the north.

By March 20, "Uncle Albert," his nickname among the troops, realized he had a fight on his hands. The obvious threat was in the southeast against the more experienced British Eighth Army. But the more dangerous threat was the U.S. Army II Corps, which, if successful, could cut through the Axis lines and reach the Tunisian coast at Gabes. This would isolate and cut off the entire Italian First Army and the *Deutsche Afrikakorps* from their supply base.

On March 21, Kesselring hopped on a plane and flew to Tunis to discuss the matter in person with von Arnim, who spent the night preparing his brief. The next morning, he presented his report. What Kesselring heard from his Army Group Africa commander did not inspire confidence in his subordinate. The field marshal recalled, "I noticed a neglect, incomprehensible to me, of the inside wings of the two armies [Fifth Panzer and First Italian]."

Everywhere in the south, the Axis forces were in danger of envelopment. The New Zealand Corps had flanked the Mareth Line by threading through the Tebaga Gap and attempted to penetrate the defenses of 164th *Leichte* Division. Farther to the northwest, Patton's II Corps rolled east. Kesselring realized that only German units could stabilize the situation. "On 21 March, the attacks of the American II Army Corps removed every hope that the Centauro Division would be able to hold the position east of Gafsa and the Imperiali Brigade that one west of Maknassy, which were actually favored by the terrain."

This worrisome realization was only the beginning. The enemy's objectives seemed clear to Kesselring. He wrote, "Although a clear or least approximate conception of the displacement of the enemy existed and conclusions could be drawn from it about the strength and direction of the Allied attacks, the Tunisia Army Group and the First Panzer Army [Italian First Army] remained in a remarkable state of apathy."[54]

As luck would have it, Patton chose an axis of advance that ran along the boundary of the Fifth Panzer Army and Italian First Army, exploiting a seam between the two commands. Therefore, it was not clear at first which command would deal with the attacking American force. North of the penetration was the Fifth Panzer Army, under the command of *General der Panzertruppe* (General of Panzer Corps) Gustav von Vaerst. Despite its name, von Vaerst's Fifth Panzer Army was mostly an infantry army. At the beginning of March, its order of battle included the Manteuffel Division (an understrength motorized division), the 334th Infantry Division, the Hermann Goering Division (which lacked its artillery component), and several ad hoc *marschbataillone*, or replacement battalions. It also had one battalion (*Schwere Panzer-Abteilung 501*) of the new Tiger tanks. However, most of von Vaerst's force was too far north to react to the incursion.

Along the southern edge of the American bulge was the famed *Deutschse Afrikakorps* under the command of *Generalleutnant* (Lieutenant

General) Hans Cramer. Unfortunately for von Arnim and Kesselring, Cramer's command had been battling the British Eighth Army since March 20. His two panzer divisions, the 15th and the 21st, were the mobile reserves for the Mareth Line. Therefore, he had nothing left to commit.

In response to American and British attacks, Kesselring ordered Army Group Africa to block the American penetration and authorized the dispatch of the 10th Panzer Division from the theater reserve to deal with the materializing threat from the southwest. *Generalmajor* Friedrich Freiherr von Broich, who had moved his division from Sousse to Mahares, Tunisia, on March 20 for such a mission, directed his command to roll out.[55]

When von Broich's unit arrived, Kesselring had already decided how he wanted the panzer division utilized. According to von Arnim, the 10th was supposed to conduct a "frontal attack" with all of its panzers against the 1st Infantry Division, which recently had captured El Guettar and was pushing eastward along the Gafsa-Gabes highway.

The field marshal recognized that the Axis needed to act decisively to prevent a complete collapse in southern Tunisia. "After the fundamental mistake had been made not to support the Centauro [Division] in the defense of the . . . strong position, a halt in the advance between Dj Chemsi and Dj Berda had to be attempted, in order to prevent an attack on the Schott Position from the rear," explained Kesselring. "That could best be carried out on that wing by a counterattack, which would endanger the northern wing on the Dj Orbata from the direction of El Guettar and in any case would make impossible a further advance along the road El Guettar—Mahares deep into the Tunisian theater of war." Kesselring chose Cramer's *Deutschse Afrikakorps* to oversee the counterattack.[56]

While serving in time as a prisoner of war, von Arnim wrote an account of his experiences in Tunisia. In it, he claimed this attack order from Kesselring was against Cramer's wishes. Likewise, in his postwar account, Kesselring challenged von Arnim's interpretation of the directive. "I do not recollect the wording of my order with regard to the commitment of the 10th Panzer Division," wrote the field marshal. "I have my doubts that the order has been rendered correctly, as I am sure I did not assign an operational objective to this half division." However, later on in his commentary, Kesselring seemingly contradicts himself. "I quite agree with the alteration of the command allegedly given by me." Regardless, von Broich had his marching orders from Cramer to strike the southern edge of the American penetration along the Gabes-Gafsa axis.[57]

Except von Broich would not have his entire division. Two of his battalions, 1st Battalion, 69th Panzergrenadier, and 1st Battalion, 86th Panzergrenadier, were headed north to stop the 1st Armored Division at Maknassy. There they would be under the command of *Oberst* (Colonel) Rudolf Lang, to form a *Kampfgruppe* (battle group) with other elements from the Fifth Panzer Army. Initially, this *Kampfgruppe* was under the direct control of von Arnim's Army Group Africa and not the Fifth Panzer Army. In short, part of the 10th Panzer Division was under the operational control of Army Group Africa, while the main body was under the control of *Deutschse Afrikakorps*. It was a tribute to Wehrmacht staff work that von Broich was able to pull this off with few hiccups.[58]

On the night of March 22, the truncated division with both of its panzer battalions rolled into its assembly area approximately fifteen kilometers east of El Guettar. With battle approaching, von Broich ordered his division to muster at its assault position at 0300 hours the next morning. Most of the German soldiers did not sleep that night. It was a full moon, so it almost felt like daylight, as the moonbeams reflected faded shadows behind the panzers. While some panzergrenadiers wrote letters, others just sat there, alone in their thoughts. Many of them were hardened veterans, and they expected victory. They believed the amateurish Americans would fold and run, as they had at Kasserine Pass.[59]

Monday, March 22, 1943
Western Tunisia
U.S. Army II Corps, 18th Army Group
General Patton's first major operation as commander of II Corps was, so far, a moderate success. Operations on March 21 resulted in the 1st Infantry Division bagging hundreds of Italian prisoners of war from the Centauro Division. The next day, March 22, most of the activity occurred north of the 1st Infantry Division, in 1st Armored's sector. There, Maj.

Gen. Orlando Ward's tankers finally captured the town of Maknassy early in the morning and continued eastward in an attempt to capture the high ground east of the town but failed to capture it by nightfall.[60]

Despite the successful capture of Maknassy, Patton was not pleased with his subordinate's progress. He wrote in his diary, "I sent Gaffey [Brig. Gen. Hugh J. Gaffey, Patton's chief of staff]. He did all he could but it wasn't enough. Ward has not yet taken Maknassy Heights. I hope that this will not be too much of a failure. I blame myself." At the end of entry, the corps commander scribbled, "I think the Bouches [pejorative term for Germans] will react this evening or in the morning. God please fix it up O.K."[61]

Further east toward the coast, the British Eighth Army hammered away at the Italian First Army defending the Mareth Line. The fighting was fierce. Colonel Dickson, the Corps G-2, wrote at 0925 hours that the "heavy fighting on [the] Mareth Line indicates bulk of Rommel's force [sic] there." To Dickson, this meant that II Corps had not achieved its primary task of drawing German forces away from the Mareth Line to allow the Eighth Army to penetrate the Axis defenses there. However, Patton's operation was far from complete. The Big Red One still had a few cards to play.[62]

0930 to 0955 Hours, Monday, March 22, 1943
Lortress, Tunisia
Forward Command Post, Danger Forward, 1st Infantry Division
At 0930 hours, Patton called Colonel Gibb over the field phone. Ward's lack of progress was souring the general's overall mood.

He asked the division operations officer, "How is everything going?"

"Okay sir," was Gibb's reply.

"Do you have the position on the right? [Djebel Berda]" asked the general.

Gibb sighed and answered, "No sir."

"Well goddamn it, get moving, and get there right away!" barked Patton, hanging up the phone.

Gibb had his orders. At 0955 hours, he rang the 18th Infantry CP. "We have to take something out there today [referring to the seizure of Djebel

Berda]. I got orders from the big chief [Patton]. I just wanted to warn you I am going down there with an artillery representative." Luckily, General Roosevelt was at Greer's command post, discussing the same issue.[63]

0945 to 1750 Hours, Monday, March 22, 1943
El Keddab Ridge to Djebel Berda, Tunisia
1st Battalion, 18th Infantry, 1st Infantry Division

General Roosevelt arrived at Greer's headquarters at 0945 hours that morning. Together with the regimental commander, the two officers sized up the situation. Thanks to their own reconnaissance, they knew the enemy was several kilometers to the southeast in the mountains and that one patrol remained on the high ground near Djebel Berda as an observer. Both men realized that to control the valley, the 18th Infantry needed to seize key terrain northeast of the Djebel Berda hill mass. On the map, it was labeled Dj el Kreroua.

Greer decided that York's battalion would draw this next mission. He wanted "1st Battalion to move forward and occupy positions to [the] right flank of 2nd Battalion." He then instructed Colonel Sternberg "to come in on [the] flank to aid 1st Battalion if necessary." For artillery support, Greer planned an artillery fire mission to commence at 1300 hours to suppress enemy defenses. Earlier that morning, the 32nd Field Artillery neutralized an artillery battery and six tanks while destroying two more tanks. These targets were just east of Djebel Berda. The question was whether the Axis had replaced those forces.[64]

York also was concerned about the objective's location. "This was another movement that I really sweated out in view of some artillery fire that we had been receiving," confessed Colonel York. "I knew that if the Germans spotted us moving across the desert to Djebel Berda that they could cut us to ribbons with artillery fire before we could reach the high ground on the other side, and frankly, at that time I did not see how in the world they could help but see us. I would have preferred to make this movement . . . at night time [sic]. Since we can't always choose our assignment, however, we had to move out."[65]

As planned, the battalion departed at 1300 hours. A Company led the way with B Company close behind them. Both units had a platoon of heavy machine guns attached to them. The infantry "moved out across the valley in a very extended formation sending one platoon out and then feeding the other platoons into the formation." Trailing behind the two lead companies was C Company and D Company, respectively.

Within minutes of crossing the line of departure, 1st Battalion approached its objective. Much to Colonel York's surprise, nothing happened. Carter later proposed a theory as to why York's command lucked out. "Actually the ground that appeared to be absolutely flat had a very gentle roll to it which was just enough to hide the column as it marched across the desert," wrote Carter.

Minutes before H-hour, Greer and Roosevelt moved to another location to observe 1st Battalion's deliberate attack. When they saw York's speedy progress, Greer's staff radioed a cryptic message to the division. "Group on right advancing. Jumped off a bit before one. Over to [the] mountain now. Took a defiladed route." To Colonel Gibb, this meant that 1st Battalion was closing in on Dj el Kreroua and was now climbing toward Djebel Berda.[66]

When A Company arrived at the base of Djebel Berda, it linked up with patrol that had left earlier and was waiting at their makeshift observation post. They were close to the objective, but they were not close enough. When York reached the front-line trace of his battalion, he discovered a problem. "The column could go no farther without exposing itself unless it moved backward and then circled over miles of very rough terrain," explained Carter.

Colonel York had a deadline. He did not want to skyline his battalion advancing toward Dj el Kreroua, but he also needed to reach it before nightfall. He decided that speed was more important. He did not like the risk, but he felt he had no other choice. The regiment was depending on him.[67] Sure enough, the German and Italians gunners spotted his column as they crested the ridge. Carter wrote, "All of his artillery and mortar fire fell along the column at a terrific rate in an attempt to halt the advance of the battalion."

Almost immediately, the unit started taking casualties. The men huddled behind whatever cover they could find. While Captain Carter hugged the ground, a messenger arrived to tell him that his company executive officer was dead and his mortar platoon leader was wounded. Thankfully, his platoon had evacuated him to safety. Carter ordered his first sergeant to assume the role of company executive officer and his mortar platoon sergeant to take command of the mortar platoon.

Despite the murderous artillery shelling and machine-gun fire, York ordered his battalion forward. He described the steel hell his men endured. "Resounding off of those hillsides and down through the valley, it made noises I shall never forget," said the 1st Battalion commander. "However, we continued to push on up along the mountain toward our objective."

When A Company neared Dj Lettouchi, another ridgeline sandwiched between Djebel Berda and Dj el Kreroua, a heavy machine gun ripped into them. One of the platoon leaders charged the position but was cut down in the attempt to remove the threat. York ordered the battalion's 81mm mortar platoon forward to silence the weapon.

Now in charge, the mortar platoon sergeant proved his mettle. He was with A Company's own 60mm mortar section when he received the order to take out the enemy gun team. Instead of going back to his platoon to use the 81s, the mortar sergeant chose to neutralize the threat with the 60s that were with him.

"The mortar platoon sergeant took one 60mm mortar, placed it just behind the crest and with direct alignment the first round fired hit the machine gun that was firing up the column," recalled Carter. "A second round was fired for good measure and the enemy machine gun was never heard from again."[68]

Meanwhile, Colonel York kept the regiment informed of his progress. At 1700 hours, his battalion reported that Axis artillery was shelling his column as they approached the objective. As fate would have it, by the time the mortar sergeant had silenced the enemy machine gun, York's patrols had found another, more concealed route through Dj Lettouchi. The rest of his command reached it shortly before sundown.

York described the spot. "When we reached the vicinity of our objective it seemed as if the terrain would just swallow our battalion. I recall uttering the statement 'All this and heaven too.'" The location, though, was not Dj el Kreroua, which was still farther to the east. Moreover, a towering peak loomed over their battalion's battle position. Carter wrote, "It was a position in a crescent but was overlooked by Hill 772 which was a wall of mountain, practically sheer, a thousand feet over our heads."

When the 1st Battalion commander informed his boss of his current location, Greer insisted that York continue his advance eastward. His subordinate responded that he had sent out three patrols to the north-east, east, and southeast to reconnoiter the enemy positions. For some unknown reason, this convinced Greer that York needed more assistance, and he ordered Sternberg's 2nd Battalion forward.[69]

At 1750 hours, Sternberg received the order to "attack [enemy] position from the rear tonite [sic]." The regimental command post then warned both battalions, "Be careful you do not shoot each other up."[70]

1615 to 2355 Hours, Monday, March 22, 1943
Lortress, Tunisia
Forward Command Post, Danger Forward, 1st Infantry Division

Colonel Gibb was well aware of Vanguard's progress that late afternoon and early evening. Around 1615 hours, a staff officer from the 18th Infantry called the division command post to inform him that 1st Battalion had made contact with Axis forces at Djebel Berda.[71] Fifty-five minutes later, General Allen called from the division observation post. He had been watching Greer's operation and could tell that the 18th had run into trouble. "Enemy is stronger than the 18th thought it was," remarked the division commander over the field phone. "East of the road, and behind the ridge are sixteen tanks, three batteries of artillery and some infantry. A patrol was shot-up. They [1st Battalion] are approaching the hill. The objective has not yet been taken."

For the next hour, the operations staff waited to hear back from their commander. Shortly at 1800 hours, the 18th Infantry reported that they had run into trouble and that a "platoon sent up was drawing fire from an Italian machine gun."

Within minutes of that call, General Allen warned them that he was running behind schedule. "I will be late," he said over the phone. "I want to see this thru [sic]. Tell Mason [chief of staff] that Sternberg is going to help York. This is a tough lot. There's a lot of accurate arty. Get word to II Corps." Allen wanted his chief of staff to know that Greer's 2nd Battalion was preparing to support 1st Battalion in the next attack. The Big Red One commander estimated the Axis strength to be two or three companies of infantry with one mortar section and two batteries of artillery—too much for one infantry battalion to handle.

Allen's staff obliged and alerted II Corps that Greer's regiment had stalled. In response, the corps staff logged the following message in the daily journal: "Going is not as good as expected. Committing a second battalion of Greer's 18th Infantry this evening."[72]

The Vanguard forward command post called shortly after General Allen's less-than-sanguine update about the Axis defenders atop Djebel Berda. Unfortunately, it was more discouraging news from the front lines. "The platoon sent up has worked itself within five hundred yards of the machine gun position," reported the regiment's operations officer. "There's strong fire and they are unable to advance. Five minutes ago, they were digging in probably against the machine gun. The battalion is sending an officer up there. We will let you know." Of course, unbeknownst to the regimental command post, York's mortar platoon sergeant had already knocked out the offending machine gun, but information did not travel as fast in 1943 as it does in the twenty-first century.[73]

Sometime after 1920 hours, Colonel Greer arrived at Danger Forward to meet with his division commander to discuss the solution to the logjam along the northeast of Djebel Berda. Allen's plan involved several moving parts. He wanted Greer to maintain control of Djebel Berda with 1st Battalion. He agreed with Greer's decision for 2nd Battalion to occupy Hill 369, "where it will extend to the left of 1st Battalion." Moreover, Allen wanted Sternberg's command to "deny" the road junction northeast of Dj el Kreroua, disrupting Axis access to El Guettar Valley from Gabes and points south.

Along the north side of the valley, Colonel Brown's 3rd Battalion would remain anchored on Dj el Mcheltat. Since the 18th Infantry's frontage now extended over ten kilometers from north to south, the division commander ordered 2nd Battalion, 16th Infantry, and one of the division reserves to conduct a reconnaissance "along the EL GUETTAR—GABES [sic] Road with a view [for] employment of 2nd

Battalion 16th Infantry in support of the 18th Infantry." To buttress Colonel Brown's 3rd Battalion, 18th Infantry, Allen decided to keep 3rd Battalion, 16th Infantry, near El Keddab Ridge, where it would serve as another division reserve. Allen assigned the entire 16th Infantry's Cannon Company and shifted one platoon from the 26th Infantry's Cannon Company to Greer's command to beef up the 18th's indirect fire and antitank capability.

For artillery support, 32nd Artillery Battalion moved forward one mile east of Dj bou Rhedja to support the operations of the 18th Infantry Regiment. When it got there, A Battery established the gun line for the rest of the battalion. From corps artillery, most of the 17th Field Artillery Regiment and A Battery, 36th Field Artillery Battalion, would perform a general support role. To provide survivability and countermobility support, Colonel Rowland's 1st Engineer Battalion allocated its C Company and one platoon from its A Company "[to] assist Combat Team 18 in organizing the defense of the area."

To reconnoiter the eastern end of the valley and the areas east and south of the 18th Infantry positions, Allen ordered Colonel Baker's 601st Tank Destroyer Battalion to perform a guard mission. Baker's main purpose was the denial of "all routes in the southern portion of the 1st Division Sector to enemy tanks." In addition, Allen ordered the 601st commander to establish two company battle positions in front of the 32nd Field Artillery's gun line, and these positions "will be dug in with front defilade." The division commander also wanted Baker to allocate one platoon for a mobile reserve.

To secure the 18th Infantry's northern flank, the 26th Infantry continued its push eastward with orders to seize Rass ed Dekrla Ridge. From there, Allen wanted the regiment to "push reconnaissance to the east in the direction of El Aiaoli and El Maizila vigorously and deny the roads leading to these points to the enemy." In addition, he wanted the 26th "[to] deny the road from Bou Hamran to Y-4173 [Dj Takadelt] to the enemy."

Meanwhile, the Rangers also had a mission. Impressed with their night-fighting capability and aggressiveness, the division commander allocated the division's northern flank to Darby's rough-and-ready brawlers. In addition to reconnoitering the villages and ridges of Sakket,

Djebel Hamadi, and Dj bou Smail, the Big Red One general authorized the Rangers "[to] attack enemy positions or strong points where found."[74]

Shortly after receiving the plan from General Allen, Colonel Gibb worked the phones to implement it. One of the first units he called was the 601st Tank Destroyer Battalion. It was 2027 hours when he reached its commander. The division operations officer did not waste time with idle chatter. "Just finished talking to the General," Gibb said to Baker. "He wants two companies deployed in front of the artillery to provide flanking fire. He wants one platoon kept in reserve."

Baker countered with his own idea. Gibb shot it down and repeated Allen's directive. "General wants two companies in front of the artillery," said the G-3, who then hung up the phone.[75]

Three minutes after Gibb spoke with the 601st, Colonel Akers from II Corps called him to find out his division's disposition. "What is the dope? Got where they are going?" he asked Gibb.

The operations officer then leaned over the map to explain his division's current state of affairs. "See where Hill 369 is?" asked Gibb. "Go northwest up to Djebel Berda—have that grid?" The operations officer probably paused so that Akers could find it on his own map. "Go a half inch from 369. We got a battalion on Hill 369."

"Any change in the opposition?" asked the corps staff officer.

His division counterpart replied, "Three batteries of artillery; one battery of big stuff—definitely well-organized positions. It's Italians." Gibb then changed the subject. "I want air support. Their guns are out of range of ours by five thousand yards," said the operations officer.

"Give us a specific time for what you want. Reconnaissance coming over there tomorrow morning," Colonel Akers assured him.

"It would be suicide to pull our guns out there," replied Gibb. "Sound and flash can't pinpoint them—it's hard for a plane to see them. We want eight planes for four hours' time."

Akers instructed, "Call back in about five minutes."[76]

It took the Assistant Corps G-3 more than five minutes, but he got the air support. At 2140 hours, Akers contacted Gibb over the field phone. "Alright we can give you all we can from 1000 to 1400," he announced to Gibb.

The two then argued over the merits of pushing out the artillery to support the 18th Infantry. Akers then asked, "How many bombing raids today?"

"About five," replied the Division G-3. "Three dive bombing, three bombing, and three strafed."

Akers inquired, "Losing many men?"

"Heavy," was Gibb's one-word reply.

"I'll see what I can do," responded Aker. "Call back."

Gibb hung up the phone and waited for more information.

Shortly before midnight, Akers came back with specifics. The Big Red One would receive three missions from the U.S. Army's XII Air Force. Each mission would have a planned loiter time of fifty minutes. He clarified the coverage. "It won't be continuous," said Akers. "You will have two and half hours when the planes are in the air; and one and half hours when the planes won't be in the air. It won't be the same planes. You'll have other planes from other missions as they come in that period. There isn't any fixed time. They may be called elsewhere."

They spoke for a few more minutes, and then Gibb thanked him and hung up the receiver. He wondered if the allocated aircraft would be enough to support the 18th Infantry and enough to scare off the persistent and pesky German Stukas. He would have his answer in the next twelve hours.[77]

2130 to 0100 Hours, Monday to Tuesday, March 22–23, 1943
Along the southern side of El Keddab Ridge (Hill 336), Tunisia
Forward Command Post, 601st Tank Destroyer Battalion
At 2130 hours, Colonel Baker received his marching orders directly from General Allen, who reiterated his desire to have two companies defend his indirect fire support assets. Baker's mission was twofold: protect the 32nd Field Artillery Battalion, which was displacing to a new location along the forward slope of El Keddab Ridge, and block a potential panzer thrust "which would cut the supply axis of CT-26 or CT-18 [CT stands for "combat team"]."

The 601st commander made a quick tally in his head of his available combat power. B and C Companies were at full strength, each with twelve tank destroyers. He had attached three 75mm guns to his Reconnaissance Company so it was above its authorized strength. However, his A Company was operating with only four tank destroyers since two of its platoons were detached to another unit as part of another operation. In total, he had six 37mm guns and thirty-one 75mm self-propelled guns ready for battle. It was more than enough to give a panzer *Angriff* (attack) a bloody nose.

For his battalion's decisive operation, Baker chose to place his B and C Companies in front of the artillery positions as directed from his higher headquarters. He ordered the two company commanders "to select, occupy positions . . . and dig in destroyers and machine guns, to establish lateral patrols and protect artillery units east of hill mass." He even specified how he wanted his forces arrayed. "Two platoons abreast," wrote Baker, "with one platoon echeloned in depth in each company. Mass of guns to be north and northeast of the GABES Road."

Baker devised a concept of operations for his shaping efforts. For A Company, the colonel ordered the one platoon "to defend pass on GABES Road, protect right flank and be prepared to move as a Battalion reserve." To provide early warning, he directed his Reconnaissance Company to send two platoons "[to] cover the movement of Companies 'B' and 'C' into position . . . withdraw to pass at daylight, assist Company 'A' and be prepared to move on Battalion order." The Reconnaissance Company's last platoon had the mission to reinforce the right flank of A Company and "be prepared to move on Battalion order." To ensure proper support, the 601st already had an ammunition dump colocated at the forward command post, east of the pass and north of the Gabes road. The main command post was several kilometers farther back and west of El Keddab Ridge.

Shortly after the tank destroyer commander spoke with General Allen and the G-3, he issued his orders verbally to his subordinate commanders. Baker was confident that if the panzers did appear, his battalion would have the upper hand because of the terrain. "East of our defensive position and north of the GABES Road are wadis and gentle rolling ridges with some knolls," wrote the commander. "It is favorable tank destroyer terrain with dry, sandy soil." Even better, for the defenders, the terrain turned any would-be attackers into a fatal funnel. "South of GABES road the terrain is very flat and around our right flank was at that time very soft and boggy," recalled Baker. "Previous reconnaissance had proved that even jeeps could not maneuver out of range around our right flank."[78]

Now, all they could do was wait. At 0100 hours, the two reconnaissance platoons pushed east and established a static screen line. Both platoons then made contact with 3rd Battalion, 18th Infantry, to the north and 2nd Battalion, 18th Infantry, to the south to ensure that they had no gaps for possible Axis infiltration. Everything was set for the division attack that morning.

"At this point," remarked the 601st commander, "the Germans seized the initiative and launched a surprise attack before dawn."[79]

0300 to 0500 Hours, Tuesday, March 23, 1943
Djebel Berda, Tunisia
1st and 2nd Battalions, 18th Infantry Regiment

The evening of March 22 and the early morning of March 23 were uneventful for the soldiers defending the southern flank of the regiment. At 0300 hours, guides from Colonel York's 1st Battalion left to rendezvous with the lead elements of Colonel Sternberg's 2nd Battalion. After they linked up, the guides directed E, F, and G Companies to their assault positions for the upcoming attack. The only enemy activities of note were random tracers and flares and some occasional harassment fire from Axis artillery.

According to Captain Carter, the D Company commander, soldiers from his battalion heard the droning sound of engine motors a few minutes before 0400 hours. The battalion command post relayed this information to his regiment, but nothing came of it.

Despite the troubling noises, 2nd Battalion moved into its assault position. At 0430 hours, Sternberg reported that his command was ready to jump off at 0445 hours as planned. His axis of advance was northeast in its orientation with E Company on the right and G Company on the left. F Company was the battalion reserve. York's Battalion also had a two-company frontage with A Company on the left and B Company on the right. Like F Company, C Company was the reserve for 1st Battalion.

At 0440 hours, the 32nd Field Artillery Battalion serenaded the Axis lines with an intense five-minute preparatory barrage. "This concentration ended with a round of white phosphorous from each gun which was the signal for the attack," wrote Captain Carter. Everything was going according to plan. And then the wheels came off.

"All of sudden at 0500 the noise in the valley to [the] north sprang into action," recalled the D Company Commander. "Luckily the trains of the 2nd Battalion had just moved into the hills to join us."

The noise was the 10th Panzer Division.[80]

CHAPTER THREE

Morning Attack

"When daylight came, the mist and dust started to rise from the valley floor, and the first thing I saw was tanks, German tanks. Straining to see under the fog, all I could see was tanks, more tanks, and more tanks."

—CORPORAL FRANK VINEY,
B BATTERY, 32ND FIELD ARTILLERY[1]

0015 to 0600 Hours, Tuesday, March 23, 1943
5000 yards east of the El Keddab Ridge (Hill 336), Tunisia
1st Platoon, Recon Company, 601st Tank Destroyer Battalion
FIRST LIEUTENANT JOSEPH A. GIOIA WAS WIDE AWAKE. SOMEWHERE out there were the Germans. He was the platoon leader for 1st Platoon, Reconnaissance Company, 601st Tank Destroyer Battalion. His platoon's job was to find the Krauts lurking in the darkness in front of his unit. Together with 2nd Platoon, Gioia's platoon was several thousand yards east of the 601st Tank Destroyer Battalion. To his southwest was 3rd Platoon, overlooking the road to Gabes.

Gioia's platoon had departed at 0015 hours and established its screen line at 0115 hours. His platoon outpost consisted of two half-tracks, mounting 37mm antitank guns, and one half-track with a 75mm gun. To guard against infantry, Gioia ordered his soldiers to dismount their .30- and .50-caliber machine guns and dig in.

At 0430 hours, Gioia spied something in the moonlight. He later recalled, "The silhouettes of foot-troops were seen and the rumbling of tanks were heard. At about the same time two men in a motorcycle and side-car came along the right into our position."

The motorcyclist yelled out, "Panzer! Panzer!"

One of Gioia's men, Technician Fifth Grade James Nelson, opened fire with a Thompson submachine gun. Bullets skipped across the ground. The motorcyclists did not have a chance, and their broken vehicle rolled to a stop. The two German soldiers, one of whom was bleeding from a bullet wound, threw up their arms and surrendered. The lieutenant reported the enemy contact to his commander, Capt. Michael Paulick. The recon platoon leader knew the motorcyclists were scouts, like him. The panzers were not far behind.

Fifteen minutes after the initial engagement, Gioia spotted the tanks. Even though it was still dark, the full moon provided enough illumination for the platoon leader to count sixteen panzers and several hundred infantry approaching his position on foot. He estimated that the mass of men comprised two companies of German panzergrenadiers. And they were only 200 meters from 1st Platoon's battle position.

"We opened fire with everything we had," said Gioia. "37mm canister on foot-troops at short ranges . . . is very effective."

Shrapnel raked the German lines. For a moment, the panzergrenadiers staggered and faltered. Paulick claimed that the initial fusillade inflicted fifty casualties. The company commander ordered his 1st and 2nd Platoons to withdraw back toward the rally point that was along the southern spur of El Keddab Ridge.

The withdrawal was not without incident. The 2nd Platoon pulled out at 0520 hours. Suddenly, a high-explosive (HE) round slammed into the platoon leader's half-track, injuring him. Moments later, another half-track caught fire.

Gioia and Paulick wondered how the German fire was so accurate at night. Searching for answers, they watched German tracer rounds crisscross through the air, scanning for targets. When a tracer bounced off a half-track's gun shield, the panzers then would open fire with their main gun at the spot where the round deflected. It was an effective technique.

By 0600 hours, 1st Platoon and the remnants of 2nd Platoon reached the rally point. Captain Paulick quickly tallied the losses. His 2nd Platoon leader was wounded, and the platoon sergeant was missing. In addition, Paulick had to abandon one of the damaged half-tracks. Even worse, one of his jeeps had run over a friendly mine, destroying it. It was not an auspicious start to the morning. Despite the mishaps, they had accomplished their mission of finding the Germans. It was time to let the tank destroyer platoons deal with them.[2]

0530 to 0615 Hours, Tuesday, March 23, 1943
Along the southern side of El Keddab Ridge (Hill 336), Tunisia
2nd Platoon, B Company, 601st Tank Destroyer Battalion
First Lieutenant Robert A. Luthi heard the warning over the radio from the Reconnaissance Company that the Germans were coming. In response, he ordered his four tank destroyers to move into their fighting positions. His platoon had arrived at 0100 hours and had only four hours to dig in. That was not a lot of time, especially when the only tools the soldiers had were shovels and they had to scratch out holes for vehicles like an M3 half-track.

Captain Henry E. Mitchell, Luthi's company commander, positioned Luthi's and the other B Company platoons in echelon across the southeast side of El Keddab Ridge to protect the artillery from probing German infantry. The 3rd Platoon, under the command of First Lt. Francis K. Lambert, was the closest to the road and was on the southern flank. Luthi's platoon was in the middle, while 1st Platoon, under the command of First Lt. John D. Yowell, was on the northeast flank.

Luthi saw the probing infantry first. "At about 0530 hours, I saw many men coming over a ridge in front of our position," wrote Luthi. "I waited until they were a thousand yards from our position, then I ordered all guns to fire. I observed our shells landing all around the enemy infantry."[3]

Although the venerable French 75mm was not great against tanks, it was lethal against infantry in the open. The gunners loaded HE rounds into the breach instead of the standard armor-piercing (AP) ones. The result was German infantry falling in droves.

Sergeant John C. Ritso was a vehicle commander in Luthi's platoon. When Luthi ordered his men to fire, he let loose with his 75. "I saw bunch of Infantry, about twenty-five, all in the same bunch so I fired on them with a couple rounds of H.E.," wrote Ritso.

Ritso described what happened after the rounds detonated. "The results were about six [German soldiers] left to get up and walk." The other nineteen lay dead or dying on the ground.

Despite the steel rain, the German advance continued. Their procession seemed unstoppable to Luthi. "The enemy infantry kept advancing under our fire, and some of them swept around our left flank," recalled Luthi.

Ritso saw the same from his position. "The Infantry kept right on coming and got within fifty yards of our gun position. Here we were in a valley where we couldn't get to them," said Ritso.[4]

Sensing that the Germans were about to flank his unit, Luthi acted on his own initiative. "I made a quick decision," wrote Luthi. "I ordered my platoon to withdraw to a hill about one thousand yards behind us, where A Company, 601st Tank Destroyer Battalion had their guns in position." The 2nd Platoon's withdrawal unhinged B Company's position, and it triggered a domino effect along the entire line.[5]

0600 to 0615 Hours, Tuesday, March 23, 1943
Along the southern side of El Keddab Ridge (Hill 336), Tunisia
3rd Platoon, B Company, 601st Tank Destroyer Battalion
First Lieutenant Lambert's platoon was the anchor for the battalion. His tank destroyers were the closest to the Gabes road in B Company. Captain Mitchell understood the importance of this key terrain, and Lambert's platoon overlooked this chokepoint along the road. Even though it looked like wide-open sand, the ground south of the highway was impassable. The mapmakers labeled it the Chott El Guettar, and the 601st Tank Destroyer's engagement area was along the edge of it. Mitchell and Baker called the sand "soft," and no vehicles, not even a jeep, could traverse it. If a driver tried, the loose powder acted like quicksand and trapped the hapless vehicle like a mammoth in a tar pit. Hence, the

German panzers and trucks could not maneuver south of the highway. Their mobility corridor was only a thousand meters wide and within range of the tank destroyers' guns.

Lambert saw the panzers before they saw his platoon. "As soon as the enemy clearly silhouetted against the skyline, I gave the command to fire," wrote Lambert. "My guns immediately opened up on the enemy."[6]

Corporal Harry J. Ritchie was a vehicle commander in Lambert's platoon. When he heard Lambert's command to engage the panzers, he ordered his gunner to unleash hell. His team had spied a Mk IV seconds before, and they hammered it with 75mm AP rounds. The first round hit the panzer. It shrugged it off. The second, though, caused the German tank to shudder and stop. Corporal Ritchie's team fired one last round to make sure it was dead. Then they turned their attention to another panzer lumbering down the road. Before the German crew could react, Ritchie's gun team plastered it four times. Interspersed among the AP rounds were ten HE rounds that Ritchie used to push back the swarming panzergrenadiers.[7]

Nearby, Sergeant James G. Horne's gun crew added their own hot steel to the fight. Unlike Ritchie, Horne had dismounted his half-track and crawled forward twenty-five meters for a better vantage point. He did not see any tanks, but he did see infantry—a lot of them.

Horne wrote, "I then gave the range to my gunner and we fired about twenty rounds of H.E. ammunition at them."

He heard clanking and rumbling over his right shoulder. "Just then to the right I spotted about ten or eleven tanks." Horne peered through the dust and smoke. He calculated the range at approximately eleven hundred yards and fed the data to his gun crew, who made the necessary adjustments on the 75. The gun barked five times. Two panzers rolled to a stop, wounded but not dead.

"We hit them low," added Horne. "It must have been the bogie wheel we hit." Although limping, the panzers were far from finished.[8]

Battlefield friction spoiled Lambert's schemes. Over the crash and thunder of explosions, the platoon leader heard over the radio the order to withdraw to their subsequent battle position along the ridge behind them. Lambert did not believe it. He called Captain Mitchell to confirm the command. Mitchell did not reply. No one did. All he heard was static.

Lambert wondered what was happening. Then he noticed his flanks. "When I looked to the left flank," wrote Lambert, "it seemed to me that all the vehicles in that sector had withdrawn, including two of the destroyers under my command. This left my two right destroyers completely exposed on the left and right."

With few options, the lieutenant from Hudson, New York, radioed the withdrawal order to the other tank destroyers. One of them hit a mine on the way out. The resulting explosion injured most of the crew while leaving the half-track a blazing wreck. Lambert was left with only three working M3 tank destroyers.

When Ritchie heard the order to fall back, he began to pull his half-track out of its fighting position. Meanwhile, his gunner, Corp. Frank Diaz jumped up on the M2 .50-caliber machine gun and laid down suppressive fire to cover their retrograde. The chugging crew-served weapon suppressed the onrushing German infantry and bought the time Ritchie needed. His vehicle reached another fighting position three hundred yards farther up the trail.

The corporal's fortune then changed. After firing five more rounds from the 75, the big gun jammed. A stray bullet had damaged the latch on the breechblock so that the crew could no longer open the breech to load another shell. When Lambert heard the news from Ritchie, he ordered the corporal to pull out of the line and head back to the rear. The lieutenant hoped that one of the battalion mechanics could fix it. To add to his frustrations, Corporal Bailey's half-track blew a tire. With Ritchie's and now Bailey's half-tracks out of action, Lambert had only one tank destroyer left in the fight. The battle was not even an hour old.[9]

0430 to 0710 Hours, Tuesday, March 23, 1943[10]
Along the southern side of El Keddab Ridge (Hill 336), Tunisia
1st Platoon, B Company, 601st Tank Destroyer Battalion
Along B Company's northern flank was 1st Platoon under the command of First Lt. John D. Yowell. The lieutenant from Dallas, Texas, com-

manded a hodgepodge force. Not only was he in charge of his platoon but, under his control, he also had one tank destroyer from A Company and three tank destroyers from C Company.

He knew the Germans were coming at 0430 hours when he heard the rat-a-tat of Nelson's submachine gun as it cut down the German motorcyclists. Thirty minutes later, he got the word that panzers were heading down the Gabes road. The platoon leader alerted his men.

"I told Sergeant [Willie B.] NeSmith to be especially watchful because he was nearest to the road," wrote Yowell. "He reported that a tank was within one-thousand yards of him. As it was still dark I told him to fire when he saw fit."

NeSmith looked over the barrel of his 75. He could not fire at the tank because he could not depress his barrel far enough to engage the target. Corporal Victor Hamel, who commanded the other gun truck, reported that he was not in position to fire at the panzer either. Yowell ordered his two tank destroyers to shift to other fighting positions.[11]

Meanwhile, other gunners were finding targets. Sergeant Adolph I. Raymond spotted three panzers plodding past his southern flank. Like NeSmith and Hamel, he was not in the right position, but he did not wait for permission to move. He acted on his own initiative.

"I backed my vehicle and faced it to our right flank and opened fire on a Mk VI," wrote Raymond. "Five rounds bounced off and the sixth one went home."

Sergeant Raymond saw Hamel and NeSmith pull out and ordered his crew to provide covering fire on a second panzer so that Hamel and NeSmith could shift to their supplementary fighting positions. Unlike the previous target, this panzer jolted and stopped after the first hit.

Before Raymond could celebrate, he came under fire from another group of tanks rolling past his original spot. The first hit ricocheted without inflicting any damage. The second, however, crashed into the M3's engine, and the vehicle began to smoke and cough. Raymond ordered his crew to bail out before it brewed up. As Raymond's men dashed across the killing ground to reach the safety of Corporal Hamel's vehicle, S/Sgt. Michael Stima, the platoon sergeant, opened fire with his jeep's .50-caliber machine gun to cover their escape. After they reached Hamel's M3, the corporal drove them back to the platoon command post. Although unharmed, Raymond's crew was out of the fight.[12]

The time was around 0600 hours. From the south, Lieutenant Yowell heard Lambert's 3rd Platoon open fire at the procession of panzers rolling past them. Sunlight was peeking over the eastern horizon, and Yowell had a better idea of what he was facing. Although the dawn's illumination was helping his aim, it also revealed how impossible his task was.

"I estimate[d] at least four to five lines with fifteen to twenty tanks in each line," Yowell later wrote. "There were over one-hundred tanks and I am sure of this statement. There were tanks in groups of 6's and also a column of tanks along the southern ridge."[13]

When Lambert's platoon began to chip away at the unstoppable panzer parade, the column reacted. Headlong, they pushed toward the source of offending fire. As a result, they exposed their vulnerable flanks to Yowell's platoon. Like most tanks, the sides were thinner than the armor on the front, and the exposed flanks faced Hamel and NeSmith's tank destroyers.

NeSmith did not disappoint. His gun team loaded an AP round. NeSmith sighted it on a panzer that was almost a thousand meters away but then ordered the gunner to hold his fire. Yowell inquired over the radio why the sergeant had not engaged the tank.

NeSmith replied, "I'm waiting until they can get a little closer and I can hit them for sure!"

The gunner finally fired when the panzer was only 400 meters away. The AP round hit the tank and popped off the turret like it was a bottle opener. Hamel remarked that the blast "sent the turret sky high."[14]

Hamel found success, too. He engaged one panzer, and within seconds, it caught fire. The loss of two tanks alerted the panzer crews that they were taking fire from elsewhere. Suddenly, Hamel heard pinging on the face of the gun shield and on the side of his half-track. His crew ducked down instinctively. The Germans had found them.[15]

Yowell recalled, "When the tanks located us they turned completely around and came back over the same route. I believe they returned because of the impassable terrain and also to put out our four guns out of action. When the tanks located our position, they fanned out and started towards us. All this time Staff Sergeant Stima was keeping a steady stream of 50-caliber machine gun bullets on the infantry and also pointing out targets with tracers."

The platoon leader needed the tracers. Raging fires and blinding dust obscured the battlefield. Even worse, German artillery used smoke shells to conceal the panzer column. Yowell needed to move to see his targets. Thin-skinned "Purple Heart Boxes" were not supposed to slug it out with tanks—that was not their mission. The half-track tank destroyers used shoot-and-scoot tactics to survive.

He ordered the remaining three gun trucks from his platoon to drive to the next ridgeline. To provide covering fire, he asked the guns from C Company to suppress the Germans while they moved. Sergeant NeSmith, Corporal Hamel, and Corp. Longin M. Meczywor then pulled out of their respective fighting positions while C Company banged away at the Germans.

The suppression failed. A 75mm round from one of the panzers slammed into NeSmith's half-track, instantly killing one of the crew and wounding the others. One soldier stumbled out of the track and headed toward Corporal Hamel's vehicle. Before NeSmith could drive out of harm's way, another shell detonated near the rear of the M3, immobilizing it permanently.

Corporal John Nowak was in Yowell's track and saw the round that knocked out NeSmith's vehicle. Four survivors climbed out of the stricken vehicle and staggered over to Nowak and Yowell's track. The lieutenant and corporal then saturated the survivors' injuries with sulfanilamide to prevent infection. The white powder made it look like they were stuffing the gaping wounds with powder sugar. After they bandaged the gashes, the platoon leader loaded the wounded onto a jeep that would bring them back to the aid station. Yowell and Nowak then removed the remaining ammunition from NeSmith's smashed M3, as they were running low in their own trucks.[16]

Elsewhere, the fighting continued. Despite their move to another position, Hamel and Meczywor could not make out targets through the smoke. "There was so much dust in the air that we waited for an [sic] half-hour so we could spot enemy tanks," recalled Hamel.

Finally, he saw a panzer through the haze. "I opened fire on the first tank and put it in flames, with my fifth round, which was a super shell on delayed fuse."[17]

Panzers were not the only targets that morning. Corporal Leo G. Cook was a gunner on one of the attached half-tracks from C Company. He saw a convoy of ten trucks in the valley and shoved a M48 HE round into the breach. Instead of the normal charge, he opted for supercharge, which gave the round a muzzle velocity of 1,950 feet per second—several hundred feet per second faster than the normal charge.

"I fired three fast rounds of Super HE into about ten trucks that had grouped together," wrote Cook. "I'm sure that two were knocked out of commission, the rest scattered in all directions."[18]

Although the panzers and trucks were dying, Yowell's was running out of ammunition and more panzers were approaching. He estimated that if each panzer required four to five rounds for a kill, he would run out of shells before breakfast. Each M3 carried fifty-nine rounds, and some of those were smoke projectiles. And more panzers were coming.

Suddenly, Yowell heard a loud thunk. Corporal Meczywor's vehicle sustained a hit. Luckily, no one was injured, but it was out of commission. The lieutenant ordered his soldiers to remove the ammunition from Meczywor's M3 and transfer it to PFC John Sauklis's vehicle, which was one of the attached tracks from C Company. Meczywor had already exhausted his supply of AP, so the only ammunition remaining were HE rounds. To make them more effective against tanks, Yowell instructed the men to use delay fuses.

The process was time consuming, and the panzer gunners took advantage of the stationery target. Without warning, a shell screamed and slammed into Sauklis's M3, shattering its White 160AX engine block. It was now a useless hulk.

Yowell realized they were sitting ducks if they remained in their current position. Hamel and the attached tracks from A and C Companies had fired all of their ammunition. Even worse, he had lost contact with his commander—not to mention that the German artillery had found the range, and shells were landing all around their position.

"The 88's on our left spotted us and started firing at us," wrote Corporal Cook from C Company. "Sergeant [Woodrow W.] Puckett's gun in back of me was hit and then they started adjusting on me. There were three vehicles about eight feet apart (Lieutenant Yowell's, Sergeant Puckett's and mine) and the 88's were coming so close, that I could feel the breeze."[19]

The platoon leader then described what he faced. "At this time we were doubly enveloped by enemy infantry and the friendly artillery had blown their guns and had gone over the ridge for at least thirty minutes. I heard and also felt a muzzle blast on my left."[20]

It was time to go. Corporal Nowak remarked, "Finally we realized that our platoon was about the only one left. It was there that Lieutenant Yowell distinguished himself. He maneuvered his platoon tracks from hill to hill always remaining in defilade. He directed the vehicles to safety and we were the last to leave the area. We didn't go as the tracks did but instead sought haven in nearby mountains. We picked up a couple of tracks from other companies on the way. All were without ammunition."[21]

With 1st Platoon withdrawal, B Company's original line was in tatters, and the attack was far from over.

0500 to 0650 Hours, Tuesday, March 23, 1943[22]
Along the southern side of El Keddab Ridge (Hill 336), Tunisia
2nd and 3rd Platoons, C Company, 601st Tank Destroyer Battalion
"An armored attack is coming down the road! Don't fire on us!" screamed a voice over the radio.

The frantic call was Capt. Herbert E. Sundstrom's first inkling that trouble was ahead. He must have thought "So much for going on the attack!" Sundstrom's command held the line between B Company to the south and C Battery, 32nd Field Artillery, to the north.

To defend his position, Captain Sundstrom established a defense-in-depth. To block the northern avenue of approach stood 3rd Platoon under the command of Second Lt. Charles N. Munn, who hailed from Jackson, Michigan. The 1st Platoon, under the command of Second Lt. Samuel G. Richardson from Tampa, Florida, was to hold down the southern flank. Behind them was the 2nd Platoon, under the command of First Lt. Lester D. Matter Jr. from Dallas, Texas. Matter's platoon "was directly behind the roadside platoon [Richardson's 1st] ready to move or back up any position." Sundstrom's executive officer was First Lt. John C. Perry from Ithaca, New York. His primary job was to supply the platoons with ammunition.[23]

Sundstrom was confident in his men's ability to defend the pass. He had learned a lot since the previous November, when his company landed in North Africa. "We went hull-down at every opportunity," wrote the commander. "If no natural feature existed we created protection by digging the destroyer in. Mutual support was by platoon. Three covering for one moving. No more than a few rounds from each position—then pull back and move to an alternate."

That morning, he felt that the terrain favored his tank destroyers. "At El Guettar, we had such natural mounds, etc. and that was our salvation," recalled Sundstrom. "Spacing of guns was not according to yards or feet but according to the terrain. Often a gun might be covering a wadi only."[24]

Several minutes after hearing the squawking on the radio, Sundstrom's company came under attack. "At about this time, a cloud of smoke enveloped the road and machine gun and cannon fire from tanks began coming from within the smoke screen," he recalled.

Lieutenant Richardson from 1st Platoon called the C Company commander and requested permission to engage the enemy. "I told them yes, if the targets were within range," replied Sundstrom.

The commander decided the best place to control the fight was with the 3rd Platoon, so he hurried north to meet with its platoon leader. Earlier that morning, he had examined the platoon's disposition and relocated each of Munn's destroyers. He was familiar with the platoon's defensive arrangements.

Sundstrom was right—from Munn's command post, he could see the vanguard of the German assault. Both counted each panzer and added the numbers in their heads. They confirmed their count of eighteen tanks with each other.

Sundstrom knew he did not have enough combat power to repel the German juggernaut. He grabbed the radio at Munn's dismounted observation post and ordered Lieutenant Matter from 2nd Platoon to reinforce 3rd Platoon with a section of two tank destroyers. The company commander then called the battalion command post to alert Colonel Baker of the German envelopment. Baker reminded him to hold the line.

The Cornhusker commander from Plattsmouth, Nebraska, estimated his ammunition needs and realized that his platoons would expend all their ordnance before the Germans ran out of panzers. He summoned his executive officer, Lieutenant Perry, and ordered him to laager the ammunition trucks at the entrance to the pass so that the platoons would not have too far to travel to restock their gun trucks.[25]

Minutes after Captain Sundstrom's conversation with Lieutenant Perry, 2nd Platoon Leader Lieutenant Matter arrived with a section of two M3s. Sundstrom escorted the section to a spot past the northern flank of 3rd Platoon.

Corporal Salvatore H. Migliaccio was one of the halftrack commanders from Matter's reserve. "Platoon commander [Lieutenant Matter] led us to our position where we were in full view of the proceedings taking place in the valley beneath us," recounted the corporal from White Plains, New York. "Keeping in touch by radio, as well as possible, we opened fire on the vehicles which were identified as tanks, using few AP, for sensing, but on the average using a preponderance of HE." Migliaccio's arrival was just in time.[26]

Lieutenant Munn described the initial German fusillade: "The lead tank of this column was laying a smoke screen through which other tanks were advancing. Two tanks were also firing tracers from their machine guns, and wherever these tracers would ricochet, they would fire a round."

The Wolverine lieutenant ordered his tank destroyers to engage the advancing panzers. Sergeant Allen Breed's M3 fired first. His aim was true, and a Mk IV panzer exploded after sustaining a hit from Breed's 75. Moments later, Corporal Kenneth D. Kalwite's and another track lit up two more.

Sergeant Robert C. McElroy from Lexington, Virginia, was a halftrack commander from Lieutenant Matter's 2nd Platoon on the northern flank. He recalled that the initial German onslaught was more bark than bite. "After the battle started, I was sent to the left flank, under a hail of machine-gun fire and artillery which I took to be an 88mm gun. Most of the machine guns [were] being fired for demoralizing effect only, I think, although some were pointing out our guns with tracers, which immediately brought down artillery fire on us."

McElroy kept driving until he found a gulch so that his half-track could have defilade from the panzers. Inside the gulch, he still could see the whole valley. "The tanks by then were covered with smoke and also being fired upon by several guns, which made sensing of shots difficult," wrote the sergeant. "We got one tank and saw several burst into flames, but [I] do not think it was our shots that caused the effect."[27]

Not far from McElroy was Bill Harper. Harper recalled the scouts' final report as they passed through their lines earlier that morning. "Let the first five through, give the rest of 'em hell," remarked the half-track driver.

After sunrise, he counted seventy-five panzers rolling toward him. "It looked like a parade," said Harper.

It was time to play hide-and-seek. "We're behind the top of the hills," said Harper, "and we'd pull up and fire and then back down."

It was the only way for the half-tracks to survive. Harper knew that if he stayed in one place too long, a Panzergranate 39 round from a Mk IV would turn his half-track into molten metal. He remembered another M3 half-track driver that suffered some hard luck. "Every time he'd pull up, they [panzers] were shooting at him before he could get up to where he could shoot, and he couldn't figure out why they knew he was there," said Harper.

The sergeant from Mount Pleasant, Texas, looked at the other track to see what was wrong. He spotted the problem. "We had about a twelve foot radio antenna mounted on the windshield, and they were seeing that antenna and knew he was coming up," explained Harper. "And each time he got up there, they relayed in on him."

Even though hell was exploding around him, Harper marveled at the bravery of the German panzer crews. "One of the things you had to admire about the German solider was, we knock out a tank and the crewmen, if they weren't hurt, they would take their machine gun off the tank and ground mount it and lay there and keep shooting," recalled the sergeant.[28]

Despite German determination and grit, the tank destroyers from 3rd Platoon continued to exact a heavy toll on the panzers. Corporal James E. Markle wounded one with a single round. Before Markle hit them a second time, two of the crew tried to escape. Sergeant Milford D. Langleis, who was manning a dismounted M2 .50-caliber machine gun at Lieutenant Munn's observation post, saw the desperate men as they climbed out of the smoldering and smoking steel trap before the fire consumed them. He depressed the butterfly trigger with his thumbs, sending a stream of slugs toward the two figures. The solid metal bullets ripped through the two doomed soldiers, killing them instantly.

Munn observed the panzers recoil and withdraw out of range of the C Company tank destroyers. Munn believed the Germans were pulling back to regroup. "This ended the first wave of the attack," wrote the platoon leader.[29]

0500 to 0947 Hours, Tuesday, March 23, 1943[30]
Along the southern side of El Keddab Ridge (Hill 336), Tunisia
1st Platoon, C Company, 601st Tank Destroyer Battalion
Lieutenant Richardson wondered why things went wrong at the wrong time. After receiving permission from his commander to open fire on the panzer swarm in front of him, he tried to raise his men over the platoon radio. He heard only static. Forced to rely on the same methods the Union army used in the Civil War, Richardson grabbed one of his soldiers and told him to run to each tank destroyer and give them the message to engage the enemy. The young GI dashed into the darkness. Several minutes later, Richardson's gun trucks opened fire.[31]

Sergeant Louis J. Bednarz from Long Island, New York, commanded one of Richardson's gun trucks. "The first thing we heard was enemy machine gun firing. The gunner looked through his sight and couldn't see anything," said Bednarz. The sergeant then peered through his binoculars, hoping to see something. "I couldn't see a thing," he recalled, "except tracers from the enemy machine guns."

Bednarz picked up his radio and called his platoon leader. Like his lieutenant, all he heard was silence. The M3 commander warned his men to keep "a sharp lookout for enemy infantry."

Finally, around 0600 hours, it was light enough to see. Bednarz saw that the hillside was crawling with enemy infantry.

"I gave my commands and my crew went into action," wrote Bednarz. "We threw out about twenty round of H.E. Normal and the infantry stopped their advance."

Shortly after dealing with the panzergrenadiers, the NCO from Long Island noticed the procession of panzers along the ridge. "We saw the enemy tanks lined up in the background. They were lined up pretty close. . . . Again my crew went into action and started firing at these tank[s]."[32]

Off on Bednarz's flank was Sgt. Henry G. Manning's gun truck. Manning was a Razorback from Fort Smith, Arkansas, where they hunted hogs. But on March 23, Manning was hunting panzers. "After daybreak and it became light, we were able to pick out targets," wrote Manning. "I picked out a tank, called my range and after a few rounds, the tank started to smoke."

With one panzer down, Manning turned his attention to another target and spotted what he thought was one of the new Tiger I panzers. "We kept firing at this tank and after several rounds, the tank stopped moving, although it was not on fire or smoking," remembered Manning. The sergeant ordered his driver to shift positions so that German gunners would not get a bead on his half-track, and they withdrew to another location.[33]

Sergeant Steve Futuluychuk also was half-track commander in 1st Platoon. Like his fellow NCO, Sergeant Bednarz, Futuluychuk reported hearing enemy machine guns first that morning at 0500 hours. Unlike Bednarz, the young NCO from Troy, New York, waited for confirmation from Lieutenant Richardson before he engaged the enemy. After hearing from the platoon leader's runner to open fire, Futuluychuk's crew obliged.

"It was still dark when we opened up, daylight just breaking," recounted the sergeant. "My gunner sent two tanks up in smoke and I another. I'm positive of three tanks going up in smoke."[34]

From his observation post, Richardson watched the panzers brew up. He tallied the German losses. He later recounted that his men and

1st Platoon, B Company, had destroyed three or four Mk IVs and three other tanks of unknown type. He dispatched a messenger to Lieutenant Yowell's platoon to check their status.

While the 1st Platoon Leader tried to regain contact with his flanks, his men loaded up on more ammunition for the next fight. Sergeants Bednarz and Futuluychuk withdrew from the ridge and linked up with Lieutenant Perry, the executive officer, near the entrance to the mountain pass. Perry was looking for Lieutenant Munn's platoon when he ran into the two NCOs and Sgt. Herman C. Bartling. Bartling's half-track was attached to Lieutenant Yowell's platoon in B Company. They all needed AP and HE rounds, so the executive officer emptied his ammunition half-track for them. Sergeant Futuluychuk recalled that Lieutenant Perry allocated more than forty rounds of HE with normal fuses to his crew. With a fresh load, he hoped it was enough to stop the next German assault.[35]

Meanwhile, the runner returned from B Company and reported to Lieutenant Richardson that Lieutenant Yowell still had two working 75s and one abandoned M3. Richardson explained, "I told the messenger to get some of the men out of the anti-aircraft section and go run the gun." The lieutenant did not know that the abandoned gun truck was probably Sergeant NeSmith's gun truck or one of the other knocked-out half-tracks Yowell's men had evacuated.

The Germans disrupted the platoon leader's plan. "As he [the messenger] and the crew started to go over the ridge, a heavy artillery barrage came down on the ridge behind us."[36]

Sergeant Bednarz felt the Germans were aiming their artillery on his gun truck. "They finally started to get a bracket on my gun emplacement," he wrote. "So, I told my driver to turn the motor over and pull into another position." His gun truck withdrew behind the nearby 5th Field Artillery Battalion.[37]

Others also felt the heat from the German guns. Similarly, Sergeant Manning explained, "They [Germans] had a bracket on the gun, so I told the driver to back around a knoll, pull in a ditch and wait to see what was going to happen."

Fate enforced Murphy's Law. As Manning's driver pulled out of the ditch, the M3 threw a track. They were stuck. And they were under machine-gun fire from German infantry.

Manning recounted what happened next. "A Field Artillery Lieutenant [most likely Lieutenant Yowell] told us to leave and get out of there, as the enemy had the range on us." The crew grabbed their weapons and abandoned their M3. For them, the battle was over.[38]

Futuluychuk's team was not far from Manning's half-track when the artillery barrage exploded on them like a sudden hailstorm. Despite bursting shrapnel, his crew kept fighting. Finally, Lieutenant Yowell, the only officer left on the ridge, ordered the sergeant to fall back. Futuluychuk was happy to obey. A piece of shrapnel had clipped the barrel on his M2 .50-caliber machine gun, making his half-track far from battle worthy anyway. Navigating the narrow defiles and passes while avoiding incoming artillery, the driver flipped the M3. Fortunately, no one was injured. The sergeant and his section abandoned it and escaped into the hills.[39]

The platoon leader and his command section were the only ones left at the battle position when the German artillery lifted. Richardson asked his messenger to go back to the southern flank to assess the damage on his platoon. When the runner returned, he reported that "all guns either gone or knocked out burning." Even worse, Richardson's radio operator could receive radio traffic from the C Company commander but could not transmit messages. What he could hear was not good.

"My radio operator reported that he heard the 3rd Platoon radio report to the Company Commanding Officer that Infantry was surrounding his position and that he was low in ammunition," recalled Richardson.

The news did not improve. The lieutenant explained, "We heard several transmissions concerning ammunition and then one which said that Infantry [*sic*] was coming around our left flank and that we were to withdraw by leap frog methods to the Battalion Forward C.P."

The platoon leader ordered his men to pull out. His small section was comprised of his half-track, a three-quarter-ton truck, and a jeep. After all the soldiers were inside their vehicles, Richardson led the way in his half-track toward the mountain pass.

"When we reached the mine field, there was a vehicle burning on the road, at the forward edge of it," wrote Richardson. The lieutenant ordered his driver to keep driving. "I ordered the driver to gun it pass the burning vehicle. We did and the momentum of the track carried us into the minefield. About four to five mines exploded beneath, but luckily no one was seriously injured."

It was almost ten o'clock when Richardson learned that the 899th Tank Destroyer Battalion was heading toward the battlefield. He realized that the minefield that had wrecked his vehicle would do the same to the 899th's tank destroyers. He decided to remove the mines himself. Together with his men, the platoon leader cleared the obstacle, opening a lane for the 899th. Richardson elected to remain behind to guide the arriving battalion through the obstacle belt. His platoon, though, was out of the fight.[40]

0510 to 0710 Hours, Tuesday, March 23, 1943
Along the southern side of El Keddab Ridge (Hill 336), Tunisia
Forward Command Post, 601st Tank Destroyer Battalion
At 0510 hours, Lt. Col. Herschel D. Baker received the first reports of a German attack from his Reconnaissance Company. Initially, he thought his battalion could deal with the unfolding situation. Using the field phone in his forward command post, Baker called the division G-3, Lt. Col. Frederick W. Gibb. "We are having an attack," he said. "Ten tanks and two companies of infantry. Think we can handle it."

By 0710 hours, the 18th Infantry reported to the division that elements of the 601st Tank Destroyer Battalion were withdrawing through their positions. Colonel Gibb felt the tank destroyers could not handle it. Colonel Greer, the commander of the 18th Infantry, requested more reinforcements to plug the gaping holes left by the 601st. Refusing to quit, Colonel Baker tried to do the same thing with his remaining forces.[41]

The 2nd and 3rd Platoons from B Company, 601st Tank Destroyer Battalion, had created the holes when they pulled out of their respective battle positions without their commander's authorization. When Baker learned of their withdrawal, he was furious. He immediately ordered

Capt. Benjamin A. G. Fuller II, the battalion S3, to organize a counter-attack to recapture the positions. Fuller relayed the order over the radio to B Company to send one platoon to accomplish the mission. The B Company executive officer, First Lt. Kenneth B. Stark, was the only one on the B Company radio net when the S3 summoned him. Several minutes later, Fuller left the forward battalion command post and hand delivered the order to Lieutenant Stark. This time, he wanted two platoons to counterattack. One platoon would reinforce C Company, while the other would block any further German attacks on the 32nd Field Artillery, which was still to the northeast of their former positions.[42]

0710 Hours toward 0800 Hours, Tuesday, March 23, 1943
Along the southern side of El Keddab Ridge (Hill 336), Tunisia
B Company, 601st Tank Destroyer Battalion
When Fuller arrived at the B Company command post, Captain Mitchell, its commander, was absent. He had left the CP to reorganize what was left of his shattered company and bring order to the chaos. Lieutenant Stark was the only senior leader left in the CP. Stark reported to the flustered S3 that B Company did not have two platoons to spare for the counterattack. They had only five operable gun trucks.

As if on cue, the Germans knocked out one of the five. Captain Paulick, the Reconnaissance Company commander, had ordered Sgt. Michael H. Dragon to establish an attack-by-fire position with his M3 along a ridge. Sergeant Dragon, the vehicle commander, wrote, "Shifting my positions upon orders from Captain Paulick, we opened fire on the right [southeast] at three thousand yards. This position wasn't very good and I was told there were some more positions to be had on the far right side of the hill. Finding a better position, I moved my halftrack and as I was directing my driver into a partial defilade we got hit in our motor." In the pattern established that day, the half-track started to brew up, forcing Dragon and his crew to abandon the dying vehicle.[43]

When Mitchell learned that he lost another halftrack, he was not pleased. His muted disdain for the Reconnaissance Company commander was evident in his after action report. "Captain Paulick, on his own initiative, placed one of the guns on the skyline to fire at a group of tanks on the south. This gun was easily destroyed," penned the frustrated B Company commander.[44]

Stark cobbled together the remaining four tank destroyers and placed them under the command of Lieutenant Lambert, his 3rd Platoon Leader. Three of the guns were from Lieutenant Luthi's 2nd Platoon (Sgt. John C. Ritso's, Sgt. Joseph J. Kindall's, and Corp. Clyde L. Holden's), and the fourth was Sergeant Horne's from Lambert's own command. The crews cross loaded the ammunition from the damaged half-tracks into their vehicles.

Since B Company had only one platoon of combat power, it could perform only one mission—not the two that Captain Fuller wanted. Stark and Lambert decided the most important was defending the 32nd Field Artillery's howitzers. Lambert hopped into his half-track and ordered the other M3s to follow him onto the ridge.

While the officers debated the merits of their course of action, the German attackers maintained their momentum. Their panzers were close enough to place effective direct fire on the trail that led to the 32nd's gun line. Lambert found this out the hard way.

"We followed the designated route in an attempt to get to the artillery," wrote Lambert. "But extremely heavy tank fire knocked out my vehicle and I ordered the guns to keep going at full speed in an attempt to get them in defilade behind a small ridge to the east."

With his men, the platoon leader dived out of the bullet-magnet half-track and scurried behind the ridge for cover. Despite the loss, Lambert persevered and proceeded to the ridge on foot with another corporal. Meanwhile, Sergeant Ritso from 2nd Platoon assumed command of the makeshift group. When his motley crew arrived at the 32nd's gun line, the acting platoon leader immediately positioned his tank destroyers between the guns and the approaching panzers.[45]

The sergeant and his men were under fire from the moment they rolled up. "I spotted a tank to my front so I fired on it but the shot landed over," recalled Ritso. "I came down on the range and got a hit with A.P. tracer. The crew started climbing out of the tank so I put a round of H.E. delayed fuze in the tank and it started to burst into flames."

The NCO targeted the escaping crew. It was cold and calculating, but he did not want to face them again in the future, gunning for him in another panzer across the battlefield. "I then put another round among the crew that were running for safety and got them," described Ritso.

Before the crew could celebrate their victory, a Mk IV panzer emerged from behind the first. Ritso ordered his men to load an AP tracer round into the 75. The gunner fired the cannon, and the projectile slammed into the tank. It sputtered and stopped. Ritso was not taking any chances, he wrote, "so to make sure I put an H.E. delayed fuze in it and set it on fire."

Yet, the panzers kept coming. A third appeared from behind the first two smoking hulks. Ritso's crew repeated the loading drill. Once the gun was up, the gunner aimed the 75.

"I fired an A.P. tracer into it, stopping same," explained the sergeant. "I had one more round of H.E. left so I fired that at the tank. I hit the tank but didn't set it on fire this time, so the tank crew kept on firing the guns at us."[46]

Despite their efforts, the soldiers of B Company were losing ground. The panzer crews were determined to capture the guns of the 32nd Field Artillery. Following close behind the Mk IVs and Mk IIIs were the German infantry, blazing away at the gun crews with their MG 34s. With no HE or AP rounds for his 75, Ritso realized that his only option was escape.

"Enemy tanks were all ready [sic] approaching us from all sides except the rear, because they couldn't get over the big hill which was behind us," wrote the sergeant. "We were trapped in our position and couldn't get any of the guns out. Two guns were already out of action, and rather than let the Enemy get the guns and use them on us, we destroyed the other two that were usable and the Artillery did the same thing."

Ritso and the remnants of Lambert's platoon scrambled over the El Keddab Ridge to safety. Although, ostensibly, they had failed in their mission to protect the guns of the 32nd Field Artillery, the German victory was a Pyrrhic one. Scattered in front of the abandoned tank destroyers were scores of burning and blackened panzers. The tanks served as temporary tombstones for many of the dead.[47]

Captain Mitchell's tank destroyer company now was a company without tank destroyers. Most of the crews had survived and lived to fight another day. The company commander spent the rest of the morning on foot, searching for a way to reach Lieutenant Yowell's cut-off 1st Platoon. He never linked up with them. He returned to the rally point to watch the arrival of the 899th Tank Destroyer Battalion.

Mitchell later wrote, "I have the highest admiration for the men of my command who remained in action against a superior force until their guns were silenced."[48]

0900 to 1300 Hours, Tuesday, March 23, 1943
Along the southern side of El Keddab Ridge (Hill 336), Tunisia
2nd and 3rd Platoons, C Company, 601st Tank Destroyer Battalion
North of B Company, the tank destroyers of 2nd and 3rd Platoons, Company C, were still in the fight. Captain Sundstrom knew the Germans had infiltrated between his 1st and 3rd Platoons. He had lost radio contact with Lieutenant Richardson, the platoon leader for 1st Platoon. Sundstrom ordered the 2nd Platoon Leader, Lieutenant Matter, to shift a section to block the German breach.

Sundstrom recalled, "We moved to counter this, but every time, we moved the guns, we seemed to run into a cross fire."[49]

The 3rd Platoon was under heavy pressure as well. Lieutenant Munn spent much of the time hunkered down in his observation post because the panzergrenadiers had discovered his location. Munn wrote, "By this time, the Germans had set up two machine guns and were constantly firing on my O.P. and destroyers."

Munn peered over the side of his hole, hoping to spot the offending MG 34s. He found one and tapped Sergeant Langleis on the shoulder. The NCO was still manning the .50-caliber machine gun and swung the M2 over and raked the German position. One of the German gunners recoiled and then slumped over the top of his weapon, dead.

Munn hoped for a reprieve, but the attackers were determined. "At this time," continued the lieutenant, "two German light tanks were able to reach a defiladed position and they proceeded to set up mortars."

Langleis spotted the observer for the mortar team, crawling among the rocks. Once again, Langleis opened fire with the M2 and killed him. Although the observer was dead, the mortar team found the range and began to bracket the open-topped M3 tank destroyers. One of the incoming rounds detonated near Corporal Kalwite's track, and the bursting shrapnel wounded two soldiers, including the driver, Technician 5th Grade Rudolph Y. Rodeffer from Crawford, Virginia. The corporal brought the two injured men to Munn's observation post, and the lieutenant administered first aid. Despite the platoon leader's efforts, Rodeffer was bleeding out.

"I realized that he would have to be taken in, if he were to live," recalled Munn.

Even more important than Rodeffer's life was ammunition. The 3rd Platoon was running out, and the lieutenant needed to resupply his platoon. To do so, he needed Lieutenant Perry. Munn wrote, "I ordered all guns to save at least twenty rounds in case the tanks closed in." He turned the command over to his platoon sergeant and left to find the executive officer.[50]

Perry was waiting for him near the pass. German panzers had occupied an attack-by-fire position near B Company's old location, and these tanks were now shelling Perry's ammunition resupply point. When Munn arrived, he jumped into the back of the executive officer's halftrack and told them where to go.

"The pass as we came out was being shelled directly by a group of tanks from the right flank [southeast], who immediately spotted our track, and gave us no easy moments, as we returned to the left flank again [the northeast]," described Lieutenant Perry.[51]

Munn, sitting in the back, wondered if he had made the right decision, switching vehicles. "The Germans must have realized that this was an ammunition halftrack, for the fire laid down on us, was quite heavy," he remarked matter-of-factly.[52]

At one point, the platoon leader could not find the way back. He asked Perry's driver to halt the vehicle, and he jumped out of the M3. He walked ahead to find his platoon. When he found his tank destroyers, he returned to the half-track and guided it to his platoon, where they unloaded the ammunition.

After they emptied his track, Lieutenant Perry headed north to avoid German artillery. There he found B Battery, 32nd Field Artillery. The red legs told him that the Germans had blocked the route to the north.

Not satisfied with the answer, Perry climbed up to the company observation post and saw the panzers. The artillerymen were right. When the lieutenant returned to his half-track, his driver reported that the M3's engine was failing. They were stuck with the artillery and German infantry swarming around them.[53]

South of Lieutenant Perry's location, the C Company commander was under similar pressure. Captain Sundstrom explained, "One of our men reported that enemy infantry was coming along the foot of the mountain." He and Lieutenant Matter debated their courses of action. Like Perry's conundrum, the Germans had closed off the southern and northeastern escape routes. Their only option was to hike over the El Keddab Ridge on foot.

"I decided my radio was of no value where it was. I ordered all vehicles immobilized and I sent the men back in group of 3's," wrote Sundstrom. Before he destroyed the radio, he ceded control of the company to Lieutenant Perry. Together with Lieutenant Matter, Captain Sundstrom climbed up the ridge and escaped.[54]

Perry and Munn were the only officers left from C Company. Now in command, Lieutenant Perry directed Munn to position his remaining tank destroyers in front of 32nd Field Artillery to protect the howitzers from the panzers. At 1100 hours, the 3rd Platoon Leader lost Corporal Kalwite's half-track when it sustained two direct hits. Several members of the crew were injured, and Private Robert B. Davis died. Two other soldiers survived but were out of the fight. Munn ordered Kalwite to withdraw his wounded track several hundred meters to the rear and out of harm's way. This left the lieutenant with two half-tracks of his own and another from 2nd Platoon (Corporal Migliaccio's).

Munn later recounted, "From this time on, (1300), the tanks never came within range, or if they did, they were defiladed, so that we could not fire on them."[55]

0630 to 1200 Hours, Tuesday, March 23, 1943
Gabes Road Pass through the El Keddab Ridge, Tunisia
A Company, 601st Tank Destroyer Battalion

First Lieutenant Frederick C. Miner commanded the only platoon from A Company, 601st Tank Destroyer. He had taken charge of the platoon on March 21, after an exploding bomb dropped from a Stuka wounded the previous platoon leader, First Lt. Lawrence R. Marcus. Unlike Marcus, who hailed from Dallas, Texas, Miner was from the small town of Seaford, Delaware.

The battalion commander sandwiched Miner's single platoon between B Company and the Gabes road, which bisected the lieutenant's unit. His mission was simple: block the German advance. If the German armored wedge penetrated his position, then the panzers would have an open road to El Guettar and the division's rear area. It would be Sidi Bou Zid and Kasserine all over again. The new platoon leader took one look at the position and decided to place three of his gun trucks north of the road and one south of the road. All were in defilade.

Thomas Morrison was north of the road. He drew a picture after the war that depicted the location of each gun truck in Miner's platoon. "Two tank destroyers [were] dug in on the top of the sand dune," wrote Morrison. "When it got too hot they could pull back down to the bottom of the sand dune until another target showed up."

In front of the sand dune was the third tank destroyer, and on top of the sand dune were Lieutenant Miner and S/Sgt. Rafael Iagulli. They were directing the battle from a dugout observation post. Morrison was #2 gunner in the third gun truck. "We had dug it in so only the gun stuck out over the pile of sand," recalled Morrison. Behind his truck were the 5th Field Artillery command post and switchboard and one A Company command vehicle. Overlooking the road to Gabes was a single 37mm towed antitank gun. Eventually, the survivors of B Company would occupy an attack-by-fire position south of the road.[56]

Like the gunners in B and C Companies, Miner first saw the Germans at sunrise. "Shortly after daylight German tanks approached us from the East traveling on the main road," wrote the lieutenant. "I waited until the leading vehicle got within eight hundred yards and then ordered my platoon up to the crest to open fire. About the same time the unit on my right flank, units in the valley and the field artillery opened up thus making it difficult to observe the results of the firing of my platoon."[57]

Sergeant Chester Karolewski was one of Miner's tank destroyer commanders. His gun truck was on the south side of the Gabes road. Karolewski recalled, "I had a good field of fire and in the morning, around daybreak, we opened fire on tanks firing about thirty rounds."[58]

The panzers were not willing participants and continued to swing to the south, where they disappeared behind a hill. Terrain, though, was not the only obstacle to mask their fire. Sergeant John J. Conway was another gun commander in Miner's platoon. He wrote, "After firing five rounds we were ordered back down to our former position because we could not observe anything due to intense dust and smoke caused by artillery fire."[59]

Nearby in his gun truck was Thomas Morrison. He watched the panzers emerge from the morning fog and smoke. One of the tanks swerved to the south into the soft sand. Morrison knew the ground was bad for panzers. Morrison remarked, "One of them pulled all the way over and he got tangled up in a salt marsh, and he was stuck out there."

Lieutenant Miner requested artillery on the trapped panzer. He also targeted the accompanying infantry. Morrison described the effects of artillery and cannon fire on the hapless panzergrenadiers. "Miner called down a high burst artillery on them and he wiped them out," said the soldier from Brewster, Ohio. "We shot into them, too. We were shooting delayed action, and it would hit the sand and it would bounce in the air and explode. So, they did a lot of damage, too."[60]

By now, the German panzers were edging farther south, trying to skirt between the Chott El Guettar and the Gabes road. The narrow mobility corridor became a shooting gallery for the 601st Tank Destroyers. Miner recounted, "At this time I counted well over thirty tanks circling to the right. I ordered two of my guns to take them under fire, keeping the other guns ready against another thrust at the pass. The combined fire of the artillery and Tank Destroyer elements on my right turned this thrust back before they had gotten one thousand yards from the hill." Still, it was not without cost. The Germans knocked out the towed 37mm antitank gun overlooking the Gabes highway.[61]

Around 1000 hours, General Roosevelt arrived at A Company's battle position. Morrison wrote that he "came strolling down the road tapping his swagger stick on the road as if he were on some quiet avenue." Morrison and the rest of his crew could not believe their eyes that a general would expose himself to such danger.

"His aid [*sic*] and his dog robber were trying to get him to return to the comparative safety of the sand dunes but he refused to go back until he had supervised the replacement of a 37mm antitank gun that had been hit early," added Morrison. "I never say much about the action I saw those days for I learned that anyone who wasn't there thought I was lieing [*sic*]."[62]

Around noon, an American half-track approached the pass, towing an unknown antitank gun. "I held my fire because I was afraid that it was Americans escaping from the battlefield," recalled Lieutenant Miner, "but when seven Germans dismounted and placed the gun in position I ordered two of my guns to open up."[63]

Sergeant Conway's gun truck responded. "We fired ten rounds and after our mission was completed we dropped back to defilated [*sic*] position where we remained overnight through to the noon of March 24 when we were relieved."[64]

Not far from Miner's platoon, Colonel Baker had seen the half-track drive up the road, and he ordered his men not to shoot the strange vehicle. "Some of my subordinates insisted on opening fire," he recalled. "I told them to wait. The gun was unlimbered on the hard surface road. About this time Company 'A' on my left opened fire with great effect. The gun and the vehicle were destroyed."

The battalion operations officer, Captain Fuller, despite sustaining a severe wound, commandeered a jeep and drove out to the smoldering half-track to see if any of the crew had survived. Fortunately, Fuller confirmed the incident was not fratricide. The towed antitank weapon was a German 75mm gun, and the charred and mangled bodies were five German soldiers. In a nearby wadi, Fuller found two more panzergrenadiers alive, and he escorted them back to friendly lines to undergo processing as prisoners of war.[65]

Deterred but not defeated, the panzers withdrew to lick their wounds. For several hours, Miner's platoon waited in the pass. "I have to give Lieutenant Miner credit for leadership at El Guettar and the way he had us dig in," explained Morrison. "When the field artillery lost its CP, he ran a phone line to his position and gave fire commands."[66] Elsewhere, the battle raged.

0500 to 0730 Hours, Tuesday, March 23, 1943
Dj el Mcheltat (Hill 482), Tunisia
Command Post, 3rd Battalion, 18th Infantry Regiment
Lieutenant Colonel Courtney P. Brown learned about the impending attack shortly after the 601st Reconnaissance Company reported it to the 18th Regiment. The command post received a terse message from the tank destroyer battalion at 0500 hours. The radio operator logged the message; it was almost verbatim First Lieutenant Gioia's report to Captain Paulick. It read, "Ten tanks and two companies of enemy coming down the Gabes road on our front."

Around the same time, the radio operator heard the message that the 32nd Field Artillery Battalion was under attack. To ease the pressure on the howitzer units, Colonel Greer ordered two attached platoons from the 16th Infantry Regiment to reinforce the red legs. The ominous messages continued. Shortly after the warning from the 601st, Brown's companies confirmed that the approaching column was bypassing 1st and 2nd Battalions, which were across the valley from his battalion.[67]

First Lieutenant Herbert A. Smith was the executive officer for M Company (Heavy Weapons). He later wrote, "At 0500 on 23 March a distant rumbling noise, similar to that made by tanks, could be heard by the 3rd battalion in the valley to the right front [southeast]."

For several minutes, the staff officers and clerks in the command post waited for more information from their line companies. Brown hoped his men were ready. Over the past few days, he had established a defense-in-depth along the southwestern side of the hill mass known as Dj el Mcheltat. To his front were two infantry companies. Company K, under the command of Clifford B. Raymer, occupied the northern flank, while Company L, under the command of Capt. Donald H. Fogg, occu-pied the southern flank. Securing the second echelon was I Company, under the command of Capt. Henry R. Sawyer. According to Lieutenant Smith, the formation resembled a horseshoe with I Company 350 meters northwest and to the rear of the two other companies. To augment his line units, Colonel Brown allocated to K Company and L Company a platoon of heavy machine guns each. For indirect support, Brown posi-tioned the battalion's 81mm mortar platoon between the two echelons. Near the mortars was the battalion command post "in the center of the horseshoe behind a rock ledge." For communication, the signalmen laid wire from the battalion command post back to the regimental command post on El Keddab, near Hill 336.

Around 0545, Lieutenant Smith watched the sky light up. He wrote, "Tracers could be seen and dim shapes of tanks and vehicles could be discerned rolling up the valley toward the hill mass of Oued El Keddab."

The light show prompted a call from Colonel Greer, who asked Colonel Brown what was happening in his sector. Brown spoke plainly. Smith paraphrased his battalion commander's response. "It sounded as if a whole panzer division was moving up the valley towards Gafsa, but that only a few tanks could be seen at this time," wrote Smith.[68]

At 0610 hours, the radio operator heard, "Tank destroyers be pre-pared to meet armored thrust." Five minutes later, a runner came into the regimental command post and exclaimed that twenty-three tanks had penetrated the American lines and were approaching Hill 336. The sudden emergency compelled Colonel Greer to request immediate air support to strike the panzer wedge.[69]

Colonel Brown and the rest of the 3rd Battalion knew that the fighter-bombers would not arrive in time. Smith recalled, "At 0630 it was light enough to see well out into the plain. The 3rd Battalion position was approximately nine hundred yards from the level of the plain and the position was marked by a great many deep ravines and rock cliffs not accessible to tanks."

Smith hoped that the severely restrictive terrain would block the panzers because he knew that not much else could. If the panzers turned their attention toward 3rd Battalion and found a way up the ridge, then it would be curtains for his unit. Still, he was in awe of the spectacle before him. As he described the scene, "We watched from grandstand seats the show of magnitude and precision put on by the 10th Panzer Division."

It was a massive display of combat power. The various company commands called back to the battalion, as if they were reporting a horse race over the radio with more information each second. From his position, Smith counted seventy-five panzers—a mixture of Mk IIs, IIIs, and IVs. (He was wrong. They were only fifty, but the Germans also had a company of nine Marder IIIs.) Behind them were the infantry. Some were riding on Sonderkraftfahrzeug (Sd.Kfz.) 251 half-tracks, and some were on foot.

"They proceeded up the valley slowly in a deployed formation. Infantryman [*sic*] walked straight up and did not seek to take cover except behind tanks," wrote the company executive officer.[70]

Unlike Colonel Baker and the tank destroyer crews who could see only what was directly in front of their positions, Smith had a panoramic view of the battlefield. From his vantage point, he observed two major columns. In the south, the heavy weapons company executive officer spied the main effort that was heading toward the 601st Tank Destroyer Battalion and most of the artillery. The column had the lion's share of the Mk IIIs and IVs from the 7th Panzer Regiment. For infantry, it had 2nd Battalion from Panzergrenadier Regiment 86. The objective was the seizure of Hill 336.[71]

Closer to Smith's location, one column broke north and headed toward his battalion. This one worried him. It comprised most of the mechanized infantry, who were riding in the back of Sd.Kfz. 251 half-tracks. This was 2nd Battalion, Panzergrenadier Regiment 69. It had three line companies, each armed to the teeth with more than twenty light machine and four heavy machine guns, three 3.7cm towed antitank guns, and two 8cm mortars. The heavy weapons company had three towed 5cm antitank guns, four towed light infantry guns, and a platoon of pioneers. Several panzers supported the attack.[72]

Around 0730 hours, the German artillery and mortar strikes began. The target was 3rd Battalion, 18th Infantry Regiment. Most of the artillery came from a battery of seven StuGs from the Panzer Artillery

Regiment 90. Shortly after the preparation barrage, the panzergrenadiers struck the forward positions with their half-tracks trailing behind them.[73]

Smith wrote, "The enemy rode up and over foxholes sometime crushing men in their holes, but the 3rd battalion [sic] fought back savagely and held firmly to its position in the horseshoe."[74]

0440 to 0659 Hours, Tuesday, March 23, 1943
Dj el Mcheltat (Hill 482), Tunisia
K Company, 3rd Battalion, 18th Infantry Regiment
K Company was ready for the Germans. Its commander was Capt. Clifford B. Raymer from Sodus, New York. Like many junior officers, Raymer earned his commission through ROTC in 1933 from Cornell University. Raymer, unlike his West Point contemporaries, had spent the previous decade as a businessman, not as a soldier. He owned three farms and ran a trucking business that hauled fruit and vegetables.

Fortunately for Raymer, his first sergeant was a consummate professional soldier. Clifford H. Mayou had been in the army for eighteen years and had spent ten of those years with K Company. He was the oldest man in the company. Mayou later admitted, "When that job was over, I felt a good bit older."

Raymer recalled the hours leading up to the attack. "That night we were pulled out of reserve and moved to Hill 382 [he meant Hill 482] and dug our foxholes and slit trenches. All that night we heard vehicles in the valley. The 1st Battalion had already gone across the road and the 2nd Battalion had followed it in an attempt to extend the Division line. We were pretty well stuck on Mcheltat."

The men in the foxholes knew something was wrong, and so did their commander. Raymer continued, "The next morning, at 4:40 o'clock, when it started getting light, the sounds were much louder. When the fog lifted, we saw plenty of tanks and halftracks and then our artillery and Jerry's artillery opened up and it was plenty vicious for a while [sic]."

The commander ordered his men to prepare for combat. "As soon as this happened, everybody in my company was alerted and we passed the ammunition and praised the lord and then sent the empty jeeps back to the battalion ammo dump. I told them to get as many grenades as they could carry."

Soon after the jeeps departed, a pair of German infantry scouts emerged from the morning mist near 1st Platoon's position. First Lieutenant Astor A. Morris, the platoon leader, and S/Sgt. Jackson Hawkins opened fire on the two enemy combatants. Morris had a Thompson submachine gun, and he killed a German lieutenant. Hawkins shot the other soldier with his M1 Garand.

As if on cue, the whole company lit up the slope. Raymer described the carnage with relish. "Everything worked according to the book," he said. "We saw the halftracks and armored vehicles moving toward the position and they came right up to the little valley we were prepared to cover. We were covering a five hundred yard front, which made it a little tough, but when the vehicles pulled up as close as they could come and disgorged the troops, we were ready for them all along the front."

It was a shooting gallery. Every bullet seemed to hit a German soldier, and every grenade exploded amongst a German squad. The commander later remarked, "We let them have it with our machine guns and antitank grenades at a range of two hundred yards."[75]

Captain Edward R. Kuehn was the Battalion S-2 for 3rd Battalion but was with the grunts that morning. He explained, "Because our communication equipment was not good in the hill area, Colonel Brown always sent his S-3 and S-2's to the companies that were involved in combat. I was with 'K' Company at that time. My M1 rifle got so hot it didn't fire, so I used another one belonging to a dead soldier who didn't need his anymore."[76]

The 1st Platoon was on the northern flank of the company. The Germans hit them the hardest that morning. The soldiers of 1st Platoon responded with rifle grenades. Corporal Harold A. Benson knocked out two half-tracks with the newfangled projectiles from his 1903 Springfield. Nearby, Technician Fifth Grade Julius Jacobs took out a Mk II Panzer and half-track. After sustaining a shoulder wound, his platoon leader sent him back to the aid station to undergo treatment. When Jacobs arrived, he refused evacuation, and, after wrangling with the medics, they released him so that he could return to the battle.

With K Company holding the high ground, grenades were the weapons of choice for most of the soldiers. "You could look in the air and see between thirty and forty grenades all at the same time," remarked Second Lt. William A. Russel, platoon leader for 3rd Platoon.[77]

To keep the Germans from overrunning 1st Platoon and the rest of K Company, M Company's mortar men were relentless. They expended more than 500 81mm HE rounds on the attacking Germans. "The mortar barrels turned a dull red color caused by the intense hea[t] created by the rapid rate of fire," wrote Lieutenant Smith. "This deadly accurate fire was, in part, instrumental in repulsing the enemy attack on the 3rd Battalion front during the morning of the 23rd March."[78]

For twenty minutes, the situation looked bleak. At 0640 hours, 3rd Battalion reported to regiment that "Company K . . . being forced back." Five minutes later, the battalion informed regiment that they were withdrawing "slightly." But, by 0659 hours, the danger had passed, and the battalion reported they were not falling back. The battle, though, was far from finished.[79]

0440 to 0659 Hours, Tuesday, March 23, 1943
Dj el Mcheltat (Hill 482), Tunisia
2nd Battalion, Panzergrenadier Regiment 69
Ernst Breitenberger was a nineteen-year-old machine gunner in Panzergrenadier Regiment 69. His weapon was the MG 34. Although not as famous as its successor, the MG 42, the 34 was still a deadly firearm and more than a match for the American air-cooled Browning M1919 machine gun. It could spit out 800 to 900 rounds a minute at a blistering velocity of 2,500 feet per second. Even worse for the Yanks, his panzergrenadier platoon had six of them, compared to an American infantry platoon, which had no organic light machine guns in early 1943. In fact, the entire company had only two M1919 machine guns. With the additional machine-gun platoon from M Company, the Americans still had only six machine guns (two light and four heavy) in the area. Breitenberger's company of panzergrenadiers had almost thirty belt-fed weapons (twenty-four light and four heavy).[80]

Early on the morning of March 23, the panzergrenadiers occupied a tactical assembly area fifteen kilometers east of Hill 482. Then they rolled out on the Gafsa-Gabes road and headed west toward the American lines. With the sun just below the eastern horizon, the Sd.Kfz. 251 halftracks turned north.

"It was rough ground, a lot of ridges and washes," recalled Breitenberger. "The ground quickly became so steep that the halftracks could go no further. Not [at] all. Just impossible. We got out, formed up, and began our attack straight north."

Major Paul Pommée was Breitenberger's battalion commander. He wanted his unit to seize Hill 482. To accomplish the mission, he had two of his infantry companies, plus a few tanks. At Kasserine, this would have sufficed, but not this day.

"Very soon we were completely stopped by the 18th's infantry," wrote the nineteen-year-old machine gunner. "Their heavy machine guns did not bother us, but we began to take losses from 'sniper' fire. The Americans had built little walls of rocks in front of their firing positions, and we had trouble seeing where the shots were coming from."

Breitenberger and the rest of the battalion kept pushing forward. The young soldier confirmed Lieutenant Russel's account of the deadly game of grenade tossing. "We worked up to within fifty feet of them and threw a lot of grenades up," wrote the panzergrenadier, "but had to just hope that the grenades were landing in the correct places."

The game continued for most of the morning, with neither side gaining ground. It was worse for the Germans. "The ground was too hard to dig in. You could get down maybe three to four inches, that's all," recounted Breitenberger. Each company had started out the attack with approximately 140 men. That number decreased as the morning wore on, and by noon, Major Pommée had little to show for it.[81]

0700 to 0730 Hours, Tuesday, March 23, 1943
El Keddab Ridge (Hill 336), Tunisia
Command Post, 18th Infantry Regiment
At 0700 hours, General Roosevelt arrived at Colonel Greer's command post. Teddy Roosevelt's son always wanted to be close to the action. He

felt that the division command post was too far away to understand the ebb and flow of the battle, so he headed out to Colonel Greer's forward CP.

From atop Hill 336, the assistant division commander saw the German forces. "At dawn the battlefield lay at my feet a circular plain about seven miles in diameter. I could see it all," he later wrote to his wife in a letter.

He continued, "The first move was a screen of German tanks to our right flank—twenty-four in all. We took them under artillery fire. On they came until they had nearly turned our position—the shells bursting around them." Roosevelt immediately saw the threat and ordered the division headquarters to send the 899th Tank Destroyer Battalion to plug the gap. Several minutes later, Roosevelt order the division's artillery "to move up" and support the counterattacking units.

Roosevelt remained at the 18th Infantry command post for another ninety minutes. At 0910 hours, the observation posts radioed that the panzers were pulling back. Satisfied that the attack had stalled and with reinforcements arriving shortly, the assistant division commander left Greer's headquarters ten minutes later. [82]

0600 Hours to Midday, Tuesday, March 23, 1943
Djebel Berda Ridge (Hill 772), Tunisia
2nd Battalion, 18th Infantry Regiment
Richard Lindo headed up a forward observer team the morning of March 23. Colonel Thompson had attached his section to Colonel Sternberg's 2nd Battalion. It was still dark when Lindo and the others realized the morning would not be a boring one. Lindo wrote, "We heard nothing, but looking back to our left rear, we could see tracers from American machine guns zipping down the valley floor and ricocheting."

The officer ordered his section to keep digging their foxholes. When they finished, they could not fall asleep. At 0625 hours, as the sun crested over the ridges along the eastern horizon, Lindo saw what had caused the early morning fireworks. "There in the mist on the valley floor, was the entire 10th German Panzers [*sic*] Division spread out—tanks, infantry, trucks, guns, as if on a table we'd look down on in a war game," described Lindo.

That was not the worst of it. The panzers were behind them. "The Germans had gone right by us to our rear, and both of our battalions [1st and 2nd] were cut from our supplies," explained Lindo.[83]

The Germans attacked the 18th Infantry's southern flank with a single motorcycle battalion named the *Kradschützen-Bataillon 10* (10th Motorcycle Battalion). The 10th had two motorcycle infantry companies, one armored infantry company mounted on Sd.Kfz 250 half-tracks, and one armored car company with a mix of Sd.Kfz. 223s and 222s armored cars. According to a prisoner of war, the 1st Company (the armored car company) had ten vehicles, while the 2nd Company (the half-track company) had twelve troop carriers. The two motorcycle companies had approximately 160 men and twelve motorcycles with sidecars in each of its four platoons. Each platoon had four light machine guns. Each motorcycle company had two heavy machine guns and two 81mm mortars for support. In addition to the four assault companies, the battalion had a fifth weapons company with three 75mm towed antitank guns and a couple of infantry guns. Finally, the battalion had six self-propelled 75mm guns most likely StuG IIIs. The battalion commander was Maj. Heinrich Drewes.[84]

The motorcycle battalion had little luck against Colonel Greer's dug-in battalions, who had the advantage of the higher ground. Most of the attacks were only probes and never seriously threatened the 18th Infantry's southern flank. Still, it was combat, and fate was fickle. Lindo wrote, "A German shell landed beside our jeep, blew out the tires, and killed Corporal Danny Sullivan of my liaison section. Danny was Catholic and I knew his folks would want to have his body taken out of there and properly buried, so we kept his body by us. With the jeep gone, we had to backpack our radio now."[85]

Phil Ault was a correspondent for *United Press*. At El Guettar, he decided to tag along with 2nd Battalion, 18th Infantry. He had been in North Africa since the invasion in November. Now, he was in a foxhole, watching the battle unfold in front of his position. "We watched wave after wave of German bombers trying unsuccessfully to clear a path for the tanks," wrote Ault. "They zoomed down on the gun positions, then raced strafing along the naked road over which big American trucks were hauling badly needed ammunition."

As Ault and the grunts watched the Luftwaffe bombers and fighters pound the American lines, they cursed the American air force. "We wondered where the American air force was," explained the reporter. "That night we learned. It was out of sight behind the hills, dealing unmerciful punishment to the Luftwaffe at its bases. It was pleasant to learn that some of those planes we saw diving bombing the troops never got home."

The 183 soldiers in G Company could do little but wait it out as the panzers headed north and west toward the division rear. Their position was atop Djebel Berda. Ault described it as "three hundred yards of almost bare rock with a scant covering of clay shot through with gravel and a few weary weeds. It was naked if ever a position was."

To protect themselves from direct fire weapons, the dogface infantry dug their positions on the reverse slope. Due to the impenetrable rock, their foxholes were less than eight inches deep and no better than makeshift graves. "Shells from field guns and tanks began to splatter on their slope," wrote Ault. "Snipers on the higher ridge beyond could see them now. Every time a doughboy raised his head, a bullet pinged past. . . . They were trapped, cut off from all help. Orders were to hold."

They wanted to fire back at the panzers, loitering below, but the Germans knew the range and maintained their distance so that they were outside the reach of the American mortars and machine guns. However, the Germans could still fire their main guns and did.

Ault wrote, "They were pinned to the ground so tightly that they couldn't leave their foxholes to make a latrine. They used helmets as toilets."[86]

1837 to 0600 Hours, Monday, March 22, 1943, to Tuesday, March 23, 1943
Base of Dj bou Rhedja (Hill 483), Tunisia
C Battery, 32nd Field Artillery Battalion
Captain Allston S. Goff still was smarting from burning his hands on March 21 while carrying smoldering powder bags. His skin was singed and resembled burnt paper. Ashamed of his pain and wanting to appear strong before his soldiers, Captain Goff refused to show how he was suffering from the wound. His solution? "I went off by myself, hid myself,

and cried. Then Doc Shapiro came and put a lot of water-soluble stuff on my hands and loose bandages," recalled Goff.

Despite the throbbing, Goff remained in command of his battery. Sometime around midnight, Major Harry H. Critz, the battalion executive officer, ordered Goff to shift his battery farther east to support the infantry attack scheduled to take place later that morning. Critz explained that the guns had to displace because "we wouldn't be able to support our 18th Infantry's advance next day down the valley."

Goff nodded. The major was right. "Since I was the Senior Battery Commander, following Major Critz's order, I took the other battery's officers out in the dark, going right onto the metalled [sic] road, then left on it and left again into the gullies in front of el Keddab Ridge."

The C Battery commander found a perfect spot in some wadis east of Dj bou Rhedja. Directing traffic, Goff guided each unit to a location along the slope. "'A' Battery, you go in here, 'B' Battery, in here, and 'C' will be nearest the main road," said the commander.

The three batteries rolled out and set up their guns. It took most of the night and no one slept. "We layed [sic] the guns pointing southeast ... and 'located' ourselves on the map, by guess and by God," wrote Goff.

The German attack surprised them. At 0600 hours, the 32nd Field Artillery reported to the division that they were "being attacked by tanks." The sudden appearance of panzers was the first problem for Goff to deal with. The second problem was communication. The initial German attack had cut the wire between his gun line and the fire direction center, leaving them without any enemy coordinates for gun calculations. As a result, they could not conduct call-for-fire missions.

Goff wrote, "We did no shooting until the Jerries were in on us, and then did just 'shooting from the hip.'"

C Battery was not only the unit on the gun line under attack.[87]

1837 to 0600 Hours, Monday, March 22, 1943, to Tuesday, March 23, 1943
Base of Dj bou Rhedja (Hill 483), Tunisia
B Battery, 32nd Field Artillery Battalion
North of C Battery were the four guns of Battery B. The move to their new positions east of the Dj bou Rhedja had been anything but smooth.

First, a German spotter plane flew over their column as it moved out toward its new firing location. Many of the men wanted to fire at it, but experience told them to leave it alone. Antiaircraft at night would have confirmed their location to the observer, circling above.

First Lieutenant Francis E. Silva Jr. was the executive officer for the battery. He recalled, "The wadis and ridges made it very rough going. The trucks had to stay in low-gear. . . . Still, we worked our way cross county, going up and down, to a position on the forward slope where we would have at least sight defilade even if not smoke defilade."

Sadly, the nighttime odyssey claimed a life. Silva wrote about it years later. "At that time we had with us a young soldier," wrote the lieutenant. "Standing orders were that no one was to go to sleep in the back of these big trucks carrying ammunition. But he did just that. Going up the bank of one of these steep wadis, the ammunition slid back on the kid, and killed him." The Germans had not yet attacked, and B Battery was down one soldier because of an accident. Silva had little time to grieve.

At dawn, the panzers rolled up on his battery. Many of the panzergrenadiers were from 8th Company, 2nd Battalion, 86th Panzergrenadier Regiment, while many of the panzers were from 1st Battalion, 7th Panzer Regiment. The German thrust clawed toward C Battery and the Gabes highway in an attempt to turn the flank of the artillery battalion.[88]

Silva knew the Germans were close—too close. Silva explained, "I was myself down to adjusting fire of one gun at Charge I, minimum range and getting overs and shorts on a German tank, even though we were firing at identical range settings each time. We had the exact range, but couldn't get a hit. I was doing the observing myself and giving the orders to the gunners twenty feet away. And the damned tank was shooting back."[89]

Nearby was a soldier named Frank Viney manning a .50-caliber M2 machine gun. He was part of B Battery, but unlike the cannon cockers who operated the 105mm howitzers, Viney's mission was local security. It was his job to prevent German infantry from overrunning the gun line.

Earlier that morning, one of his squad mates had asked the battery commander, "Is this going to be a rest area?" Viney could not believe the question. German artillery and Stukas had hounded them for more than twenty-four hours. It had to be the prelude for something big.

The battery commander snarled, "Dig in! This isn't any rest area!"

Viney and the rest of the machine gunners dug in. That morning, they were thankful they had heeded the captain's orders. "When daylight came," recalled Viney, "the mist and dust started to rise from the valley floor, and the first thing I saw was tanks, German tanks. Straining to see under the fog, all I could see was tanks, more tanks, and more tanks."

Within moments, the panzers opened fire on his position. Despite the cacophony of earsplitting explosions and whistling bullets, Viney kept a cool head. His machine gun was useless against tanks, especially Mk III and IV panzers, but it was deadly against soft-skinned vehicles like trucks. After several minutes, he spotted one. "There was a Volkswagon [sic] with a flat bed on the back of it going around delivering ammunition to these big tanks. One big German tank stood out," recalled Viney.

He readied the gun and then noticed that the tank had two soldiers perched on top of it. The machine gunner grabbed a pair of binoculars. He later wrote, "We could see two GI's sitting on that tank. The GI's must have been prisoners of the Germans. The two of them got off the tank and came up towards the shallow ridges we were hidden in."

Dumbfounded, he took his fingers off the butterfly trigger and watched the odd spectacle unfold. He continued, "The Germans must have just let them go. German soldiers were standing around these two before they left the tank, but no one took any action about their leaving at all. Who they were, or what outfit the GI's belonged to, I have no idea."

Viney did not have time to ponder the whereabouts of the two mystery soldiers. The Germans were relentless. He chugged away with his M2, hammering at enemy infantry wherever he saw them. His assistant gunner tapped him on the back, and Viney looked over his right shoulder. The young soldier from Allegheny, Pennsylvania, could not believe his eyes.

"At one point," began Viney, "some lieutenant came up on our right, on top of one of these ridges along side ours, and stood up there looking through his field glasses, no cover or anything. All of sudden there was a 'WHAM!' and no more lieutenant. . . . It was quite a ways from their tanks, but you could see the guy standing there, and boom!"[90] He hoped that the Germans did not have a bead on him.

0600 to 1100 Hours, Tuesday, March 23, 1943
Base of Dj bou Rhedja (Hill 483), Tunisia
Antitank Platoon, Southern Flank of C Battery,
32nd Field Artillery Battalion

Private Walt Smith sensed the German panzers were on the backside of the hill in front of him. He could hear the crack and thunder of the guns, booming over the crest of the ridge. Unfortunately, his weapon was almost useless against the approaching enemy goliaths. He was a driver, and his vehicle towed an M3A1 37mm antitank gun. His platoon had six of them.

Malcolm Marshall, a friend of Smith's, explained, "These little guns had long necked-down brass cartridges which gave good velocity, but the armor-piercing shell itself you could put your thumb and forefinger around. Such shells were too small to penetrate anything but armored cars. They would simply bounce off German medium tanks."

The M3A1 was practically worthless. Its round, the M51 APC (Armor Piercing Cartridge), could penetrate only 61mm of armor at 500 yards. In comparison, the newer and heavier M1 57mm towed antitank gun could penetrate 100mm of armor at 500 yards. The M3A1's performance was so poor that commanders ordered the crews to fire at targets that were within 400 yards or less. For protection, the only option was concealment since the gun shield was capable of stopping only shrapnel and small arms—not a 75mm round from a panzer. The hapless crews relied on hope—hope that the German tankers would oblige them with flank or rear shots, where the armor was thinnest. The gun was far from ideal, but it was all the 32nd Field Artillery had the morning of March 23.

Smith was aware of the gun's limitations. "We knew that the guns wouldn't stop much armor," he said, "but we called ourselves 'The Ring of Steel!' We got the biggest kick out of that!"

Because of its shortcomings, Smith's section leader positioned the antitank gun in a wadi, facing toward the Gabes road. The obsessive search for perfect concealment meant that the gun had no targets when the panzers rolled up the highway. However, the gun crews did encounter panzergrenadiers. Smith recalled an incident. "At about 11 o'clock that morning when the Kraut tanks were spread out across the valley and the Kraut infantry was about into our firing positions, Sergeant Red Pierce came around and took out the breech blocks from our guns so they'd be useless to the Germans. He never came back."

Left with only rifle grenades, the antitank crews prayed that the Germans would not press the attack. Smith later reasoned, "Our gun was in position only to cover this one wadi, so even if we could have fired, it wouldn't slow up many infantry."[91]

0600 to 1050 Hours, Tuesday, March 23, 1943
Base of Dj bou Rhedja (Hill 483), Tunisia
A Battery, 32nd Field Artillery Battalion
Raymond Kociuba was cannon cocker for the #2 gun in A Battery. His battery occupied the northern flank of the 32nd Field Artillery Battalion position. "Our new positions were in a draw, hidden from the Germans to our front," wrote Kociuba.

They did not remain hidden for long. When the attack began that morning, A Battery was far enough north of the road to escape the attention of the panzers. However, the panzergrenadiers found them. With the enemy infantry closing in, the howitzer crews lowered the barrels and turned the weapons into shotguns. "We took out the greater part of our powder charge," explained Kociuba, "lowered our barrels, and fired at 'minimum' range."

The soldiers of A Battery wondered how long their ammunition would last. The enemy infantry kept coming up through the wadis, like army ants. As the morning wore on, Raymond observed GIs straggling back to the rear. At 0820 hours, Colonel Greer ordered 3rd Battalion to remain in position to protect the 32nd Field Artillery, but despite the efforts of L Company, Germans swept past its southern flank and headed toward the artillery positions.

Kociuba wrote, "Captain Whittemore got on the phone from the battery command post and ordered us to leave the guns and pull back to the new infantry line. So, we all took our .03 rifles (bolt action, single shot) and ran back."

The red legs grabbed their gear and began to withdraw. It was not a rout but an orderly process. As the soldiers fell back, many encountered injured men from other units. "I passed a wounded Infantryman, who was waiting for a medic," wrote Kociuba. "I got his M-1 Garand rifle, since I had none, and we ran up on top of the ridge and flopped down facing the Jerries. We, plus part of the 3rd Battalion, 18th Infantry, made up a firing line."[92]

Near A Battery's original position was its forward observer, First Lt. Gerard T. Clarke. He recalled the German attack. "On that plain near El Guettar were thousands of infantry and what seemed hundreds of tanks advancing on our infantry," wrote Clarke. "I found a rock foundation of an old house, raised a few feet from the plain, for an observation post, giving me a good field of view. I called many fire missions, raising hell with the panzers."

Later in the morning, the panzergrenadiers approached his observation post. Clarke grabbed an M-1 Garand from one of the soldiers in 3rd Battalion, 16th Infantry, and started to plink away at the encroaching infantry. Several times, his aim was true, and he "picked off several Germans who got too close." His shooting revealed his position, and a panzer blasted at his location. Fortunately, none of the rounds hit him.

The near miss did give Clarke pause. "As I looked around me, I could see bloodstains there from previous forward observers who had been at the same spot and weren't as lucky as I was," remarked the lieutenant.

After his battery withdrew to join 3rd Battalion, 16th Infantry, along El Keddab Ridge, Clarke remained at his post and continued to call fire missions on the enemy. At one point, he spotted a juicy target. "There were the German cook tents, serving meals, hundreds of men waiting in line for their chow, communication tents full of men and equipment, gasoline storage areas, ammunition dumps, tank and truck maintenance areas," recalled Clarke. "What a turkey shoot! To my dismay and outrage, my guns of the 32nd FA couldn't fire. They had been overrun by German grenadiers." Eventually, Clarke left his position and linked up with the rest of his battery on El Keddab later that afternoon.[93]

0430 to 1107 Hours, Tuesday, March 23, 1943
El Guettar, Tunisia
Headquarters, 1st Infantry Division (Danger Forward)
The soldiers and staff officers of the G-2 were always prepared for the worst. It was their job. They needed to think like the enemy. They would log even the strangest reports because the action might indicate something new and sinister. At 0430 hours, the field phone rang. It was someone from the 18th Infantry Regiment, reporting arcing amber flares and artillery rounds near their positions. The soldier jotted down the report and filed it in the journal. Fifteen minutes later, the intelligence section heard the phone drone again. Again, it was the 18th Infantry. This time it was more serious: motorized patrols and enemy activity. Before the analysts could digest the information, the 601st Tank Destroyer Battalion chimed in to alert them of a panzer attack rolling down the Gabes road. This was the real thing.[94]

At 0510 hours, Danger Forward received a call by field telephone from Colonel Baker, the 601st commander, confirming the earlier reports of the German attack. Fifty minutes later, the 32nd Field Artillery called in to inform division that they, too, were under attack from panzers. Colonel Gibb, the Division G-3, took the reports in stride. He did not want to commit valuable assets until he had more information. At 0625 hours, Lt. Col. John H. Mathews, the commander of 3rd Battalion, 16th Infantry, alerted Danger Forward that the Germans were about to envelop his command, which was on Hill 336 and behind the 32nd Field Artillery.

This latest report spurred Gibb to act. Mathew's battalion was to backstop the artillery. If the enemy bypassed these forces, they would be behind the division artillery and on their way to another victory. Gibb grabbed the field phone and rang the 16th Infantry Regiment command post. He ordered Col. D'Alary Fechet, its commander, to "move your antitank company up right away. When trucks arrive move [the] rest of your outfit by infiltration. Go no further than El Guettar." Thirty minutes later and after a short planning session, Colonel Fechet issued the movement order to his command.[95]

At 0645 hours, the division artillery reported thirty panzers at grid zone 3268. This meant the German column was four kilometers east of

Hill 336. Seven minutes later, Gibb requested the corps artillery to pound them. "Get long-toms on them," he said over the phone.[96]

The G-3's "long-tom" was the unofficial moniker for the 155mm M1A1 howitzer, part of the corps' artillery battalions. The M1A1 was one of the best American weapons of World War II. It had a maximum range of 23.2 kilometers and was deadly accurate. Supporting the 1st Infantry Division were two battalions of M1A1s, two battalions of 105mm howitzers, and one battalion of 8-inch howitzers.[97]

Meanwhile, several other members of the G-3 staff coordinated air support to strike the column. The first sortie would come from the 81st Fighter Group, which was comprised of Bell P-39 Aircobras. The P-39 mounted a single 37mm cannon in the nose of the aircraft, similar to the German BF-109. In addition, it had two .50-caliber machine guns behind the propeller and four .30-caliber machine guns mounted on the wings, and it could carry a single 500-pound bomb underneath the fuselage. As a fighter, it was unspectacular, but as a fighter-bomber, it excelled.

Brigadier General Paul L. Williams, commander of the XII Air Force and thereby the 81st Fighter Group, wrote, "The P-39 with its (deck) speed and tremendous firepower, proved the most effective for straffing [sic]. Its sturdy construction enabled it to complete its mission even though often hit badly by Anti-Aircraft fire." Williams described how the Aircobra stalked its prey: "The P-39 tactics were to fly from the airdrome to the target at minimum altitude, attack from an angle and turn away without ever having passed over the target."[98]

The Aircobras had plenty of targets. At 0650 hours, the G-2 section alerted the command post that the enemy column along the Gabes road stretched more than ten kilometers. Twenty minutes later, Colonel Greer, the 18th Infantry's commander, confirmed the report when he relayed the message from his 3rd Battalion that "the whole road [was] lined with vehicles. [Makes] good air mission."[99]

Shortly after eight o'clock, II Corps headquarters assured Danger Forward by phone that help was on the way. The unknown staff officer told Colonel Gibb, "Stuff on the way now, four P-39s. More [is] coming. Also, light bombers [are] alerted."

The command post was buzzing. Discordant voices and not-so-distant explosions, punctuated by the chatter of machine guns, made the simple act of thinking almost impossible. However, these times determined the success of one's career.

Gibb suddenly remembered the 899th Tank Destroyer Battalion. Roosevelt had ordered them into the fight, and the G-3 had not heard of their whereabouts. At 0815 hours, he picked up the field phone and called Colonel Greer. "What is the story on the 899th?" he asked. According to Gibb's memory, they had rolled out forty-five minutes before. Since they had priority, they should have arrived at the pass by now. Greer did not have the answer.

Gibb asked, "Let us know when they go by." He then promised Greer that 16th Infantry's antitank company was heading his way.[100]

General Allen stood in the background and gave guidance to Gibb when he felt he needed it. So far, Gibb was in control. The division commander's most important job was to remain calm and imperturbable. Allen did not know the 10th Panzer Division was in the area, but he had sensed something was wrong the previous night. "I knew something was fishy," he said after the battle to a friend, "and we were ready for anything, weren't we?"[101]

Sometime between 0700 and 0800 hours, Roosevelt contacted Allen over the phone. The assistant division commander was still with the 18th Infantry Regiment. He told Allen, "German infantry units had reenforced [*sic*] the Italian defenders on the Djebel Mcheltat (in the center) and on the Djebel Berda (on the south flank), and there German units were then pressing hard against the 18th Infantry Battalions, that had attained the forward slopes of these two objectives. Also, probing columns of German infantry and tanks had infiltrated behind 3rd Battalion, of the 18th Infantry Regiment, in the Division center; and had overrun some of the field pieces of the 5th and 32nd Field Artillery Battalions (operating in support of that Regiment)."[102]

Roosevelt's report was sobering. Thoughts of Kasserine were not far from their minds. For some of the officers huddled inside the command tent, the approaching panzers seemed too close for comfort. (They were approximately four kilometers from Danger Forward.) One of them had the temerity to suggest to Allen moving the forward command post to a different location to prevent the panzers from overrunning it.

Allen scowled, "I will like hell pull out, and I'll shoot the first bastard that does." With that warning, Allen settled the issue. No one was retreating.[103]

Around 0820 hours, the 18th Infantry reported over the radio that the German attack had stalled. "Tanks [are] withdrawing on right, leaving two apparently disabled. Things [are] running smoothly."

At 0830 hours, the first P-39s were over the battlefield. From his position, Greer could see the warbirds and radioed Danger Forward, "Request strafing mission on enemy reinforcements coming up road."[104]

Eleven minutes later, Colonel Greer called over the radio and alerted the division that his command post was under mortar fire. This meant the Germans were close. However, he also added, "General withdrawing of armor from sector. Our arty is raising hell." The last sentence was a boon to the morale in the division headquarters. For the moment, the fortunes of war were smiling on the American army.

For the next hour, Colonel Gibb shuffled units across his chessboard. He called the 26th Infantry Regiment. He needed them to shift forces to the south so that they could secure the northern flank of the 18th Infantry Regiment near Dj Ank. Gibb said over the field phone, "Your southernmost battalion [must] push vigorously until contact has been gained with the 18th."

The G-3 soon learned that one company from the 26th Infantry had cleared Hill 536. The report from the company commander was positive. According to the log, it was "not running into much stuff. Some enemy south of them."[105]

Ten minutes before eleven o'clock in the morning, Colonel Mason received a call from Brig. Gen. Clift Andrus over the field phone. Andrus was the division's artillery commander. His news was, at best, mixed. "One battery of the 5th cut off," he began. "32nd has had a hard time but still firing. Some of them told to move out. Cannot get anything up there now. All communications out. I have radio communication with some of them. Things going much better."

Andrus then repeated the common refrain that morning. "Short of ammo. We can't get it. Trains back in Gafsa waiting to be filled except for the 5th Field Artillery, which is [still] on the road."

However, not all was lost. "The 105s will be able to get some [ammo] for a while yet but not a lot," reported Andrus. "The long-toms won't get any until 1500. They're not quite out yet."[106]

Mason and Gibb knew ammunition was the decisive point. If the guns could keep firing, they had a chance to beat back any German attack. That the batteries still had ammunition was the result of Allen disobeying a directive from Patton. Mason later revealed, "General Patton's personal contribution to the initial assault of the German force was his direct order that no artillery ammo was to be dumped on the ground at gun positions. Pleas by Division for reconsideration were refused on grounds that the Division would get overrun and thus provide the Germans with ammo for the guns they would capture. The time-distance back to Corps ammo dumps made resupply during a battle wholly impractable [sic]."

Mason recalled Allen's response. "In any case," wrote Mason, "the order was disobeyed, probably with General Allen's unofficial knowledge, but had this non-authorized extra artillery ammo not been present at the gun positions, most likely the 10th Panzer Division's attack would have succeeded."[107]

Ammunition was not the only problem facing the 1st Infantry Division that morning. The artillery strikes knocked out the landlines, and radio communications were intermittent with units out on the perimeter. At 1055 hours, Greer called the division headquarters over the phone. He needed air support. "Looks like they [the Germans] are prepared for a counterattack in front of 3rd Battalion," said Greer. "Our 1st and 2nd battalions I ordered to withdraw but I can't get messages through to them. They are still south of the road, running short of ammo."

Greer updated the division on Colonel Brown's status. "3rd Battalion on left of the road. 5th and 32nd are on hill mass we are on now. They are in front of that. We must get ammo to them. We will try to get some up to them."

"Tanks between us and them," explained the 18th Infantry's commander. The presence of panzers was complicating the resupply issue.

If the panzers remained at their current location, then resupply trucks would be unable to reach the trapped units.

Greer offered a solution. "We are registering on the tanks now," he said. "7th and 17th [Artillery] are firing on them at position Four . . . Five . . . Six . . . Five."

He concluded his report with his personal observation. "I don't know the size of the force. The whole plain is covered with tanks and vehicles in large groups," said Greer. He added, "I got that from the Cannon Company OP too." Although the attack had stalled, it was far from finished. Unbeknownst to Greer and the others, it was only an interlude.[108]

At 1107 hours, Mason called the corps headquarters over the field phone. He felt his corps was underperforming. He needed more ammunition, and he needed air support. He was getting little of either. Several A-20 Havocs and B-25 Mitchells had struck the German positions earlier that morning, but Mason felt the bombing run made little impact on the German forces. Moreover, German Stukas were hitting their positions.

Mason even asked, "If you can in any way influence keeping fighter support over us we would appreciate it."

The nameless voice responded, "They are short. We gave your request. Trying to do what we can," it said.

Mason growled. "It does not take a whole sweep. Some on reconnaissance can contest the air is what we want. They can hang back off the horizon and wait until the planes go out again and then knock out things."

"We will take it up again," the voice assured him. It did not assuage Mason. Corps then asked, "How many targets were hit this morning?"

Mason shook his head. "I don't know," answered the chief of staff. "We have trouble with the phone lines. I think things are getting reorganized on both sides. We'll need the air support after a while and badly. I want to get it lined up in advance so when we call for it, you will know what is going on up this way. Fighter support is the main thing we are asking for."[109]

He would have to wait before the fighters came.

For now, the skies belonged to the Luftwaffe.

0947 to 1600 Hours, Tuesday, March 23, 1943
Gabes Road, just to south of Hill 336, Tunisia
B Company, 899th Tank Destroyer Battalion
Unlike the 601st Tank Destroyer Battalion, which had makeshift vehicles, the army outfitted the 899th with its latest weapon, the M10 Tank Destroyer. This tank killer mounted a 3-inch gun, which meant that the rounds had a larger diameter than the M3's 75mm gun. Therefore, it had better penetrating power. At 500 yards, the M10's gun could penetrate up to 98mm of sloped armor with its standard M62 APC. At a thousand yards, it could penetrate 90mm of sloped steel.[110]

The 899th was a latecomer to the party in North Africa. It was still stateside at Fort Dix, New Jersey, as late as New Year's Day 1943. It left the United States on January 13 and docked at Casablanca, where the troops disembarked on January 26. While the men bivouacked and acclimatized to North Africa, they learned that they would receive the newest weapon in the U.S. Army inventory—the M10 GMC.

The unit historian described the reaction of the men, "Not since the battalion had been activated on July 1, 1940, were the men and officers so elated as they were with the news. At the time of leaving Camp Hood, Texas, all had hoped that the battalion would not have to fight with the 75mm S.P.'s. but it seemed to [*sic*] much to expect M10's, which were a novelty even at Camp Hood."[111]

The commander of the 899th was Lt. Col. Maxwell A. Tincher, a member of the West Point Class of 1937. Like many battalion commanders in World War II, Tincher was young. He was born on September 6, 1914, in Minnesota. On graduation from the U.S. Military Academy, he commissioned in the infantry. With war fast approaching, his promotions came quickly. He attained the rank of captain on September 9, 1940, and the rank of major on February 1, 1942, and earned the rank of lieutenant colonel that same year on September 3. Several months later, he assumed command of the 899th.[112]

The up-and-coming Tincher did not impress the top brass when he arrived with his troops that January. The 899th hosted several important visitors, including Gen. George C. Marshall. The Army Chief of Staff did not find the 899th to be ready for combat. When Marshall returned to the United States, he wrote a letter to Maj. Gen. Andrew D. Bruce, who was the post commander of the Tank Destroyer School at Camp Hood. In the letter, he said of Tincher's 899th, "What I want to draw to your personal attention is that this unit displayed a lack of disciplinary leadership and training that was glaring and meant that it was not useable for any battle against the Germans until it had been reconstituted. The men were all right, the training was seriously wrong."

Marshall did not hold back. He continued to thrash the 899th and the Tank Destroyer School: "As this is the second time there has come to my attention a deficiency in the ordinary fundamentals of discipline in tank destroyer units I am communicating with you direct to get your comments. Such procedure is unacceptable to me. I know there are many difficulties. However, I find the other units in this instance, even the casual units, displayed a much better disciplinary set-up than this tank destroyer organization of yours."[113]

The 899th had other issues besides poor training and discipline. They had little time to train with the new M10s. They received thirty-six of them only three days before shipping out to Tunisia. After loading the armored vehicles onto railcars for transport, the crews hopped on trucks and left Morocco on March 1, 1943. They arrived in Tunisia on March 14 after traveling more than 1,400 miles. The Germans counterattacked at El Guettar less than ten days later. In response to Roosevelt's orders, this ragtag unit, short on experience, was charging headlong at the bloodied and battle-tested veterans of the 10th Panzer Division.[114]

Before reaching the battlefield, the 899th's commander linked up with his counterpart in the 601st. Baker tried to set him up for success. "I ordered that he [Tincher] employ one company immediately to counterattack north and northeast with a mission of assisting Companies 'B' and 'C' 601st TD, to defend the exposed artillery batteries," wrote the 601st commander. "I pointed out friendly minefields on the ground and described how they were marked." The incoming commander acknowledged the information and returned to his unit to formulate his own course of action.[115]

Thanks to Baker's input, Tincher's plan was straightforward. B Company, under the command of Capt. Kirk E. Adams, would lead the attack while C Company, under the command of Capt. Clarence A. Heckethorn, would occupy a support-by-fire position along the slope of Hill 336. Tincher's A Company, under the command of Capt. Thomas W. Hawksworth, would be the reserve. At 0947 hours, the two vanguard companies passed by the division artillery command post. Eight minutes later, B Company crested the intervisibility line along the Gabes road.[116]

Nearby, machine gunner Frank Viney watched the action unfold from the slopes of Hill 336. "A group of our tank destroyers came into view along the main road to our right, maybe four or five of them," wrote Viney. "They looked like Sherman tanks with short 75mm guns. They all stopped. The first tank fired at a dug-in German tank and missed. He fired another shot and another shot and missed again."

Viney did not like what he saw, wondering who was aiming the gun. He knew the panzer crews were waiting for the perfect shot before they returned fire. Unlike the rookies in the 899th, the 10th Panzer gunners would not miss three times.

He continued, "Then, our tanks with the short, 75mm guns, went forward two abreast. You could see the whole bloody thing. All of sudden this dug-in German tank put his gun on them and just picked them all off, one by one. Knocked them all out."[117]

Bill Harper also witnessed the 899th's unforgiving baptism of fire. "I really felt sorry for them because evidently this was their first combat," he remarked. "Their first platoon that was in combat . . . went through the pass, down the road, and they were wide open. All four of their tanks [were] knocked out. I don't think they . . . fired a shot, because they came through the pass and as soon as they came through the pass . . . the Germans let them have it."[118]

Second Lieutenant Gerald G. Coady was a platoon leader in the 899th. The young man from Cheyenne, Wyoming, was twenty-four years old when he first experienced the horrors of combat. Instead of wilting under the strain, he rose to the occasion. His platoon suffered some of the first casualties when German panzers knocked out two of his tank destroyers. Moments later, Coady watched another destroyer brew up, killing his fellow officer, Second Lt. Alvin F. Koch. Coady wanted to maneuver his platoon, but an American minefield hamstrung his unit's ability to shift laterally. His only option was pushing forward into the panzer kill-sac.

To understand the tactical situation, the intrepid platoon leader hopped off his vehicle and dashed around the battlefield, coordinating the fires of his remaining vehicles and those from the other two platoons. The entire time, the Germans pounded the area with cannon, mortar, and machine-gun fire. Despite the dangers, Coady led three more attacks that day, and the army later awarded him the Silver Star for his bravery.

Corporal Thomas V. Wilson was a tank destroyer commander in B Company. Shortly after cresting the ridge, his M10 suffered two hits and caught fire. Instead of withdrawing to safety, Wilson ordered the driver, Technician Fifth Grade Michael J. Pallotta, to keep the vehicle in the fight. Wilson then ordered his gunner, Technician Fifth Grade Stephen Kurowski, to continue firing the vehicle's 3-inch gun. This was more remarkable, as the first two hits had wounded Kurowski in the legs. Despite the pain, the soldier from Long Island City, New York, kept firing the gun, and the army later credited him with destroying two gun emplacements, one artillery piece, and several machine-gun nests.

Eventually, Wilson's luck ran out. A third hit punctured the fuel tank on the M10. The corporal ordered his men to abandon the vehicle, and, together with Kurowski, he remained with the stricken tank destroyer until a recovery team could tow it off the battlefield. He did not want the Germans to capture the newest American tank destroyer for its technical intelligence value. Wilson, Kurowski, and Pallotta each received a Silver Star for their courage under fire that day. They were not the only soldiers to earn such praise.

Sergeant Charles D. Lum from Rochester, New York, was in charge of a company reserve section. When panzer fire neutralized Captain Adam's half-track, Sergeant Lum volunteered to drive into the maelstrom with a new vehicle for the commander. With him were PFC Fred M. Foster and Privates Earl F. Desbien and Orrie C. Gymer.

After handing off the vehicle, Private Foster saw one of his company's M10s sustain a direct hit. Without a second thought, Foster, with Desbien and Gymer not far behind him, ran toward the smoking vehicle on foot. When Foster arrived at the M10, he realized that he needed a stretcher to carry the wounded, as they could not walk. The quick-thinking soldier from Buffalo, Wyoming, fashioned a makeshift stretcher from equipment that was latched onto the side of the destroyer. The Germans continued to fire at them and hit the smoldering hulk three more times while the three soldiers evacuated the three wounded crew members. Ultimately, they rescued all the survivors and carried them off the battlefield. For their actions, the army awarded Lum, Foster, Desbien, and Gymer each the Silver Star.

Despite the acts of heroism, Colonel Baker was less than impressed with the company's overall performance. "This company [B] moved very slowly and stopped on the pass where they drew intense enemy fire for about ten minutes," wrote Baker. "The leading M10 cut off the road too soon and hit the mine field causing more delay. The rest of the company passed the mine field [sic] safely, but failed to reach their objective. The Company Commander later claimed he was pinned down by enemy fire. In my opinion he maneuvered poorly making an easy target and after losing three or four M10's took up a defiladed position where he remained until withdrawn to a supporting position at about 1600 hours."[119]

The battle of El Guettar was the 899th Tank Destroyer Battalion's first major battle. Seven men lost their lives, and another thirteen men were wounded, most of them from B Company. Four M10s were lost. The Germans had knocked out three of them, while the fourth struck a mine. It returned to the battlefield twenty-four hours later. All were from B Company.[120]

Allen N. Towne was a medic in the 1st Infantry Division. He had seen the new M10s rumble past his aid station the morning of March 23, 1943. After the battle, the battalion maintenance teams towed the shattered machines back to a temporary repair site located near Towne's location.

The medic recalled, "I looked them [M10s] over and saw where the German 88mm shells punched holes clean through the 3-inch armor plate and then exploded inside the tank destroyer. Some shells even went out the other side. These tank destroyers were not like tanks because the turrets were open at the top. This made it easier for the men to get out if the tank destroyer was hit and started to burn."[121]

Lieutenant Goady and the rest of B and C Companies continued to battle the Germans for another six hours. The rookies from the 899th did not know they were beat and refused to leave. However, the Germans did not have plans to withdraw either.[122]

0500 Hours to Midmorning, Tuesday, March 23, 1943
Oasis south of El Guettar, Tunisia

A. J. Liebling was a veteran reporter for *The New Yorker*. Like all good war reporters, Liebling wanted to be where the action was. He wanted to smell the gunpowder from spent bullet casings and share the dangers with his fellow American soldiers. He believed in the cause. In fact, he was a believer before Pearl Harbor. Prior to America's entry to the war, he had reported the German blitzkrieg through France from Paris in May 1940, he saw firsthand the ruins of a blitzed and bruised London in the spring and summer of 1941, and he sailed on a Norwegian tanker across the U-boat–infested North Atlantic the following winter.

And on March 23, 1943, he was sound asleep, nestled in desert oasis, when a voice interrupted his dreams. "Baker reports German tanks threatening to overrun Field Artillery," cackled the voice over the radio.

Liebling stood erect. He was a guard dog, and his ears perked up when he sensed danger. Liebling recalled, "Half awake, I realized that it was no dream voice; then as I became fully conscious I knew it came from inside a half-track equipped with radio which was parked about ten yards from me."

Moments later, the radio squawked again. "Baker recommends infantry on lower slope ground fall back toward soft ground and resist tanks with rocket guns."

The inquisitive reporter now had a story. He started asking questions of those around him. He was with the headquarters defense platoon with several officers, including one man from the G-2 section. The nameless officer remarked to Liebling, "They think they can push us over and laugh at us because Americans can't stand up to German armor." It was obvious to the journalist that the sting of Kasserine still stung, but the soldiers of the 1st Infantry Division were determined to expunge that stain from their record.

From all the different incoming reports, he soon divined the German plan. "Apparently, the German intention was to come around the rear of the American position in the north . . . and cut the main road back to Gafsa, then retake the town and thus leave the First Division stranded. If the maneuver succeeded, the entire disposition of Allied forces designated to contain the German Army in Tunisia while the Eighth Army smashed its way through the Mareth line would be upset," explained the reporter. Liebling felt the stakes could not have been higher.

The intrepid correspondent decided to find a better vantage point to watch the contest. With him was a liaison officer named Troup Howard Matthews from the 1st Armored Division. Together, they found a mud brick wall to crouch behind, and there, they watched the battle unfold like spectators at a sporting event. In fact, Liebling described the battle-field as a "football stadium" with each ridgeline as the stands. Matthews had a pair of binoculars, and he used them to report on the battle's progress while the journalist jotted notes.

Liebling wrote, "Matthews looked through the binoculars and saw a couple of small dots creeping hesitantly towards us like lice across a panhandler's shirt front. He said they were tanks. They came nearer, very indirectly and with frequent halts, until they got as big as bedbugs on a wall, and then geysers of black smoke and dirt began to appear near them."

The two realized that between them and the panzers was open sand. Both hoped that the combat engineers had laid a minefield because without it the German tanks would roll over them. All the headquarters platoon had to stop them were the useless 37mm peashooters. It was not a comforting thought. Liebling estimated that the Germans were only two miles from their location.

Despite the approaching danger, the liaison officer continued to dictate and the reporter continued to scribble. "Then the howitzers got to them," he wrote. "Four tanks were shot through. Their clumsy black bodies, belching dark smoke, remained on the field right below the command post now. You could see them with the naked eye, and they had outgrown the bedbug stage. They were about as big as caramels."

For a moment, the attack stalled. Satisfied that the danger had passed, the two men went to breakfast.[123]

0558 to 1145 Hours, Tuesday, March 23, 1943
Feriana, Tunisia
II Corps Headquarters
The first word of trouble reached the corps headquarters at 0558 hours. Danger Forward reported ten panzers and two companies of infantry. Forty-two minutes later, the phone rang again. Now, the Germans were advancing and had reached a point three kilometers east of Hill 336. At 0700 hours, 1st Infantry Division reported thirty tanks east of the Djebel Berda hill mass. By mid-morning, that number had increased to fifty panzers, and they occupied an area more than six square kilometers.[124]

The Germans had caught the Corps G-2 flat-footed. Thanks to signals intelligence, they knew that the 10th Panzer Division was heading south. They did not know it was about to make a right turn and head west. In his nightly periodic report, Col. Benjamin "Monk" Dickson, who was the Corps G-2, concluded that the Germans were withdrawing toward the coast along the Gabes road after receiving reports of eastbound "heavy traffic." He predicted that the Germans were executing a defense in the north against the 1st Armored Division, near Maknassey—and certainly not a counterattack at El Guettar. Fortunately, the 1st Infantry Division was fighting hard.[125]

Amidst the ringing phones and radio chatter, General Patton arrived at the headquarters fully dressed. He later wrote in his diary that he had slept in "full pack, except shoes and coat." Around 0630 hours, the cocksure corps commander received a call from 1st Infantry Division. Patton recalled, "Terry Allen phoned that he was being attacked by one hundred tanks." Even worse, wrote Patton, "[because] his division was advancing he was not well disposed to meet an attack and they [the Germans] broke through the 18th Infantry and overran B Battery of the 32nd Field Artillery and battery of the 17th getting twelve guns." When Roosevelt requested the 899th Tank Destroyer Battalion, Patton immediately approved it. In addition, he ordered a battalion of infantry from the 34th Infantry Division and a battalion of 155mm howitzers to Allen's beleaguered command.[126]

Close air support was aloft, and the fighter-bombers and spotter planes were sending back reports to the II Corps Headquarters. The first came in at 0815 hours, and it confirmed Allen's report that the Germans had amassed a large panzer force. More troubling was the location; it was only eleven kilometers from Allen's command post, and closing. For forty minutes, the officers debated amongst themselves what was happening. They could do nothing but wait. Shortly after half past nine, Air Support Command relayed from their spotter plans that German panzers were still near El Guettar, but they were no longer advancing. By 1100 hours, Patton felt the tide had turned.[127]

Allen subsequently claimed that they had "knocked out" twenty panzers. Patton was dubious. He scribbled in his diary, "I doubt it. Perhaps ten or fifteen." The corps commander felt Allen exaggerated. In fact, when Allen had reported a hundred tanks earlier that morning, Patton added his own note in the next sentence, as if mocking Allen. He wrote, "Actually there were fifty."

Patton also criticized Allen's tank destroyer tactics. "We had unduly heavy losses in A.T.SP [Antitank Self-Propelled] guns due to faulty employment and very unfortunate terrain," wrote the corps commander. He noted that air support was too slow in reacting. He recalled that it took one hour and forty minutes for the first aircraft to reach El Guettar. Still, for now, it was a victory of sorts. His soldiers were holding firm and not retreating pell-mell to the rear.

Throughout much of the morning, intelligence reports filtered up to the corps headquarters. Sometimes the numbers were accurate, but, more often, they were inflated. Sometime between 1145 and 1153 hours, 1st Infantry Division reported seeing more than 200 tanks and other vehicles several kilometers southeast of the Gabes road. These reports fluctuated all day, muddying the intelligence picture. Was the 1st Infantry Division facing one panzer regiment, one panzer division, or something more? By noon, the Corps G-2, Col. Benjamin A. Dickson, still did not know exactly who was attacking the Big Red One.[128]

CHAPTER FOUR

Afternoon Attack

*"It is a good thing to have teamwork when you're playing Notre
Dame. It is good to have a division functioning as a unit when you're
on the five-yard line. I would like to quote a couple of lines from the
First Division song: We're a hell of gang to tangle with: just stick with
us and see. The First Division will lead the way from hell to victory."*
—MAJOR GENERAL TERRY DE LA MESA ALLEN,
COMMANDER, 1ST INFANTRY DIVISION[1]

All Day, Tuesday, March 23, 1943
El Guettar, Tunisia
Aid Station, 18th Infantry Regiment, 1st Infantry Division
THE AID STATION TENT HAD A HUGE RED CROSS EMBLAZONED ACROSS
it, but the Luftwaffe continued to attack the area around medic Allen N.
Towne. He was in the battle. Towne wrote, "The Germans had control of
the air and strafed and bombed often. . . . When they identified a possible target, they would drop canisters full of small bombs. These canisters
would open up in the air and spread the bombs over a large area."

For protection, Towne and the other medics dug slit trenches near
the tents. These trenches became their cots when they were not working
inside the aid station. "You could not have a peaceful sleep unless you
had a covered hole," recalled the medic. "Sleeping in a small, covered
foxhole is not pleasant because the dirt keeps trickling down on you
and your blanket."

Lying in the hole, Towne wondered, "What if a bomb lands nearby? Will the hole collapse and smother me?"[2]

On March 23, Towne and other medics were busy. Casualties rolled in throughout the day and within a few hours, the butcher's bill overwhelmed them. By mid-afternoon, Towne realized that the wounded were not just from the 18th Infantry but also from other units, including German ones. "We had so many wounded that we had to put them in the field near the tent," wrote Towne. "At one time, we had forty or fifty wounded men at our aid station with more coming in all the time. Even with all twelve ambulances taking the wounded to the clearing company, the number kept building." Only the wounded who need a surgeon to sew up a sucking chest wound or tie off a gushing artery received immediate medical attention. During the forty-eight-hour period of March 22 through 24, the division clearing station processed 305 battle casualties.[3]

The grim business of triaging the wounded became a game of statistics. Surgeons were supposed to determine who had the best chance of living and prioritize who received medical care. Some of them could not do it. "We also had a problem with some of the doctors because they would spend so much time with the worst cases (who could not live)," wrote Towne. "We had to select the ones to be worked on. It was bedlam."

The memory of the crying and wailing wounded stuck with Allen decades after the battle. They haunted his memories. "One young soldier had been severely shot in both of his legs by a strafing German plane," recalled the medic. "He was crying, 'My father lost both of his legs in World War I and now I am going to lose my legs.' All we could do for him was to stop the bleeding, put sulfa and dressings on his wounds, give him a shot of morphine and send him back to the clearing company." The young medic later learned from one of the surgeons that the soldier would likely lose both legs.[4]

1500 Hours, Tuesday, March 23, 1943
El Keddab Ridge, Tunisia
A Company, 601st Tank Destroyer Battalion, 1st Infantry Division
It seemed as if the battle would never end. "The attack had started at daybreak and had kept going all morning without a let up," wrote gunner

Private Thomas Morrison. "Most of our equipment had been knocked out in the first encounter."[5]

Colonel Baker knew his battalion had taken a beating. According to radio reports, most of the B and C Company guns were no longer operable. "Many officers and men of my units were coming out on foot reporting their actions and losses," wrote the battalion commander.

Miner's A Company platoon was still in the fight. At 1500 hours, he ordered Sgt. Fred E. Swartz to withdraw his gun truck behind the dune to refuel and restock its ammunition for the next fight. Morrison, the gunner, climbed out of the half-track and into his foxhole. "I was in a hole making coffee for us when the M3 got a direct hit within the right rear gas tank," wrote the private.

The explosion rocked the ridgeline, and flames engulfed the half-track. "I doubt if [Theodore S.] Kordana or [Charles M.] Hird ever knew what hit them," theorized Morrison. "Swartz was getting some instructions from the Captain so he didn't get hit either." Now, without a truck, Morrison no longer had a purpose on the front line. Lieutenant Miner ordered him to the rear to wait for a new crew and half-track.

"Years later, while working for General Motors I heard a fellow worker describing how his outfit went in to relieve another outfit that had been wiped out," wrote the private. "It turned out he had been with the 899th that day at El Guettar. He let me understand that the 899th thought we were stupid to go up against a panzer with nothing but M3's."[6] Unfortunately, the last few surviving half-tracks had one more panzer thrust to blunt.

1245 to 1643 Hours, Tuesday, March 23, 1943
El Guettar, Tunisia
Headquarters, 1st Infantry Division (Danger Forward)
At 1245 hours, Colonel Greer called over the radio. It was good news. "18th still in position and doing fine," he reported. A sigh of relief came over the headquarters.

Greer continued. His voice was staccato to shorten the messages. "Enemy tanks probably are covering their withdrawal. Sternberg [2nd Battalion] is okay. Brown [3rd Battalion] is at original position. General

Roosevelt ordered counterattack to restore positions of 5th and 32nd [field artillery battalions]. Crawford is going northeast [2nd Battalion, 16th Infantry]. We need trucks and guns. 1st and 2nd Battalion are still on line. 3rd is on objective three . . . eight . . . six . . . eight. 32nd and 5th in front of me up north. We need ammo and guns."

The men in the headquarters jotted the information on pieces of paper. Others began to make calls to help Greer's beleaguered 18th Infantry. The division chief of staff, Colonel Mason, picked up the radio and informed Greer, "We've called the corps on the ammo situation and we're getting it up to you."

General Roosevelt chimed in from somewhere on the battlefield. His feisty voice made him sound like a coach giving a pep talk. "18th is doing a grand job. Also the 17th Field Artillery Battalion," he said over the radio static. "Big battle is going on in front. Twenty-four tanks. Some knocked out. Counterattacking with 2nd Battalion. I sent two companies to restore positions of 5th and 32nd. Rangers to take over positions of 2nd Battalion."

The assistant division commander reported good news. "One hundred Germans captured from the 580th Reconnaissance Unit and some from the 7th German Infantry. 1st Battalion knocked out halftracks and some tanks."

Roosevelt closed his communication with the following recommendation: "Two important things: keep lines to division open. Get ammo up."[7]

The counterattack force that Roosevelt ordered was 2nd Battalion, 16th Infantry Regiment. It was under the command of Lt. Col. Joseph B. Crawford. He assembled his battalion to move out from its attack position at 0915 hours, and he established his forward command post two kilometers due east of Hill 336 at 0950 hours. He knew that the Germans had overrun at least six howitzer positions of the 5th and 32nd Field Artillery Battalions. It was his mission to recapture the guns. Crawford's plan was to counterattack with F Company in the north, E Company in the center, and G Company in the south. The improvised operation began sometime around one o'clock in the afternoon.[8]

At exactly 1300 hours, someone from the 1st Ranger Battalion called over the field phone to confirm Greer's report. According to the nameless staff officer, the panzers were withdrawing. Fifteen minutes later, the radio squawked. It was Colonel Darby from 1st Ranger Battalion. "Our trucks are dragging three damaged TDs back from the front of our OP," said Darby. "One other just hit a mine and will also be recovered. Enemy tanks previously reported looking north from Bir Mrabott reported by our OP to have apparently withdrawn further to [the] east. Everything looks quiet now."[9]

Twenty-five minutes later, the field phone clanged. It was Lt. Col. Russell F. Akers, a staff officer in II Corps' G-3 Section. He asked for Colonel Gibb.

Akers did not waste time with small talk. "You have two bombing missions coming up this afternoon," he informed Colonel Gibb. "Also, a battalion of tanks will be moving closely to you. An LNO [liaison officer] will be up to see you. 84th Field Artillery Battalion is going to be attached to you."

Gibb replied, "We're using them for something else."

"If you have to use them then pull them out," said the corps staffer. The G-3 nodded and said, "Okay."

Akers knew air support was important. Now, it was time for information. "Give me a summary of the situation," said Aker.

"We lost no positions," said Gibb. Apparently, the six howitzers did not count in his assessment.

"The big, big chief is pleased to hear that," said Aker. Both sides routinely spoke in code because radios were unencrypted and the opposing side often tapped phone lines. The "big, big chief" was most likely Patton himself.

Gibb described the current state of operations to the staff officer. The 18th Infantry had reconnoitered much of the Dj el Mcheltat and Djebel Berda hill masses. Its forward line of troops extended from Hill 482 in the north to Hill 369 in the south. In between the two high points were the El Guettar Valley and the panzers. Elements of the 26th Infantry had cleared the ground around Hill 609, which was northeast of the 18th Infantry Regiment's positions. Farther to the west, the attached 3rd Battalion, 16th Infantry, was digging in atop Dj bou Rhedja (Hill 483), while the 1st Ranger Battalion was securing 3rd Battalion's southern flank. Finally, Crawford's 2nd Battalion had begun the counterattack to recapture the lost artillery positions.

"Any report on the bombings?" inquired Akers.

It was a sore subject for Gibb. "No," he replied.

Akers could not detect Gibb's expression over the phone and pressed the issue. "What about smoke?"

Gibb snapped, "We have none. How about some goddamn fighters?"

The staff officer assured the irate division operations officer, "We have some coming up this afternoon."[10]

The operations officer acknowledged the message and hung up the phone. The Germans seemed to control the airspace and bombed them at will. Although the P-39s and A-20s were helpful, the Stuka problem required air cover, and the Big Red One was not getting it.

Twenty minutes later, Akers called back. "Stuff we have in the air is coming down. Should be there now," he told Gibb. "Another one just took off. Maybe we'll have two more this afternoon."

The phone never seemed to stop ringing. At 1400 hours, Greer called Gibb to update him on the 18th Infantry's situation. "I request a bombing mission on tanks out there," began the regimental commander. "Grid Three . . . Nine . . . Zero . . . Six . . . Nine . . . Zero." The target location was less than a kilometer south of Dj el Mcheltat.

Greer continued to describe how he wanted the planes to strafe, as if he was directing them personally. "Move up this way a little bit, so change it a little bit this way. I estimate four thousand yards. Most them are Mark VIs."

Gibb replied, "There are two missions on the way. One of them just took off. There are two more after that."

"If we don't stop them, they are going to be here pretty soon," predicted Greer.

Gibb wanted confirmation. "That coordinate gives the location of the tanks, the Mark VIs," he said.[11]

Greer acknowledged the message and ended the call. The division operations officer had little time to catch his breath and gather his wits because four minutes later the phone rang again. He picked it up. This time it was Akers.

"Outfit of Talbot's will be one and half miles northeast of Gafsa," he told Gibb. Talbot was the commander of 2nd Battalion, 66th Armored Regiment. His name was the code for his unit. The 66th Armored Regiment was part of the 1st Armored Division, and their mission was to seize a mountain pass east of the town of Meknassy.

Akers had other news. "More field artillery coming up; arty ammo and replacements," he announced to Gibb. "What else you want?"

The operations officer yelled into the handset, "Fighters!"

The corps staff officer was dumbfounded. For a moment, he was speechless. Finally, he stammered, "They should be there now; although you don't see them." The answer did not assuage Gibb.

"We'll be dive-bombed in about ten or fifteen minutes," the G-3 claimed.

"Goddammit . . . something should be done about that. Call me if you do," Akers tried to share Gibb's sentiment, as if to mollify him.

The division's operations officer barked, "I will . . . from my hole," and he slammed the phone down onto the receiver.[12]

While Gibb and Mason worked the phones, General Allen entertained a gaggle of thirty reporters who had shown up at his command post to hear about the morning's battle. Allen's aide, Maj. Kenneth Downs, led the reporters to an almond tree where Allen met them. Liebling was among the correspondents and wrote, "The affair resembled a mass interview given by a football coach right after winning a big game." All of them waited to hear what Allen had to say, their pens poised on their notepads, waiting.

"I think the division has done fairly well today," the general announced. "And I want to stress the idea that whatever it did was due to teamwork. Everybody in the division deserves credit. The artillery deserves credit, and so do the engineers, the tank destroyers, and the Ranger battalion—and don't forget the medics and the birds who drive the trucks. I don't want anybody to think I'm sore about air support. I guess the Air Force here has a lot of demands on it. I guess maybe there was some other division on the front that was attacked by two or three Panzer divisions and the Air Force had to help them first." Allen's voice dripped with sarcasm.

"General, may I ask how many tanks you had in the battle?" asked one of the journalists.

"None," replied Allen.

According to Liebling, another reporter then inquired if the 1st Armored Division, which was on Allen's northern flank, had relieved some of the pressure. Allen responded, "I guess they had motor trouble."

The division commander changed the subject. "There is one thought I would like to leave with you gentlemen, and that is that this teamwork is due to having the division together as a unit," said Allen. "It is a good thing to have teamwork when you're playing Notre Dame. It is good to have a division functioning as a unit when you're on the five-yard line. I would like to quote a couple of lines from the First Division song: We're a hell of gang to tangle with: just stick with us and see. The First Division will lead the way from hell to victory." With those final words, he ended the press conference.[13]

Despite the deluge of outgoing howitzer shells and Allen's bluster, the Germans were far from beaten. At 1450 hours, twelve Ju-87 Stukas dive-bombed the division headquarters around El Guettar. Luckily, the howling banshees missed their target, but they were only the beginning.[14]

At 1515 hours, II Corps called. The voice on the phone said to Colonel Gibb, "We have positive information that the 10th Panzer Division will attack at 1600 today, with 1st and 2nd battalions, 86th Panzergrenadiers, with 1st and 2nd Battalions, 7th Regiment, and the 2nd and 4th battalions of the 90th Artillery Regiment." Most likely, the corps had intercepted a German tactical radio communication, signaling the impending operation.[15]

Thirteen minutes later, division called the 18th Infantry Regiment to alert them of the attack. It was clear what unit was behind the morning's festivities. The soldiers of the 10th Panzer Division were out for revenge, and Colonel Greer sensed his command would be the target of their vengeance.[16]

Gibb and the rest of the division staff did not sit on their hands, waiting for the German attack at 1600 hours. They kept working the phones and radios, preparing the reception party. At 1601, Maj. Robert N. Tyson, the commander of the 5th Field Artillery Battalion, called Colonel Gibb on the field phone.

"We have six guns that are out of action. I think six prime movers, also. Casualties are slight," reported Tyson.

Gibb asked, "What is the position of your guns?"

"The same positions as the attack this morning," answered Tyson.

"Can you get to them?" Gibb did not want the Germans to capture intact American artillery, nor did he want to spike the guns.

"Yes, we're pulling them out now," said Tyson.[17]

The 5th Field Artillery's bad day could have been worse. That morning, contrary to Tyson's report, they lost only four prime movers in D Battery to enemy artillery. In addition, B Battery lost four howitzers. Their crews had destroyed the tubes to prevent German forces from capturing them. At 1130 hours, Tyson ordered his battalion to pull out and was still withdrawing when the next attack kicked off.[18]

Ten minutes after four in the afternoon, II Corps reported that the Germans were delaying their attack to 1640 hours. The information was the result of Allied signal intelligence that had intercepted and broken the German radio code. Allen could not hold back. He ordered his signal company to transmit a message on the German radio net at 1615 hours.

The division commander's message was "What the hell are you guys waiting for? We have been ready ever since 4:00 PM." The message was signed "FIRST DIVISION."[19]

As Allen's message went out over the German radio net, Gibb was on the phone with Lt. Col. Robert A. Hewitt, the II Corps G-3. Gibb had not had all the information regarding his losses from the morning. Now, he did.

"We have lost all the guns of B and C companies of the 601st Tank Destroyer Battalion and lost seven guns of the 899th Tank Destroyer Battalion. Two are recoverable of the ones that the 601st lost," he informed Hewitt.

The Corps G-3 asked Gibb, "What did you get?" Losing two tank destroyer companies would be a bitter pill to swallow if the Germans had not paid a handsome price for them.

Gibb replied, "We got thirty tanks with a possibility of forty."

Hewitt's boss, General Patton, was never satisfied with remaining on the defensive. His operations officer understood his commander's intent and asked, "Are you pushing?"

Gibb grimaced and replied, "We have nothing to push with. What are we going to do if something hits us, and we need those tank destroyers?" The division's operations officer wondered if his corps counterpart was on the same battlefield.

"Grab the tanks you have at Gafsa. They are yours. I thought that Akers told you that. Your mission is to defend the town. Go to the assembly area and grab those tanks," said Hewitt.

"Okay, that is a different picture," Gibb replied.

Hewitt realized that even with radios and telephones, battlefield friction had caused a breakdown in communication. Fortunately, he had a solution. "Akers is on the way to the town to push everything to you," he notified Gibb.

"Fine," said Gibb, who then hung up the phone.

At 1643 hours, observation posts from the 601st Tank Destroyer Battalion reported panzers approaching from the east. Their current location was southwest of Dj el Mcheltat and northwest of Djebel Berda. This corroborated an earlier message from a division observation post that reported seeing the same thing. Estimated panzer count was three Mk VIs and eight Mk IVs. This meant the panzers had bypassed the three infantry battalions again.[20]

1600 to 1640 Hours, Tuesday, March 23, 1943
5000 yards east of the El Keddab Ridge (Hill 336), Tunisia
3rd Platoon, A Company, 1st Engineers Combat Battalion
When the panzers withdrew to lick their wounds from El Guettar Pass earlier that afternoon, combat engineers from the 1st Engineer Combat Battalion moved in behind them to reseed and extend a minefield. If the panzers returned, they would roll right into trap.[21]

In 1943, the engineer combat battalions had three lettered companies, a headquarters and service company, and a medical detachment. The battalion staff habitually attached each lettered company to one of the regimental combat teams. For example, A Company usually was with the 16th Infantry Regiment, while B and C Companies were with the 18th and 26th Infantry Regiments, respectively.

Each combat engineer company mirrored the battalion organization. It had a triangular structure with three platoons, and, like the companies, the commander habitually attached a platoon to one of the infantry battalions (1st Platoon with 1st Battalion and so on). The main mission of the combat engineer company was the removal and emplacement of obstacles, such as minefields and booby traps. Since the army considered engineers combat support, they were short of heavy weaponry. The battalion's most casualty-producing weapon was the nine 37mm towed antitank guns. Being a combat engineer was a dangerous job, but it was crucial if the infantry or armor wanted their freedom of maneuver on the battlefield.[22]

Constituted on December 31, 1861, the 1st Engineers was one of the oldest units in the division. During the Civil War, it participated in the Peninsula campaign, Antietam, Fredericksburg, Chancellorsville, the Overland campaign of 1864, and the siege of Petersburg and was present at Appomattox, when the war ended. In 1898, it fought at Manila against Spain and then remained there to quell the Philippine insurrection through the turn of the century. In World War I, it fought at St. Mihiel and the Meuse-Argonne.[23]

The commander of the 1st Engineer Combat Battalion was Lt. Col. Henry C. Rowland. Born on February 4, 1913, in France, Colonel Rowland earned his bachelor's degree in engineering from Yale University in 1937. He was commissioned shortly after graduation as a second lieutenant in the combat engineers on September 20, 1937. He made first lieutenant on September 9, 1940, and was promoted to captain thirteen months later on October 10, 1941. Thanks to the outbreak of hostilities on December 7, 1941, Rowland was a lieutenant colonel and a battalion commander, leading his unit at El Guettar less than twenty-four months after he had been a captain.[24]

The day before the German attack, the engineers had been busy. "On March 22, we laid 3254 mines in front of El Guettar, south of the Gafsa-Gabes road," recalled Rowland. "That was the weak zone of our defense and it was all broad terrain, good inviting land to the Panzer tanks. When the attack was launched on the 23rd, our mine fields were ready to direct the attack into channels the Division was prepared to police." Rowland's minefield extended from Hill 336 and curved to the southwest.[25]

Later that afternoon, Colonel Rowland received word from the division of the impending attack sometime before 1600 hours. He alerted A and D Companies to move out to close the gap between the Dj el Mcheltat and Djebel Berda hill masses. He wanted a blocking obstacle comprised of antitank mines. After completion of the minefield, he ordered the two companies to dig in and serve as infantry on the southern flank of 3rd Battalion, 18th Infantry. If the Germans were coming, they would be in for a nasty surprise.[26]

Second Lieutenant William M. Kays was the platoon leader for 3rd Platoon, A Company. He recalled hearing about the upcoming late afternoon German assault. Shortly after getting the word over the field phone, Lieutenant Kays welcomed a motorcyclist who was serving as messenger for his company commander, Capt. Charlie Murphy.

"Bring up the 2nd and 3rd Platoons and the two truckloads of mines," ordered the motorcyclist.

Kays and the others had learned that Germans had postponed their attack until 1640 hours. He thought to himself, "It sounds like Custer's last message: 'Benteen, bring up the packs.' Fine and dandy; we and the whole 10th Panzer Division would arrive at the same place at the same time."

After several minutes organizing his platoon of vehicles, Kays hopped into the cab of his lead truck. In the back were hundreds of mines. He hoped that the Germans would ignore his olive canvas–covered tinderbox on wheels. Shortly before 1640 hours, they rolled out for the front.

"We followed a fairly straight paved road over absolutely flat desert for several miles and soon got to an area with artillery batteries scattered over the desert to the right and various vehicles moving about," wrote Kays in his memoir.

He recognized two soldiers standing on the south side of the road. They were waving their hands, signaling for him to decelerate. "As we pulled near him [Lt. William Barnum] he suddenly started to wave his arm frantically," recalled Kays. "I glanced to the left and saw a whole line of Me109s skimming over the desert and coming towards us about thirty feet off the ground. It was exactly 1640."[27]

The 109s were not alone. Behind them were ten JU-88s. The soldiers of Battery B, 105th Coastal Artillery Battalion, swung their guns into action, and a steady stream of crumping sounds echoed in the valley as puffs of smoke began to appear in the sky. The Germans' planes braved the barrage and kept flying toward them.[28]

"I grabbed the door handle, leaped out of the truck, and headed for the ground on the shoulder of the road," explained Kays. "As I went down I glimpsed the wings of a plane go overhead and a pair of bombs sailing below it. The noise of the machine-gun fire was so intense that I have no recollection of the sound of the bombs. It was all over in a second, and then I heard people screaming 'medic, medic' all around me."

Kays described the carnage around him: "A great flood of blood was oozing from the back of a guy a few feet away. Another guy was running around in circles holding his left arm. Gasoline was pouring out of the ruptured gas tank just behind me, the tires were flat, and my cab door was riddled with holes. The truck following mine was on fire."

Kays and the other engineers ran to the burning truck and pulled what they could from the wreck while others attempted to put out the fire. Kays's plan was to transfer the gear and men from the damaged truck to the other vehicles in his platoon.

"At that moment I heard whistles blowing and the anti-aircraft noise started again," recalled Kays. "I looked up and the sky seemed full of Ju88s coming down at us. I simply ran as far as I could to get away from the vehicles and the mines, glancing upwards all the time, hit the dirt, and then looked up and watched almost in fascination as what looked like a school of sardines dropped out from under each plane. The bombs were silver and seemed to twinkle."

The platoon leader wondered if this was the end. "At the last second I buried my head in my hands and an instant later the earth exploded around me," wrote Kays. "A moment later I looked up and all was smoke and dust and the smell of TNT."

Kays touched every part of his body, hoping he was okay. He was still alive but realized the road was the worst place he could be. He searched for safety. He found a nearby slit trench and scurried into the foot-deep hole, laid on his stomach, and burrowed into his helmet, a turtle retreating into its shell.

"It was none too soon," explained Kays, "because once again the whistles sounded and the 40mm guns and machine guns began their deafening racket. Another huge flight of Ju88s was diving down on us (actually, it was the artillery they were after). I watched once more in fascination as the twinkling sardines appeared, and then ducked at the last instant. The earth bounced and it seemed like I was somewhere in the depths of hell."

The one strafing and two bombing runs had scattered the two platoons of A Company. It would take some time before Kays and his company commander, Capt. Charlie Murphy, brought order to the chaos. By then, the minefield was no longer necessary. It was too late for digging obstacles. For the rest of the battle, the engineers would be infantrymen.[29]

1520 to 1640 Hours, Tuesday, March 23, 1943
Along the southern side of El Keddab Ridge (Hill 336), Tunisia
Forward Command Post, 601st Tank Destroyer Battalion
At 1520 hours, the commander of the 601st received word that the Germans would attack at 1600 hours. The situation was far from ideal. Colonel Baker had only three platoons left to stop the impending German panzer attack: Miner's platoon from A Company, Yowell's platoon from B Company, and Munn's platoon from C Company. That was it. Most of the destroyers were damaged or wrecked beyond repair, scattered detritus across the valley.

Munn's last report was bleak. "He reported that he had one serviceable gun and nine enemy tanks were 1100 yards of his position in a defiladed position," wrote Baker in his after action report. "I told him to use his own judgment as to whether or not he should abandon his gun and come out on foot, thereby saving valuable trained personnel."

Later that afternoon and before the attack, Baker heard from Lieutenant Yowell, 2nd Platoon, B Company. His situation was not much better than Munn's. "He reported that he had two serviceable guns and seventy rounds of ammunition," recalled the battalion commander. "I advised him that he move north and northeast after dark and try to contact friendly infantry."[30]

When Baker learned the German command delayed their attack until 1640 hours, "we thought it might be another Nazi trick and that they had meant us to intercept." However, it was not. The Germans were punctual. Baker wrote, "At 1640 to the minute two battalions of German infantry formed some four thousand yards to our front and moved on our positions."

Baker grabbed his binoculars and scanned the horizon, searching for the panzers. He found them. "Their tanks formed behind them, as if to follow the infantry. However, the armor merely milled around and created dust and confusion. The tanks did not advance any farther, staying out of our effective range," said the commander.[31]

The 601st commander estimated the distance to the panzers was roughly 5,000 yards. This meant the panzers were likely an exploitation force that had the mission to follow a successful infantry penetration. Without their armor protection, though, the panzergrenadiers were sitting ducks. Baker wrote, "The infantry attacked in extended formation, generally abreast of the Gabes road. The men walked upright, moved slowly, and made no attempt at concealment or maneuver."

The surprised and dumbfounded officer could not believe his eyes. Before him was a massive, slow-moving target. He continued, "The tank destroyers held their fire and let the infantry come in standing up. Our silence apparently gave them confidence."

It was Pickett's charge in Tunisia. Baker played the role of Brig. Gen. Henry J. Hunt commanding the Union artillery along Cemetery Ridge at Gettysburg. On July 3, 1863, he ordered his guns to cease-fire after a lengthy Rebel bombardment. This ruse deceived the Confederates. They thought they had neutralized the Union cannons when, in fact, the Union artillery crews were husbanding their ammunition for the expected Confederate infantry assault. When Maj. Gen. George Pickett's men marched toward the Union lines, they marched toward their doom. Hunt's artillery decimated them. The deadly fusillades from Hunt's batteries whittled divisions into brigades, and those same brigades were regiments by the time they reached the Union lines.

Now, the approaching German infantry were Pickett's men, marching toward slaughter. Baker waited for the right moment to open fire. "We cut them down at fifteen hundred yards," said the colonel. "It was like mowing hay. The tank destroyers fired rapidly, employing all arms. The heavy-caliber high explosive shells were the most effective."

Colonel Darby made the same comparison when he saw the Axis attack from his position. "The infantry leading was followed by some sixty tanks in what looked like an attack in the American Civil War," wrote the Ranger officer. "The Germans took no cover, seeming not to be aware of the almost certain deathtrap into which they were moving. I was never so wildly excited as when watching this mass of men and vehicles inching towards us."[32]

Colonel Baker remembered one of his soldiers in particular. "One gun sergeant bracketed rapidly and fired as fast as he could, making five-mil deflection changes," explained Baker. "He dropped high explosive shells at seven yard intervals across the German lines." The effect was devastating.[33]

Darby corroborated Baker's account on the artillery's effectiveness. "When the Germans were within 1,550 yards, the Yankee artillery boomed one salvo on top of another," said Darby. "The shells were concentrated dead on the enemy troops. Soon the eerie black smoke of the time shells showed that they were bursting above the heads of the Germans. Then a hole would appear in the oncoming carpet of the attack."[34]

Despite the bloodshed and carnage, the German panzergrenadiers weathered the steel rain and pushed ahead toward the gun line of the 32nd Field Artillery and the infantry of 3rd Battalion, 18th Infantry. Between the advancing enemy and American howitzers were the vestiges of Lieutenant Munn's tank destroyer platoon.

1605 to 2300 Hours, Tuesday, March 23, 1943[35]
Along the southern side of El Keddab Ridge (Hill 336), Tunisia
Remnants of 3rd Platoon, C Company, 601st Tank Destroyer Battalion
One gun truck and several ancillary vehicles were all they had. By late afternoon, 3rd Platoon no longer had the ammunition for the one gun truck. Lieutenants Perry and Munn knew the German attack was coming at 1605 hours when Colonel Baker warned them of the impending

panzer *Angriff* (assault). They learned of the thirty-minute delay shortly thereafter. Neither knew what to do. Munn confirmed Baker's account. "We then asked Colonel Baker for instructions," recalled the platoon leader. "He gave us two plans and told us to use our judgment as to which we should use." Perry claimed the radio message was, "Wait until dark and try to bring out the vehicles. If it gets too hot destroy the vehicles and come out on foot."[36]

At 1640, the two officers watched a flight of German bombers as they flew over their position to bomb the artillery to the rear. In the valley, following behind the aircraft, were the panzers. It was now or never.

Munn and Perry did not want to leave the one gun truck or the other vehicles behind. The two officers asked volunteers to drive them down from the mountains. They knew it was a risky proposition, at best, and they did not want to order the men to participate in a possible suicide mission. The remaining crews had a better chance of survival if they climbed over the ridge on foot. That was the plan.

Corporal Clifford E. Maclean offered to drive Munn's command track off the battlefield while Corp. Thomas Langan volunteered to do the same for the last reconnaissance truck. To ensure that the Germans could not salvage the weapons, they dissembled the breechblocks from the guns and loaded them on Maclean's vehicle. Perry also ordered the radios loaded onto Maclean's truck to prevent their capture.

The survivors split up with the officers leading most of them on foot over the mountains. Harper remembered their flight over the ridge. "So we took off and evidently we had bad information . . . because we never saw any German infantry."[37]

It was a different story for the vehicle operators. Maclean discovered that infiltration was out of the question because German infantry blocked the roads. He eventually found a nameless captain from the 32nd Field Artillery who ordered him to torch his half-track. Maclean complied and escaped on foot. Corporal James E. Markle, another section leader in the platoon, decided to drive his truck out at the last minute. He ordered his section to leave him and escape over El Keddab Ridge without him.

"A job he knew, [*sic*] to be almost sure suicide," Munn later wrote. "To the best of my knowledge and investigation, Corporal Markle was killed in this action. Sergeant [Frank] Seiffert saw a man dead behind the wheel, but he could not be sure if it was Corporal Markle. On the 25th of March, I again went to the scene of the battle, where I saw Markle's track riddled with holes and the body had been removed."[38] He later commented in an article that his corporal from Norfolk County, Massachusetts, was "one of my best men, too."

Most of the men were thrilled to be alive. "All of us were pretty happy about getting back," remarked Munn. "But we were still plenty sore about one thing. There was a German officer riding back and forth in one of our jeeps, using it as an ammunition carrier. The boys would have given six months' PX rations if they could have recaptured that jeep—and what was riding in it."[39]

1640 Hours, Tuesday, March 23, 1943
Base of Dj bou Rhedja (Hill 483), Tunisia
B Battery, 32nd Field Artillery Battalion

First Lieutenant Frank Silva wondered what would happen next. The Germans were coming, and his battery was not far from the front lines. In fact, it was too close. "Then we got shelled by one of our Corps artillery 155's from our rear," wrote Silva. "All kinds of concussions and stuff flying around at that point. . . . We got a hell of a pasting before it stopped."[40]

At 1640 hours, the final German assault began. Almost immediately, panzergrenadiers scrambled up the hill toward B Battery. Captain Charles H. Cooke, the battery commander, ordered his men to spike the guns and withdraw westward toward El Guettar. According to Silva, Cooke issued the command because they did not have enough men to operate the howitzers.[41]

Silva was one of the last to leave with an unnamed lieutenant from an attached antiaircraft battery. Suddenly, bullets ripped through the air. Both officers dived into a nearby gully, but before they were safely behind cover, one burst struck the nameless lieutenant. Silva looked around and spotted a German machine-gun crew crouched behind an MG 34 on a bipod.

"I got up again with a submachine gun. . . . I fired on the two Germans and we didn't see them again," remarked Silva.

The battery executive officer, with the wounded lieutenant leaning on him for support, stumbled and staggered for fifty yards. The injured man said, "Go on. Leave me."

Silva shook his head. "I'm not leaving you," he replied.

"Then he collapsed," recalled the battery executive officer. "No pulse or breathing. The best I could do was fold his arms over his chest and put his helmet over his face. Took his wallet and field glasses and went on to the rear."[42]

Together with the survivors of the 5th Field Artillery Battalion, the cannon cockers from the 32nd started their reorganization that night east of El Guettar. Linking up with them was the 84th Field Artillery Battalion, a corps asset. General Andrus, the division's overall artillery commander, believed that the lack of infantry protection was the reason behind the abandonment of so many guns. In his after action report, he wrote, "Infantry must furnish close defense of battery position . . . against hostile infantry. Twenty-four guns were lost because this was not done."

Unbeknownst to Andrus, few infantry were available. Those who were nearby had their hands full.[43]

1640 to 1740 Hours, Tuesday, March 23, 1943
El Keddab Ridge (Hill 336), Tunisia
Command Post, 18th Infantry Regiment
Captain Henry B. Middleworth was the regimental S2 in the 18th Infantry. He recalled the events leading up to the late afternoon attack. "That afternoon we sweated out the second attack and at 4:40 it came. The German infantry rode up on the back of their tanks and our mortar fire was very effective. The colonel [Greer] was like a schoolboy at a picnic. He sat at this observation post and watched the boys stop Jerry. 'Let them come in closer,' he'd holler 'and we'll knock the hell out of him.'"[44]

At 1710, the regimental command post alerted the division that the German main effort was approaching 3rd Battalion. Brown's men reported at least three companies of enemy infantry with panzers climbing and scampering up the slope. Ten minutes later, observers in 1st Battalion, from their position atop Djebel Berda, warned that the Germans had surrounded 3rd Battalion.

The same voice over the radio then said, "Several hundred German troops are moving into our rear area, using the same route we took coming up here."

At 1737 hours, the news worsened. Panzers and panzergrenadiers had reached the gun line, forcing A Battery, 32nd Field Artillery, to abandon their positions. Three minutes later, the call went out over the net to 1st and 2nd Battalions. "Hold everything. Fight it out," was the message to the men in the foxholes.[45]

Despite the hazards, Middleworth claimed Greer never lost his composure. "The colonel was confident," said Middleworth. "He was king of the hill. His only worry was how Brown's battalion on Djebel Mcheltat would make out and the reports kept coming in and Colonel Brown's boys were making out fine."[46]

1635 to 1744 Hours, Tuesday, March 23, 1943
Dj el Mcheltat (Hill 482), Tunisia
Command Post, 3rd Battalion, 18th Infantry Regiment
Staff Sergeant Andrew J. Kukucka worked at the battalion headquarters as a member of the S-3 section. During the attack, he was with Colonel Brown. "My toughest job is keeping up with the old man. And that day was tougher than any," recalled Kukucka.

"At 4:35, I was talking with Captain Donald Fogg, CO of Company L on the field phone," said the operations sergeant. "I called him up and told him that we got word from Regimental that the attack would open at 4:40."

"We ain't gonna budge an inch," replied Fogg.

"Neither am I," said Kukucka.

As the two continued to psyche each other up for the upcoming battle, the German air raid began. "What was that?" Fogg asked the sergeant.

"That was a siren," he answered. By now, ME109s were strafing the area, and right behind them were Ju88s, plastering the valley with bombs. The NCO decided it was time to go and said, "Pardon me while I hang up." Later, Sergeant Kukucka saw Captain Fogg. Fogg admitted "that he had more fun that day than he'd had in a long time. I guess it was the same way with me."[47] Despite the dangers, the men were caught up in the excitement and adrenaline of the battle.

First Lieutenant Herbert Smith, the executive officer for 3rd Battalion's heavy weapons company, described the effects of the American artillery on the approaching panzergrenadiers. "Infantrymen could be seen moving steadily forward ahead of the tanks," wrote Smith. "With the first move of the enemy armor, the first shells of the remaining artillery pieces began to erupt on the valley floor. Our artillery, previously ranged in, smothered the attackers with time and point detonating fire."

The artillery and mortar fire was so rapid that it sounded as if it was "automatic artillery" to Smith. The impact was devastating on the German soldiers. Smith recalled, "What had been a well-organized attack became the movements of a disorganized mob."[48]

1655 to 1830 Hours, Tuesday, March 23, 1943
El Guettar, Tunisia
Headquarters, 1st Infantry Division (Danger Forward)
At 1655 hours, the division observation post called in on the field phone to alert them that the expected attack finally had begun. A minute later, someone from II Corps called. Colonel Gibb picked up the phone. "We are sending King [701st Tank Destroyer Battalion] down with a new tank destroyer battalion tonight," the voice announced. "I want Herschel Baker [601st Tank Destroyer Battalion] to bring his crowd back here tonight. An officer will be sent to you tonight after dark."

At that moment, Gibb did not care about tank destroyers. Once again, the Luftwaffe had strafed and bombed his division. "Can we get a fighter plane up here?" he asked.

The corps staff officer declined to answer the question about air support. Instead, he told Gibb, "I talked with the LNO who was outside of town [El Guettar]. And he told me that Talbot [2nd Battalion, 66th Armored Regiment] was going into a bivouac area there. I told him to get a LNO to you there so don't be surprised if you see him coming up the road." Gibb acknowledged the message and hung up the phone. Tanks were nice, but fighters would have been better.

Simultaneously, Colonel Mason was on another phone with Colonel Greer. The regimental commander alerted the division chief of staff that his A Company was under attack. "Planes are coming now," he said. "Tanks are moving up. It looks like the attack."

Mason replied, "I'll call corps and get protection if possible."

Two minutes later, he was on the phone with his corps counterpart, Brig. Gen. Hugh J. Gaffey. "The attack has jumped off. There's been strafing and bombing. We have no air cover and we need it right away. We also need some bombing," said Mason.

"I'll see what I can do," Gaffey replied.[49]

Fourteen minutes after five o'clock, General Andrus from the division artillery command post called on the phone. They had located another panzer column "advancing up the valley." Unfortunately, he did not have direct communication with the 32nd Field Artillery. Andrus wanted Danger Forward to relay the fire mission to the fire direction center. The grid location placed the enemy column west of 3rd Battalion, 18th Infantry, and heading west on the Gabes highway toward its regimental command post on Hill 336.[50]

At 1730 hours, Colonel Greer from the 18th Infantry Regiment called the division over the command net. "Request Taylor [26th Infantry Regiment] help out Brown [3rd Battalion, 18th Infantry]," said the voice.

Gibb radioed back twenty-five minutes later with the answer. "Taylor is helping Brown. Bombing mission was approved," said the G-3.

Greer needed it. "Enemy infantry is attacking all of our positions. They are going around the left of Crawford [2nd Battalion, 16th Infantry]," he reported over the division command net.

With the command net buzzing with activity, General Patton called General Allen over the field phone. "How are things going?" asked the corps commander.

"We got a lot of air punishment," Allen replied. He wanted Patton to know that the Allied air forces were not in the fight. "The 18th Infantry is isolated," he added.

Patton changed the subject. "I don't understand the loss of so many tank destroyers." Allen then listed a litany of reasons, including air attacks. The answer did not satisfy his boss, who ended the conversation shortly afterward.[51]

Around 1800 hours, the G-3 decided to call Col. George A. Taylor on the landline to find out what was happening on the 18th Infantry's northern flank. Taylor was the commander of the 26th Infantry.

"George," said Gibb, "do you have the 2nd Battalion in hand?"

Taylor replied, "They're still in the position they had reached this morning [east of Hill 536]. They are covering the mission that they were sent out to do and have remained on the flank of the position."[52]

Gibb looked at the map that the staff had spread out on a table in the headquarters. He then said, "We have got to shorten our lines. Pull them back to the town you are in [Bou Hamran]. Send them back to us. Send an LNO to us, and we will show him where to go [El Guettar]."

"I'm sure that we can move them in a minimum of about three hours," the 26th Infantry's commander responded. Gibb thanked Taylor and hung up the phone.

Meanwhile, Colonel Mason rang his counterpart at corps. "We just had another Stuka reconnaissance fly-over. They'll take another sock at us. We need fighters to stop it," complained Mason.

"I'll call and see what they're doing," said Gaffey.

"We need high fighter protections to keep the Stukas off us," requested Mason.

Gaffey inquired, "What's the status of the attack now?"

The division's chief of staff offered a grim assessment. "They're in front of our final positions. We must have air support."[53]

For thirty minutes, battle reports flowed into the division command post. Despite the artillery barrages, the Germans were still attacking. At half past six, a staff officer from II Corps called Colonel Gibb on the field phone. "We got air for you," the officer announced. "We just had a big sweep of about twenty-five planes. Can you try and get someone to report on our air activity to us? That should be SOP. We got Hurricanes, bombers and fighter cover."

The G-3 nodded and told II Corps the unsettling news. "They [The Germans] are still moving forward on us. We estimate thirty-eight tanks in one particular group. The new tank destroyer battalion called us from outside Gafsa. We are getting radio communication with the 18th. [The attack is] much heavier than we expected."[54] Most of the reporting was coming from 3rd Battalion, 18th Infantry Regiment.

1710 to 2040 Hours, Tuesday, March 23, 1943
Dj el Mcheltat (Hill 482), Tunisia
K Company, 3rd Battalion, 18th Infantry Regiment
Exposed on the northern flank, K Company bore the brunt of the German attack on 3rd Battalion. In fact, it bore the brunt for the entire division. "About 5:30 or 6 o'clock we saw ten halftracks and three light tanks moving against the 1st Platoon," recalled Captain Raymer. "At dusk they began their assault, running their halftracks over the entire position and shooting down into the foxholes."[55]

Early that evening, Company K still had all four of its platoons intact. To the north was 1st Platoon, in the center was 3rd Platoon, and in the south was 2nd Platoon. In addition to these three infantry platoons, K Company had a weapons platoon with three 60mm mortars and two M1919 machine guns.

The 2nd Platoon was the most vulnerable of the three infantry platoons. They overlooked a road that anchored the southern edge of 3rd Battalion's entire battle position. The platoon leader was Second Lt. Francis H. Tripp. Born in 1917, Lieutenant Tripp was a real estate salesman before he joined the New Jersey Army National Guard on September 16, 1940. His platoon sergeant was S/Sgt. Roland G. Inman from North Carolina. He was one year older than Tripp and had been with the company since before the war.[56]

At the time of the battle, Tripp's platoon had forty-two men. His command, like all infantry platoons in the army, had three squads. Each squad had one Browning Automatic Rifle as the squad's most casualty-producing weapon. Fortunately for Tripp's platoon, it was nearly at full strength so that each squad had a sergeant for a squad leader and a corporal for the assistant squad leader. In addition, it had a platoon sergeant and one medic.[57]

Walter David Ehlers was a mortar section leader for one of the 60mm mortars in Company K's weapons platoon, and during the battle, he found himself on the southern flank, not far from 2nd Platoon's battle position. The army had transferred Ehlers and others from the 3rd Infantry Division to the Big Red One only a few weeks before El Guettar to replace soldiers lost at Kasserine Pass. Now, he was in the thick of it.

"Company K has this hill to protect, which had a place where the Germans could have come in and got behind our lines through a pass there," said Ehlers in a postwar interview. "So we're up there on this hill to stop them from coming through there. They were attacking the hill and they come up there with Germans in halftracks."

By this point in the battle, K Company had exhausted much of its ammunition, including mortar rounds. Ehlers grabbed his M-1 rifle and raced down to 2nd Platoon's front lines. He became a rifleman.

He liked what he saw. "We had a pretty good defensive position because we had a big bunch of rocks up there on the hill that you would get behind," recalled Ehlers.

He quickly learned the value of holding the high ground. "And so the Germans assaulted that [position] and . . . that was kind of a mistake," commented the old veteran. "And they kept on coming up there and we were just shooting them down. And I went out there on the front, shooting at them."[58]

Not far from Ehlers was Captain Kuehn, the Battalion S-2. "In the midst of the fighting I came upon the Regimental Commander's anti-tank gun that had been abandoned by its crew except for a corporal crouched behind the gun," recalled Captain Kuehn.

He looked over the gun shield and spotted two panzers, parked near an intersection in the valley below. Two of its crew members were outside the vehicles and "talking and smoking cigarettes."

"Our 18th Infantry gun was aimed at the two Jerry tanks and I asked the corporal if he knew how to fire the gun," said Kuehn. The corporal nodded his head. The S-2 then ordered the man to prepare the gun.

"I gave him the distance and the range and he fired the gun," described the captain. "It hit the track of the tank on the right and also hit the driver. He had difficulty maneuvering to the other side of the tank to get into it and the tank also had difficulty moving to get out of range." Kuehn and the corporal then hurried to load another round, but it was too late. The panzers pulled out of range.[59]

Along the southern edge of his company's battle position, Captain Raymer positioned one of the M1917 machine guns from the heavy weapons company to secure 2nd Platoon's and the company's southern flank. At some point during the battle, the gunners abandoned the position, leaving the cumbersome, water-cooled machine gun unattended. Raymer needed the M1917 up and firing because of its vital location.[60]

Two privates volunteered to operate the weapon. One of them, PFC Raymond F. Villeneuve, was a company runner. The other was Private J. L. Burlazzi. Both soldiers were K Company veterans who had served with the unit since before the war. Villeneuve was the son of French Canadian parents and grew up in Tupper Lake, New York. At the time of El Guettar, he was twenty-one years old.[61]

Villeneuve and Burlazzi set out for the machine gun. "Creeping and crawling under heavy artillery, grenades, and small-arms fire, the two privates finally obtained the gun and placed it in action," read the citation. Villeneuve was the gunner, and Burlazzi acted as the assistant gunner, feeding the voracious belt-fed M1917.

Villeneuve started to swing the gun back and forth, raking the Axis lines. The impact of the weapon was immediate. Within minutes, two German machine guns were down, and the hillside began to fill up with German dead. Chastened, the panzergrenadiers withdrew. The two soldiers lifted the hefty and unwieldy piece and carried it to another position to keep the pressure on the enemy.

Then disaster struck.

"We had an artillery observer with us from the artillery and he called in the coordinates for our . . . artillery to fire on the Germans," said Walter Ehlers. "We're sitting there on the hill and we can see our guns down there practically in the valley," continued Ehlers. "We saw the smoke from the artillery. They fired the guns off and all of sudden we're under the barrage."

Major General Terry de la Mesa Allen, pictured here when he was the commander of the 1st Infantry Division. A veteran of World War I, General Allen was loved by his men but barely tolerated by his superiors. PHOTO COURTESY OF UNIVERSITY OF TEXAS, EL PASO.

General George S. Patton Jr. The photo was taken at the Desert Training Center near Indio, California, in 1942. At the time of the photo, Patton was a major general. The tank in the background was an M3A1 Stuart light tank. Patton assumed command of II Corps in March 1943, replacing the disgraced Maj. Gen. Lloyd Fredendall. Patton's command style, though abrasive to the soldiers of the Big Red One, was a shot in the arm for II Corps. PHOTO COURTESY OF REAL WAR PHOTOS.

Field Marshall Albert Kesselring, the commander of *Oberbefehlshaber Süd* (German Army Command South). Allegedly, it was his decision to commit the 10th Panzer Division to southern Tunisia to blunt Patton's II Corps. PHOTO COURTESY OF REAL WAR PHOTOS.

General Allen (on left) pictured with Brig. Gen. Theodore Roosevelt Jr. (middle) and Brig. Gen. Clift Andrus, Chief of Division Artillery (right). General Roosevelt was Allen's assistant division commander. PHOTO COURTESY OF UNIVERSITY OF TEXAS, EL PASO.

General Allen (last man on right) and General Roosevelt (left of Allen) speak with Lt. Gen. Omar N. Bradley (standing in the center with glasses). On the far left is Allen's chief of staff, Col. Stanhope Mason. Bradley acted as Patton's eyes and ears before assuming command of II Corps at the end of the North African campaign. Bradley relieved Allen and Roosevelt of their commands at the end of the Sicily campaign in August 1943. PHOTO COURTESY OF UNIVERSITY OF TEXAS, EL PASO.

The terrain around El Guettar was rocky and unforgiving. Still, the Allied and Axis forces managed to scrape foxholes out of the terrain. This Italian observation post on Hill 369 overlooked the Gabes-Gafsa highway. Nearby, the Italians had positioned a battery of 100mm and 75mm artillery pieces. PHOTO COURTESY OF FIRST DIVISION MUSEUM.

The self-propelled 75mm tank destroyer mounted on an M-3 GMC (Gun Motor Carriage) half-track was a stopgap measure thrown together by the U.S. War Department to field tank destroyers so that U.S. Army units in North Africa could fight the panzers. Soldiers called it the "Purple Heart Box" for a good reason. With no overhead cover and thin side armor, it was a deathtrap, but it was all the 1st Infantry Division had the morning of March 23, 1943, when the 10th Panzer Division arrived. COURTESY OF L. L. GILL, TANK DESTROYER ASSOCIATION HISTORIAN.

The officers and soldiers of the 601st Tank Destroyer Battalion. The photo was taken on July 25, 1942, while the battalion was preparing to ship out to Europe. The location was the army staging area at Indiantown Gap, Pennsylvania. Lieutenant Colonel Herschel D. Baker is the bald man, directly at the center of the photo. He ably led the battalion during the battle of El Guettar on March 23, 1943. PHOTO COURTESY OF PAUL STEVENS.

In the spring of 1943, the Allies did not have complete control of the sky. As a result, Luftwaffe air raids were common. In this photo, American soldiers are ducking behind a truck, trying to find cover as enemy aircraft strafe the Gabes-Gafsa highway. PHOTO COURTESY OF FIRST DIVISION MUSEUM.

American artillery played a pivotal role in the American victory at El Guettar. The gun pictured here is a 155mm M1918A1 howitzer. The photo was taken on March 21, 1943, during the fighting around El Guettar. The M1918A1s served in the division's medium artillery battalion in a general support role. This battalion had twelve tubes of artillery. The 5th Field Artillery Battalion was the general support battalion at El Guettar. PHOTO COURTESY OF FIRST DIVISION MUSEUM AND THE FIELD ARTILLERY JOURNAL 34, NO. 1 (JANUARY 1944).

Because of the Luftwaffe, American forces needed protection. One defense was mounting .50-caliber and .30-caliber machine guns on half-tracks, jeeps, trucks, tanks, and just about everything that moved. The vehicle, a Dodge Weapons Carrier (WC) 51¾-ton truck, in this photo appears to have twin-mounted M1919 .30-caliber machine guns. The M2 .50-caliber machine gun also proved to be very effective at defending vehicles from low-level strafing attacks. The wooden contraption behind the vehicle appears to be a well. PHOTO COURTESY OF FIRST DIVISION MUSEUM.

Most regimental combat teams in the 1st Infantry Division had one light artillery battalion in direct support. These artillery battalions had twelve M2A1 105mm howitzers like the one pictured here. This photo was taken on February 20, 1943, during the battles for Kasserine Pass. PHOTO COURTESY OF FIRST DIVISION MUSEUM.

This photo shows the mountainous terrain that dominates western Tunisia. Control of the Dorsals became paramount for both sides. Battles centered on the various passes and valleys that snaked their way through the ridges. In this photo, soldiers from 2nd Battalion, 16th Infantry, march along a road near Kasserine Pass sometime in early 1943. PHOTO COURTESY OF FIRST DIVISION MUSEUM AND REAL WAR PHOTOS.

Contrary to popular belief, the weather in Tunisia in the late winter and early spring of 1943 was cold and rainy, not hot and dry. Mud was a constant problem for vehicle mobility. Most of the roads were not all-weather, and a rainstorm could turn trails into quicksand. To keep out the elements, soldiers wore whatever they could. In this photo, these soldiers are from 2nd Battalion, 16th Infantry Regiment. The photo was taken on February 26, 1943. Patton would have fined most of the men in this photo because of their unfastened chinstraps. PHOTO COURTESY OF FIRST DIVISION MUSEUM AND REAL WAR PHOTOS.

Spring 1943. The terrain in Tunisia was bereft of dense vegetation. Hence, if the American soldier wanted cover and concealment, he had to make it himself. In this photo, soldiers walk by a series of two-man foxholes scraped into the side of the hill. The holes were all the GIs had to defend themselves against German artillery and the Luftwaffe. PHOTO COURTESY OF FIRST DIVISION MUSEUM.

Spring 1943. The valleys in Tunisia became highways for both sides as the conflict seesawed back and forth amongst the Dorsals. In this photo, American soldiers have dug their foxholes on the reverse slope of a hill. A reverse slope provided the defender cover from direct fire. In the distance, a wide valley awaits. On March 23, panzers filled El Guettar Valley as the 10th Panzer Division attacked the 1st Infantry Division. PHOTO COURTESY OF FIRST DIVISION MUSEUM.

Photo of captured German vehicles in a motor pool in Algeria in the spring of 1943. The two vehicles in the middle are the vaunted Panzer IV F2. The Panzer IV F2 variants were the first MK IVs armed with the long-barreled KwK 40 L/43 gun, which outranged most Allied guns in the North African theater. Fortunately, for the 1st Infantry Division, the majority of the panzers in the 10th Panzer Division were the smaller Mk IIIs. Still, the few Mk IVs available to the 10th Panzer Division on March 23 were more than troublesome for the 601st Tank Destroyer Battalion and the Big Red One. PHOTO COURTESY OF FIRST DIVISION MUSEUM.

Photos of destroyed vehicles after the battle of El Guettar, March 23, 1943. The battle of El Guettar was the first American victory against the German war machine in Tunisia. The only clearly recognizable German vehicle is in P1. It is a Panzer Mk IV F2 in the center, its turret pointed perpendicular to the road. To the right, another panzer lies upside, like a capsized ship. In P2, the vehicle suffered a catastrophic explosion that popped off the turret. Hence, it is difficult to determine what type of tank it is. Judging by the rear plate, it is most likely a Panzer Mk III, which was far more common in the 10th Panzer Division. Unlike these wrecks, the German mechanics on the evening of March 23 managed to extricate the majority of their damaged tanks from the battlefield. Many of these recovered panzers fought again. PHOTO COURTESY OF FIRST DIVISION MUSEUM.

Photo of G Company, 2nd Battalion, 18th Infantry, August 1941, Fort Devens, Massachusetts. G Company battled the Germans from *Kradschützen* Battalion 10 atop the Djebel Berda. On the night of March 24, 1943, the Germans overwhelmed the valiant soldiers of Company G, who fought bravely but eventually had to withdraw. Despite the German success against G Company, Axis forces were unable to force the two battalions from 18th Infantry off the hill mass. In August 1941, the commander of Company G was First Lt. Robert H. York. By March 1943, he was a lieutenant colonel and was the commander of 1st Battalion. PHOTO COURTESY OF TIMOTHY L. BOWLES.

The Bowles twins. The Bowles twins served in the 18th Infantry. Thomas Bowles is on the left. Henry Bowles is on the right. Henry was a member of Headquarters Company, 2nd Battalion, while Thomas served in G Company. Henry earned a Silver Star for his actions at El Guettar. Thomas was a mortarman in G Company, and he escaped when the Germans overran his company on the night of March 24, 1943. PHOTO COURTESY OF TIMOTHY L. BOWLES.

Lieutenant Frank W. Jakob. Lieutenant Jakob was the commander of G Company when the Germans attacked on the night of March 24, 1943. His men fought hard, and they inflicted grievous casualties on the German attackers. In the end, it was not enough, and Jakob issued the order to withdraw. The chaos of battle garbled his message so that some of his men thought he had issued the order to surrender. Many of them ended up in prisoner-of-war camps in Germany and sat out the rest of the war. PHOTO COURTESY OF TIMOTHY L. BOWLES.

This is a sketch of Staff Sergeant Raffael Iagulli (left) and First Lt. Frederick C. Miner (right), a platoon leader in A Company, 601st Tank Destroyer Battalion. The artist was PFC Thomas E. Morrison, who served in A Company and was there at the battle. He drew several sketches that reflected the chaos and ferocity of the battle. Miner's platoon blocked the Gafsa-Gabes highway, and as result, the Germans focused their attack on his platoon. PHOTO COURTESY OF THE U.S. ARMY HERITAGE AND EDUCATION CENTER.

General Allen pinning an award on the chest of a 1st Infantry Division soldier in the early summer of 1943. After the Allies had won the battle for Tunisia, Allen and his Big Red One did not have much time to savor their victory. On July 10, 1943, the 1st Infantry Division landed on the shores of Sicily as part of Operation Husky.

The scars of war. In the foreground is a two-man foxhole, a visible scar from the battle of El Guettar, scratched into the side of a hill. The photo is from May 28, 2010, nearly seventy years after the battle of El Guettar. In the background are U.S. Army officers participating in a battle staff ride. Just beneath the desert rock and Tunisian sand lies the flotsam and jetsam of war. Rifle cartridges, shell fragments, bits of uniform, and unexploded land mines remind visitors that war has not left North Africa. PHOTO COURTESY OF RICK SCAVETTA, U.S. ARMY AFRICA.

General Allen presenting the Distinguished Service Cross to Lt. Col. Ben Sternberg, the commander of 2nd Battalion, 18th Infantry, on August 8, 1943. The medal was for Sternberg's actions during the battle of El Guettar. After the war, he continued to serve in the army and eventually rose to the rank of major general and took command of the 101st Airborne Division in the 1960s. PHOTO COURTESY OF FIRST DIVISION MUSEUM.

This is a photo of Lt. Walter David Ehlers receiving his Medal of Honor for his actions in June 1944. Ehlers served in a mortar crew during the battle of El Guettar. PHOTO COURTESY OF FIRST DIVISION MUSEUM.

"One of them burst right next us," said Villeneuve. "And I could feel something sharp hit me in the face. It smarted, but it didn't knock me out." Villeneuve had no idea that the artillery that had exploded on top of his position was possibly from his own guns.

The blast blinded Villeneuve. "A lieutenant noticed I was hit and crawled with me until we were out of range of fire," recalled the stricken soldier. "He told me to keep going straight and left me to return to his gun. I kept going nearly one hundred yards when the medics met me and got me back to a field station."

The barrage killed Villeneuve's assistant gunner, Private Burlazzi.[62]

The friendly fire also hit Ehlers's location. "I was over here on the right side, right at the edge of the hill where they'd be coming through with the tanks," recalled the mortar section leader. "And I'm firing at these Germans and I'm right out there in the open, and a shell landed by me. I went up in the air and came down, and I lay flat on my face."

Ehlers survived the war and fought at places like Sicily and Omaha Beach. Yet he said, "It was the loudest shells I ever heard."

Lying on his stomach, he glanced to his side. "I feel something hot beside my arm and I look over there and here's a red piece of an artillery shell, laying there, red hot. That's how close it came to me, and my ears kind of bled a little bit from the concussion, and of course, I've had hearing problems ever since."

The soldiers of K Company immediately shot flares while officers screamed into the radio, begging the fire direction center to silence the guns. Seconds later, the howitzers stopped booming. For many, though, it was too late. "We lost about thirty-seven people up there," claimed Ehlers.

Later, the mortar section leader explained what had happened. "The guy [forward observer] got it in reverse. . . . He called in on our coordinates instead of on the Germans, and so that's how we got hit." Fortunately for Ehlers, his brother Roland in 1st Platoon survived the disastrous fire mission that wounded and killed so many brave soldiers.

Several weeks after the battle, Lt. Col. Percy Thompson, the commander of the 32nd Field Artillery, wrote that he knew of "several instances of friendly artillery fire falling on our infantry." However, he believed that the fratricide was the result of the corps artillery not coordinating with the direct-support artillery battalion during offensive actions. Ultimately, we will never know what happened to K Company.[63]

The extraordinary efforts of 2nd Platoon and the rest of Company K paid off. By 2040 hours, the Germans had withdrawn, and Colonel Brown ordered Raymer's command to fall back to reconsolidate and organize. K Company would remain in reserve for the next two days. General Roosevelt and Colonel Greer broadcast their gratitude to all the battalions over the radio. "Congratulations and appreciation for a job well done," said Roosevelt and Greer.[64]

For the victors, it came with a heavy price. The 2nd Platoon was devastated. Only eight enlisted men from Tripp's command survived the battle. The others were either dead or prisoners of war. Overall, the company's losses were nine dead, twenty-one wounded, and thirty-two missing, most of them from 2nd Platoon. Later that evening, the 69th Panzergrenadier Regiment reported they had captured thirty-one American soldiers. One of the prisoners was Lieutenant Tripp, who spent the rest of the war languishing in a prisoner-of-war officer camp near Schubin, Poland. The Germans sent the enlisted men, including Sergeant Inman, to either Stalag 2B, near Czarne, Poland (Hammerstein, West Prussia), or Stalag 3B, near Fuerstenberg, Germany.

For its efforts, K Company received a Presidential Unit Citation for its actions on March 23, 1943. For their individual efforts, the army awarded Captain Raymer and PFC Villeneuve each a Distinguished Service Cross.[65]

"It was the sweetest running thing I've ever seen," recalled Raymer. "Morale was almost feverish—the boys had one thing in mind—to keep the enemy away. Nothing could have got through them on that day."

The next day, First Lt. Gilbert E. Guth, the weapons platoon leader, searched the area in front of K Company and found approximately fifty dead German soldiers. Captain Edward R. Kuehn, the Battalion S-2, confirmed Guth's findings. "After the battle, I walked out in front of our defenses and found many dead Jerries and an officer, dead on his knees with his 38-caliber pistol in his right hand facing our lines," said Kuehn.[66]

Early Evening, Tuesday, March 23, 1943
Dj el Mcheltat (Hill 482), Tunisia
2nd Battalion, Panzergrenadier Regiment 69

Ernst Breitenberger participated in the fruitless assault on K Company's position. "We made no progress all day," wrote the machine gunner. "[We] just lay there."

Later that afternoon, the panzergrenadiers watched the Luftwaffe pound the American lines. After the raid, the men dusted themselves off and rushed Dj el Mcheltat again. Despite the bombing, the result was the same. Breitenberger's company had started the day with 140 men, but by the end of the attack, he estimated his company had suffered fifty to sixty casualties.

"Even though we were close to the Dj el Moheltat [*sic*] we could not see it," remarked Breitenberger. "Below us on the plain, whenever one of our halftracks did go out on the main road, American heavy machine gunners would pick it up and shoot at it. Since our halftracks had good, slanted armor, however, no damage was done."

Colonel Heinrich Nolte, who was the *D.A.K.*'s chief of staff, was on hand to watch the second attack. From his vantage point, he determined the continuation of the assault was pointless and supported Maj. Gen. Friedrich Freiherr von Broich's decision to suspend the operation. Breitenberger and the rest of Panzergrenadier Regiment 69 hopped onto their half-tracks and headed back to their assembly area, nearly fifteen kilometers east of Hill 482.

On March 29, 1943, cut off from his main unit, Breitenberger and the rest of his company surrendered to American forces not far from Dj el Mcheltat. When he marched past the American depots at Tebessa on his way to an Allied prison camp, he realized how the Americans had stacked the deck against the German army. "There we saw this enormous American supply dump—everything—ammunition, gasoline, food, tanks, artillery pieces—and it took our breath away," described the captured machine gunner. For him, the war was over.[67]

1845 to 1848 Hours, Tuesday, March 23, 1943
El Guettar, Tunisia
Headquarters, 1st Infantry Division (Danger Forward)
At 1845 hours, Colonel Greer called Danger Forward and gave them
the good news. Gibb answered the phone. "This thing broke just about
amounting to the schedule," Greer informed Gibb, as if he were telling a
meteorologist that his weather report was spot-on. "Instead of arty they
sent dive-bombers which did very little damage. Troops started appear-
ing from everywhere, even out of tanks in most places. They hit the AT
Company [regimental antitank company]. They hit Brown's battalion."

Greer's voice then became excited, almost giddy, "Our arty crucified
them. 17th Field Artillery Regiment crucified the infantry with HE and
antipersonnel shells. They were falling all over the place, dropping like
flies. The tanks seem to be moving to the rear—those that can move."

Gibb asked, "How about the left flank?"

"Ranger Battalion is going out to protect Brown's flank. Brown was
practically surrounded," revealed Greer. "But Brown and the Rangers
drove them off."

The G-3 smiled and sighed. Greer continued his update. "York [1st
Battalion] crucified them. Sternberg [2nd Battalion] did not get any [Ger-
mans] over there, but helped out. We have reports of tanks on our right."

Greer then paused. He heard voices in the background talking to the
regimental commander, who then continued the conversation after he
received the new reports from his staff. "The tanks are definitely moving
to the rear," he informed the G-3. "We should fill in the gaps between
Brown and the rest of my outfit. Brown's right flank is high."

Hearing the news, the division's operations officer looked at the map.
Between 3rd Battalion and the rest of Greer's command was the valley.
Earlier, it had been full of panzers. Now, it was empty.

But Greer was right. Brown had an assailable southern flank that the
Germans could and would exploit again.

"The 18th must be rested," he pleaded.

Gibb agreed, but he was running out of units to shuffle. He asked the
commander, "Can you get up to York and Sternberg?"

Greer was a broken record. "The 18th must get relief," he repeated. Changing the subject, he discussed the issue of roving tank destroyers cutting landline wires.

Then Greer asked, "Where is the air?"

"Lambert [Corps G-3] says we had five sweeps over the area today," assured the G-3.

Mollified, Greer hung up the phone.

General Allen heard Greer's report from Colonel Gibb, and he liked the news from his G-3. He grabbed the phone and called Brig. Gen. Hugh J. Gaffey, Patton's chief of staff. Allen boasted, "The enemy tanks are withdrawing. The enemy attack has been driven back."

The division commander stood over the map and outlined the results. "From right to left: York is in good shape. Sternberg is in good shape. 3rd Battalion has maintained contact with the Rangers, and they are intact in their position. More prisoners are coming back. Colonel Rowland reports infiltration where Fechet [16th Infantry] should just about hit it."[68] Gaffey congratulated Allen and the rest of the 1st Infantry Division.

Not far from the division headquarters, Patton had watched the battle from an observation post. He was with General Bradley and his aide, Capt. Chester Hansen, who was also Bradley's diarist. Hansen later wrote, "This time our troops were waiting. As the long lines of infantry advanced across the valley floor, artillery held its fire until they came within range. Then in mass concentrations of fire, it showered them with air burst."

The commander of II Corps was dumbfounded. "General Patton, from a vantage point in the 1st Infantry position, shook his head as those enemy lines thinned and then wavered," wrote Hansen.

"They're murdering good infantry," Patton exclaimed. "What a helluva way to expend good infantry troops."[69]

Echoing Patton's sentiment, Brig. Gen. Clift Andrus later praised the effectiveness of the American howitzers. "Massed indirect observed fire from determined and skillful artillery can break up and destroy an armored attack," summarized Andrus. "The battle on 23 March was a tank-artillery duel, pure and simple." Against German infantry that late afternoon, it was a massacre.[70]

Axis soldiers agreed with Patton and Andrus. A German soldier, captured several days later near Maknassey, wrote on March 26, "The American fires like mad with his artillery on our positions. We've had no sleep for forty-eight hours already."[71]

Despite the maelstrom of artillery, the Germans refused to yield. They would try one last time and remind the Americans who were the masters of Tunisia.

CHAPTER FIVE

Spoiling Attack

"It was unbelievable that people who have the say-so would let us stay on that hill and take that kind of beating. It didn't make any sense to me. You have to remember I'm not trained in military strategy as to why we were up there but to me it didn't make any sense."
—CORPORAL ARTHUR L. WINTERS, G COMPANY,
2ND BATTALION, 18TH INFANTRY[1]

0830 Hours, Wednesday, March 24, 1943
Bletchley Park, Milton Keyes, Buckinghamshire, England
Hut 3, United Kingdom's Government Code and Cypher School (ULTRA)
BLETCHLEY PARK WAS A COUNTRY ESTATE NORTH OF LONDON. BY THE early spring of 1943, the unassuming mansion and its surrounding property had become a beehive of activity. Sprawled across its lawns were wooden huts that housed various military personnel, charged with the decryption, translation, and dissemination of coded Axis messages. Hut 3 was where analysts translated Engima messages that Heer and Luftwaffe personnel sent to the various units scattered throughout Europe and the Mediterranean.

Peter Calvocoressi was a senior translator and an Royal Air Force intelligence officer who worked in the building. He said, "Hut 3 revolved round its watch. Imagine a room about thirty-forty feet across, roughly square and pretty bare except for a large horseshoe table. The head of the watch sat in the middle of the horseshoe, with some ten members of the

Watch facing him from the outside. They all knew German and that is the one thing they had in common." The translators came from various occupations. Some staffed museums or were professors at universities, while others worked in business. Many were women.[2]

Inside the makeshift wooden hut that particular morning, a Bletchley code breaker grabbed an intercept that required translating. Within minutes, she discovered it was from the operations section of the 10th Panzer Division. According to the communiqué, the previous day's battle had left the battered division with only a handful of serviceable panzers: nine Mark IVs and seventeen Mark IIIs. The same message indicated that one of the panzergrenadier battalions was "very exhausted" and that both battalions that participated in the attack were of "medium strength." The division had sustained more than 300 casualties during the fighting on March 23.

The author of the document painted a grim picture for the once proud panzer division. He wrote, "Today's heavy attacks in mountainous terrain with weak forces and inferior artillery will mean a further large using-up of forces. Even in the event of success hoped for being achieved . . . forces remains strained to the utmost."

He finished the report with a dire prediction. "Continuation of the enemy [Allied] attacks is probable on the whole front. Forces are not available to cover the mountain passes east of Bou Hamran [location of the 26th Infantry Regiment] if to-day's [sic] attack should not succeed. . . . The bringing up of new forces is therefore urgent."

Despite the prospect of failure, the 10th Panzer Division could not afford to give the Americans time to reconsolidate and organize for an attack. Therefore, *Generalmajor* Friedrich Freiherr von Broich ordered his commanders to conduct spoiling attacks to secure key terrain along the ridges and to keep the Americans off balance.[3]

0655 to 1230 Hours, Wednesday, March 24, 1943
Djebel Berda, Tunisia
E Company, 2nd Battalion, 18th Infantry Regiment,
1st Infantry Division
That morning, the Germans wanted E Company for breakfast. Shortly after sunrise, they attacked the southernmost company in the regiment.

The direction of the attack was from the south and southeast. The enemy infantry had discovered the location of the battalion's southern flank and hit it hard. Within minutes, Colonel Sternberg alerted regiment that his command was under attack at 0655 hours.[4]

Ten minutes later, the 18th Infantry headquarters contacted the division command post and informed them of the German effort. However, they did not want to alarm them and said, "[We] think we can handle it."[5]

During one of the German barrages, bursting shrapnel cut the land-line between the battalion headquarters and the E Company command post. Private First Class Henry Bowles, a member of Headquarters and Headquarters Company, received the order to repair the line. Together with his friend, Blake Owens, the two men moved out with a large spool of wire and a phone receiver to check the line once they had fixed it.

It was a circuitous journey over a hill and down into a wadi and up another hill. Finally, they saw men they thought were E Company soldiers near the bottom. "We started laying up the line to E Company on this hill," recalled Henry Bowles, "and they started shooting at us. And we're waving our hands at them and everything else and they stopped."

Thankful that the soldiers stopped shooting at them, assuming they had recognized them as fellow Americans, the two signalmen continued to climb down the slope. "They shoot at us again," continued Bowles. "We stopped a couple of times and they stopped."

Bowles and Owens finally realized the soldiers at the base of Djebel Berda were Germans, and they ran for cover. Henry continued, "By the third time they started shooting, we got up there where there were some old rocks. I remember I got behind one rock and another rock behind me was a little bigger . . . and they were digging a hole in the rock behind me. They were shooting right over it [the first rock]."

With bullets whizzing over his head and flecks of rock pelting his back, Henry Bowles grabbed the phone and called his headquarters company to report the bad news. The voice on the other line replied, "E Company is not up there. The Germans already took that hill up there."

Bowles and Owens had climbed up the wrong hill. They were now within several hundred meters of the German position. "But we're on the open slope going down through there," described Henry, "[and] it was a quarter of mile from the hill down to the bottom."

"I told him what was happening," said Bowles, referring to the man on the other line.

"Wait a minute here. The liaison officer is right here. I'll let you talk to him," replied the voice.

The artillery liaison officer got on the line and asked the two head-quarters signalmen, "Can both of you direct fire on that up there if we throw you some artillery up there?"

Bowles nodded and said, "Yeah, it's the only chance we have of get-ting out of there."

Several minutes later, the two men heard the familiar high-pitched whistling sound as two artillery rounds screamed over their heads and then detonated short of the intended the target. Bowles saw the impact and did some quick calculations in his head. "Well, go ahead and raise it up two hundred yards like that," he estimated.

A minute later, a few more rounds landed, and this time they were on target. Bowles called back and told them the good news. "All right then, when you hear them coming in, get out of there," warned the artillery liaison officer.

Within seconds of the call, the two soldiers detected the incoming storm of artillery. They got up and scrambled back up the hill. Behind them, the world exploded.

Several months later, the army awarded Henry Bowles the Silver Star for his action. Bowles later remarked, "To me, it wasn't . . . bravery. I was just trying to save my own neck."[6]

At the time of El Guettar, Henry Bowles was twenty-one years old. The young man from Alabama was far from home, but he was not far from his family. His identical twin brother, Thomas, served in the same battalion in G Company. Both had enlisted in the army in March 1940 after graduating from high school. After initial entry training, Henry became a rifleman, while the army selected Thomas to be mortarman.[7]

Thomas Bowles's twin was not the only soldier from Headquarters Company to receive a Silver Star that day. Sergeant Salvatore DeSantis worked in supply. Around noon, Maj. Elisha O. Peckham, the battalion executive officer, ordered DeSantis to return to the regimental supply area to secure ammunition for the battalion. It was a six-mile trek from Djebel Berda to El Guettar. To the twenty-four-year-old former truck driver from Brooklyn, the mission seemed like a "suicide dash," but the soldiers were running low on bullets. If they did not receive more ammunition, the Germans would roll up the battalion.

DeSantis looked at the map. The shortest route crossed the open valley to the Gabes road. It was the most exposed, but it was the quickest. The sergeant estimated he would save three hours on each leg by utilizing that route instead of the longer, safer one. Resolved, he ordered his section to pull out.

"As soon as we left the mountains at noon the tanks opened up on us," recalled DeSantis. "But we dashed right through the middle of them."

The panzer crews were stunned to see a small convoy of four jeeps in their midst, but soon, they leveled their machine guns and opened fire on DeSantis's group. "All I could see was tanks on every side," said DeSantis. "The closest one was two hundred yards away. They had to be awful careful in firing at us because of the danger of hitting each other. We didn't go in any order, but just drove like hell, and the man with the heaviest foot got there first."

Amidst the cyclone of machine-gun and cannon fire, a mine knocked out one of DeSantis's jeeps. The force of the blast blew its two crew members out of the vehicle. Another jeep crew raced over to the dazed soldiers and picked them up in their vehicle. The three remaining jeeps continued their trek and reached the regimental supply area. The total travel time was nineteen minutes. The army later awarded Sergeant DeSantis the Silver Star for his actions that day.[8]

All Day, Wednesday, March 24, 1943
Djebel Berda, Tunisia
G Company, 2nd Battalion, 18th Infantry Regiment,
1st Infantry Division
Private Thomas E. Bowles was thirsty. Unfortunately, he had little potable water left to drink. His company had not received any resupply since the

previous day because the Germans had isolated 1st and 2nd Battalions atop Djebel Berda when they attacked on March 23.

The only water source was a fetid pool at the base of the hill. Bowles later admitted he and his comrades were the ones who had polluted the pool and made it unpotable. "We used to go sit down there, eat our rations, smoke cigarettes, and throw them in the pool and wash our socks and everything else," said Bowles.

Despite the risk of sickness, the parched soldiers began to draw water from the putrid source. "On the third day we were drinking that water. We couldn't get water up there anymore."[9]

Water was not the only problem. German snipers still were perched on the crest of the hill that overlooked G Company's position. According to the survivors, the Germans wore American field jackets so that some of the GIs thought they were friendly. The green tracers and a few casualties later told them otherwise. (American rifles fired red tracers.)

Accompanying the snipers were forward observers for the German mortars and artillery. Private Raymond Oliver described the effectiveness of the enemy's indirect fire and grenades. "I could look up and see those 88 shells going six inches over my head," said Oliver. "Later a concussion grenade hit at the edge of my foxhole while I was lying prone with my rifle. It made me turn a complete flip and threw me out of the foxhole."[10]

Thomas Bowles added, "They dropped mortars on us all day long. And that's what's done most of the damage up there because they had the observation . . . to see where they were putting them things. You could take a mortar gun and in about three shots you could put it close to where you want it."[11]

Bowles knew how effective mortars were because he served on a 60mm mortar crew in G Company, 2nd Battalion, 18th Infantry Regiment. His company occupied a battle position, dominating the southern half of the El Guettar Valley. To the south was E Company, while to the northwest was B Company, 1st Battalion. Behind his position was the battalion headquarters and Company F, which served as the battalion reserve.[12]

Thomas Bowles's immediate supervisor was Corp. Arthur L. Winters, and his squad leader was S/Sgt. Nels J. De Jarlais from Minnesota.

His platoon sergeant and acting platoon leader was S/Sgt. Bobby Dees from DeKalb, Mississippi. Winters had known Dees since he had enlisted in the army in November 1940 at Fort Wadsworth, Staten Island. Dees taught Winters how to shoot a rifle. They met each other again at Fort Devens, Massachusetts. Winters was a corporal, and they had become good friends.[13]

"He was a soldier," recalled Winters about Dees. "I was a civilian but he was a soldier. He looked like a soldier and acted like a soldier every moment of the day."

Even in combat, Dees never stopped instructing Winters and the rest of weapons platoon. When G Company marched up Djebel Berda to their current positions, Dees told Winters's gun team to stop bunching up. He did not want one well-placed mortar round to take out an entire mortar crew. Dees replied sardonically, "Well, you have to remember sergeant misery likes company." It was the last time Winters saw Dees alive.[14]

The Germans pounded G Company all day with artillery. During one of the barrages, shrapnel wounded the company commander, and twenty-five-year-old Lt. Frank W. Jakob from Collingswood, New Jersey, assumed command. Jakob was a graduate of the Pennsylvania Military College, Class of 1941. Originally, he commissioned as a chemical officer, but wartime demands required more infantry platoon leaders. His classmates called him Jake, and in his college's *1941 Sabre and Sash Yearbook*, he was described as "sincere and determined in whatever he sets out to accomplish." Thanks to the fortunes of war, he was a company commander.[15]

"The shelling got worse throughout Wednesday," recalled Jakob, "and we could see the German infantry beyond getting ready to attack us. The Germans were hauling up ammunition in captured American trucks and halftracks. We just had to lie there and take it."[16]

Even worse, he did not have artillery support. "Our communications were broken," said Jakob, "and we couldn't contact our artillery to return fire."[17]

By the end of the day, the constant shelling and sniping had taken its toll on Company G, and many of the soldiers were wounded. One of the casualties was Sergeant De Jarlais. Tom Bowles and his friend Giacomo Patti left their positions to secure a stretcher from the battalion headquarters so that they could lug De Jarlais off the hill. The headquarters was a quarter of a mile behind G Company. Unbeknownst to Tom, his brother, Henry, was under heavy fire only a few kilometers south of his position.[18]

0725 to 1100 Hours, Wednesday, March 24, 1943
El Guettar, Tunisia
Headquarters, 1st Infantry Division (Danger Forward)

At 0725 hours, Assistant Division Commander General Roosevelt was at the 26th Infantry command post. He heard a commotion over the command net about the attack on Djebel Berda. He picked the field phone and called the G-3. Gibb answered the ringing handset.

"Roosevelt here," the former president's son announced. "I plan to send two companies of Rangers to reinforce 1st and 2nd battalions of the 18th Infantry."

Gibb nodded and added, "Rangers have twenty-four trucks. Is the situation bad?"

Roosevelt replied, "They don't report much in front, but they are counter battering. They [the enemy] are working up to the hills on our right and going around our right flank. Sternberg and York are where they always have been. They want to clear up the hilltop with the Rangers. 3rd Battalion, 26th Infantry was out seven hours and couldn't find him [Colonel Crawford and 2nd Battalion, 16th Infantry]."

Gibb looked at the map. "Let me know where you are in relation to Hill 482."

Colonel Mason, the chief of staff, chimed in and asked if the Ranger Battalion was better suited to defend Hill 482 along the northern flank where 3rd Battalion, 18th Infantry, was. Initially, Roosevelt agreed with Mason, but after several minutes of debate, he changed his mind.

The general directed, "I will take the Ranger Battalion . . . on top of the hill on the right flank [Djebel Berda]. I think I should start right now working Crawford up, taking over from Brown." The general wanted 3rd Battalion, 26th Infantry, to link up with Crawford's 2nd Battalion,

16th Infantry, somewhere near Hill 482 and relieve Brown's battalion. Roosevelt wanted the aggressive Rangers to clear Greer's (and the division's) southern flank of Germans. Shortly after 1100 hours, Darby's men moved out to take down the Germans atop the crag.[19]

1150 to 1155 Hours, Wednesday, March 24, 1943
El Keddab Ridge (Hill 336), Tunisia
Command Post, 18th Infantry Regiment
Around noon, Generals Patton and Allen arrived at Colonel Greer's command post. Patton wanted to see the carnage from the previous day's battle, and Allen was there to serve as the corps commander's escort. The drive to Greer's headquarters was not without incident. Several artillery shells had landed close to the convoy, and, Patton recalled, "a few small fragments hit [the] car."

After he arrived, the scrappy and pugnacious Patton scanned the valley. He saw the detritus and debris of a great contest. He wrote in his diary, "The whole battlefield of yesterday was visible and covered with destroyed vehicles, mostly ours."

Many of the panzers vanished thanks to a supreme effort on the part of German maintenance crews who towed the vanquished beasts off the battlefield. Their crews performed miracles of mechanical resurrection—the Allies would face the Lazarus panzers again.

Patton counted his losses. He tallied two dozen M3 gun trucks and seven of the new M10 tank destroyers. Fortunately, since the Americans owned the field, many of the destroyers that Patton saw scattered like wrecks after a demolition derby would similarly be up and running within a few days.

Still, the losses nagged at him. He returned to his theme of poor tactics when he scribbled, "Clearly, the tactics of those vehicles [tank destroyers] is wholy [*sic*] wrong. I told them what to do but their faulty training crapped up in the heat of battle."[20]

Meanwhile, General Allen was busy directing his division. From Hill 336, he could see the movement of troops and trucks up and down the valley. Although he was outside of his command post and away from its communications hub, he still had situational awareness thanks to the excellent observation point.

He called Gibb on the telephone at 1155 hours. Speaking in code, the division commander declared, "Neither one of Fechet's 1st and 2nd Squads are going to relieve Greer's squad. Crawford has already relieved Brown." To Gibb, that meant Allen wanted 18th Infantry's remaining battalions to remain in the field near Djebel Berda. He only wanted Crawford's 2nd Battalion, 16th Infantry, to relieve Colonel Brown's 3rd Battalion, 18th Infantry, which had taken a drubbing in the past twenty-four hours.

Looking through his binoculars at the Djebel Berda hill mass, Allen continued, "Rangers, I presume, are where they belong. I see trucks down there. Crawford has started to relieve Brown. Cunningham [1st Battalion, 16th Infantry] and Mathews [3rd Battalion, 16th Infantry] have not started to relieve Sternberg and York [2nd and 1st Battalions and 18th Infantry, respectively]."

He put down the field glasses. "It is not entirely necessary. It will take several hours, and we would have the 18th exposed for a job that really belongs to someone else. The 16th is not disposed to follow the 26th. I think we should hold it up until we get a little more info."

Suddenly, a few artillery rounds exploded in the distance, close enough to cause the crowd of general officers to duck instinctively but not close enough to cause any harm. Allen resumed, "We are having some light artillery fire up here and I think a battalion moving would draw attention. So hold on until I call you again."

Allen arrayed his division thusly: Still in the north was the 26th Infantry. In the center would be the 16th Infantry. To the south was the 18th Infantry. The 26th secured the Gumtree road that ran between Dj el Ank and Bou Hamran. On its right and in the center, the 16th Infantry would occupy the El Keddab and Dj el Mcheltat ridges. Anchoring the southern flank would be the entire 18th Infantry on Djebel Berda. Joining them would be the Ranger Battalion, which later would occupy a position to the south of Greer's 2nd Battalion. Ultimately, Allen's decision meant that the men of G Company, despite the constant sniping and shelling, would remain at their current position.[21]

2000 to 2125 Hours, Wednesday, March 24, 1943
Djebel Berda, Tunisia
G Company, 2nd Battalion, 18th Infantry Regiment,
1st Infantry Division

Darkness brought little respite for the men of George Company. Major Heinrich Drewes, the commander of the *Kradschützen* Battalion 10 opposite Company G, decided that a night attack offered the best chance of success. Like General Allen, the German commander favored the advantages of concealment over the risk of fratricide.

His men were tired. The battalion had been on the move since March 19, when it left Kairouan, Tunisia, and headed south to Sfax. From there, it traveled west and joined the rest of the 10th Panzer Division along the Gabes–El Guettar highway. On March 21, the battalion occupied a battle position north of the highway. On Tuesday, March 22, it headed toward Djebel Berda, its current position.

Drewes's plan was simple. He moved his heavy weapons to a support-by-fire position to plaster the American position with mortars and heavy machine guns. For the assault element, he committed his two motorcycle companies. With more than 300 men involved in the attack, he was confident that his grenadiers could seize the high ground and push the Americans off the hill.[22]

Shortly after dark, a single soldier in the G Company listening post heard the enemy grenadiers skulking up the hill. He alerted the men that the Germans were approaching. "[It was] the last we heard of him," remarked Thomas Bowles.[23]

At 2000 hours, the attack began. "A flare went up and those guns pounded the devil out of us for fifteen minutes. Then there were two more flares, and the artillery stopped," remembered Lieutenant Jakob.[24]

Thomas Bowles, who had only recently returned with the stretcher for Sergeant De Jarlais, recalled that the flares were so bright that it turned night into day atop the hill. The wounded squad leader asked, "Bowles, do you think we can hold them?"

Bowles tried to sound confident. "Yeah, we can hold them." He left his squad leader to join the rest of his gun crew.

The twin and his comrade, Giacomo Patti, began hanging mortar rounds and kept up a steady rate of fire with their 60mm tube while Corporal Winters located targets. Within a few minutes, though, they expended the last of their ammunition. "There was so much shelling that it was more confusion than actual fighting, but we did fight back," said Winters.[25]

During the barrage, hot shrapnel hit one soldier who cried out for help. Sergeant Dees scrambled out of his hole to give first aid to the wounded man. Thomas Bowles knew the German gunners had zeroed in on the location and shouted to his platoon sergeant, "Dees! Don't go over there!" Dees did not heed the warning. While he leaned over to administer first aid to their fallen comrade, another artillery shell screamed in and detonated, killing both men. For his selfless bravery, the army awarded Dees a posthumous Silver Star.[26]

From his position, Lieutenant Jakob had excellent observation, but his viewpoint only revealed the hopelessness of the situation. "We saw infantry swarming up the hill at us from three sides," described Jakob. "They outnumbered us at least two to one. We were still in our foxholes and had nothing left to fight with except rifles and grenades. The barrage had knocked out our last mortar and last machine gun."

Private Zoltan Papik operated the last 60mm tube in De Jarlais's squad. He recalled how the Germans knocked it out within five minutes of the attack while the last machine gunner in the weapons platoon was "sliced in half by German machine-gun fire."

Private Clark Ingrahm, a member of the ill-fated crew, found a Browning Automatic Rifle and exacted his revenge on the attackers. "I got quite a few," he recalled. He kept firing until it jammed, leaving him weaponless.

The Germans maneuvered in four-man teams up the hill. One man would carry an MG 34 machine gun or an MP 38 submachine gun, while the second and third men tossed grenades. The last man carried the ammunition. The machine gunner would suppress the American defenders while the grenadiers chucked potato-mashers into the foxholes. The small teams proved effective.

Corporal Jacque Bayer described the attackers. "Those guys wore black uniforms. Some had helmets on and some just field caps. They were all firing machine guns or throwing grenades or stabbing with bayonets. We threw grenades back. I think we got more of them than they got of us."

Despite the ferocity of the American defense, German numbers began to tell. Soon, the grenadiers were bayoneting G Company men trapped in their foxholes. Private Paul Meierle watched one man who tried to surrender, but the enemy soldier ignored his outstretched hands and shot him. The mortally wounded soldier crumpled like paper and slid back into his hole to die.

"I was firing my rifle and hit some of them," recalled Meierle. "It tickled the hell out of me when I heard those sons of bitches give that death scream."[27]

Corporal Winters was wounded in the arm thanks to shrapnel from an artillery shell. It hung at his side, lifeless. "I couldn't do anything," said Winters. "I couldn't fight. I couldn't talk, and I couldn't even think. I just laid there."[28]

Seeing the carnage around him, Lieutenant Jakob ordered the remaining survivors to fall back to friendly lines. "There was nothing else to do. We were overwhelmed. I ordered the men to withdraw to save useless loss of more lives," said Jakob.[29]

His order did not reach all the men trapped on Djebel Berda. Others thought that they heard the commander wanted them to surrender. Giacomo Patti was one of them. "Bowlesie," he shouted to his friend, Thomas, "the lieutenant says he's going to surrender! Let's get out of here!"[30]

Bowles later remarked, "Well, when the officer's going to surrender, you can do what you please. You're on your own, then."

Luckily, unlike the other men who had been on the hill for several days and had little idea as to their own whereabouts, Bowles and Patti knew the way back to headquarters, even in the dark. "So Me and Patti," recalled Thomas Bowles, "had just come back up with that stretcher so we knew which way to get out of there."

The escape was not without incident. They slid down a steep escarpment and into a pool of water before they reached the battalion headquarters a quarter of a mile behind their company position. Panting and wheezing, Bowles counted thirty-six survivors. Despite the drubbing they took from the Germans, the remnants of G Company did not want to leave their comrades behind to die or become prisoners of war.

"They wanted to get reinforcements and go back up there," recalled Bowles. "But there wasn't enough of us to do anything."[31]

The men left behind were still in danger. Corporal Winters, hearing the order to surrender, struggled to his feet and raised his hands. "The blood was running out of my hands I was bleeding so bad," he recalled.

One of the German officers saw the wounded Winters and ordered a panzergrenadier to escort the corporal to their first aid station. "While we were walking down to the first aid we were both hitting the ground once and awhile because shells were flying and we didn't even know where the shells came from," said the corporal.

When Winters stepped into the aid station tent, he saw the result of the dogged American defense. "They had a lot of wounded there. They took a lot of casualties on that hill. It wasn't an easy task for them. We gave as much as we took, and we took an awful beating," declared the mortar section leader.[32]

Thinking that the doctors might leave him to die since he was an enemy soldier, Winters was stunned at the generosity of the German medical staff. "When I got to the first aid station . . . they took care of me right away, bandaged me up . . . cleaned up my arm," he recalled. "I was amazed. They never spoke to me. They never spoke one word. They just did their job." Ten minutes later, Corporal Winters was on an ambulance, heading north to a German hospital in Bizerte. For him, the war was over.

Long after the conflict, he wondered why they had remained on the hill. As a corporal, he was not privy to the rationale behind the division commander's decisions. He did not know Allen's concerns. Still, even though tactical logic dictated that the two battalions hold Djebel Berda, it was little solace to the men of Company G.

"It was unbelievable that people who have the say-so would let us stay on that hill and take that kind of beating," said Winters. "It didn't make any sense to me. You have to remember I'm not trained in military strategy as to why we were up there but to me it didn't make any sense."[33]

At 2100 hours, the regimental headquarters finally received word that 2nd Battalion was under heavy attack. The radio log mentioned that the Germans had "pushed" G Company off the hill while capturing much of the company's equipment. Twenty-five minutes later, another report confirmed the earlier one. "2nd Battalion attacked by a considerable force of infantry," the clerk wrote in the radio log. "High ground held by G Company lost [to the] enemy."[34]

———

Not far from where G Company made its last stand was Henry Bowles. He could see G Company's battle position from his location on the ridge. He sensed his brother, Thomas, was in trouble. "They're firing mortars and everything down where he [Thomas] was located," recalled Henry.[35]

After the fireworks stopped, Henry decided to find out what happened to his twin brother. He grabbed Private Robert L. Sparks and another soldier to accompany him. Because it was cold, they wore ponchos to keep warm. However, they were not wearing the U.S. Army–issued rain gear. Instead, they had thrown on captured German ponchos.

Thomas explained, "Well, every time we'd get one of them we'd keep it because it was better than our raincoats." Unbeknownst to Henry and his two comrades, the German ponchos saved their lives.[36]

The three intrepid grunts fumbled and stumbled their way through the darkness, walking up the same path that Thomas and Patti had used earlier to transport the stretcher. As they approached the G Company positions, Henry saw several figures emerge from the blackness. He then walked ahead to find out who they were and asked if this was Thomas's unit.

Suddenly, Henry heard strange sounds. The voices were speaking in German. Despite the danger, he remained calm. He turned around and walked back to Sparks and the other soldier.

"There's nothing but Germans up here," Bowles whispered to the two other soldiers.

"Let's just go down the way we came," he murmured to the two other men. He then wheeled about and led the trio back down the escarpment.

The enemy never suspected that they were American soldiers. Thanks to the German ponchos, the three looked like the panzergrenadiers, so they never aroused suspicion. The next morning, Henry found his twin, Thomas, alive and well.[37]

2150 to 0110 Hours, Wednesday to Thursday, March 24–25, 1943
El Guettar, Tunisia
Headquarters, 1st Infantry Division (Danger Forward)
At 2150 hours, Dog Tag (the radio call sign for the 18th Infantry) called Danger Forward on the field phone to give them the bad news. "G Company was driven from the hill," the staff officer reported. "There is a wedge in the line. The rest of the group is holding." For twenty minutes, the division staff debated courses of action.

Finally, Colonel Gibb reacted. He picked up the phone and called 1st Ranger Battalion. "Send this message to Darby [the commander]. You are attached to Greer. Effective immediately. York and Sternberg are being attacked."

Five minutes later, the G-3 called the 18th Infantry command post on the phone. "You can get in contact with Darby thru his radio, by calling Dazzle," he said. Dazzle was Darby's radio call sign.

At 2330 hours, Darby had his men moving. He radioed the division headquarters. His message was terse. "Darby coming to help Sternberg," he said.

Around midnight, Colonel Gibb called Colonel Greer on the phone. "Did Anderson see you?" he asked. (Anderson was Captain Anderson, the division liaison officer.)

Greer replied, "Yes."

"Can you get orders to Sternberg and Salty?" inquired Gibb. (Salty was probably another name for Colonel York, the 1st Battalion commander.)

"We got the message to Red [1st Battalion]. We have a radio," answered Greer.

Gibb nodded and then asked, "How is everything?"

Greer corroborated the earlier report. "Germans occupied G Company position. We are going to move our CP across the valley."

The G-3 acknowledged the new information and ended the call. Since 2nd Battalion, 16th Infantry, had relieved 3rd Battalion, 18th Infantry, on Hill 482 earlier that day, the majority of Greer's regiment now was on the southern rim of the valley. For better command and control, the regimental commander decided to move closer to his units.[38]

Seventy minutes after midnight, Greer rang Gibb on the field phone. "Things look all right," he said. "We have rectified our lines. All tightened up and bound into one another. We are much better than we were. We are all dug in and fully confident that they can stop them where they are."

Gibb was relieved. Shortly after speaking with Greer, he called his counterpart at II Corps to report the good news. Colonel Akers answered the phone. "18th Infantry has consolidated what they have on the ground," Gibb announced. "Everything has seemed to have died down. Communications by radio with everything reorganized and in good shape with no reaction on the 26th Infantry side [along the highway to Sfax]. We think the enemy is still there, however. I think they are going after the enemy in the morning. At the present, they haven't taken any ground from us. They [26th Infantry] had better positions prior to the consolidation but they had too much ground for the troops to cover. They are now confident they can hold anything sent against them."

Akers then told Gibb, "We are sending up a lot of air at first light."

Gibb hung up the phone. Elsewhere, the battle continued.[39]

0300 to 1400 Hours, Thursday, March 25, 1943
Djebel Berda, Tunisia
Southern Flank of the 18th Infantry Regiment
Meanwhile, Colonel Greer continued to shuffle his troops in the dark. Shortly after 0300 hours, he ordered 1st and 2nd Battalions to withdraw nearly 2,000 yards westward so that they would be atop the crest of Djebel Berda. Serving as the rear guard was D Company, 1st Ranger Battalion, which also was preparing for an enemy assault along its eastern crest. Unbeknownst to the company commander, E Company was the unit approaching him. After avoiding a fratricide incident thanks to the "rapid explanations" from the E Company commander (who could

not clarify why he did not know the daily password), the two infantry company commanders sorted it out before the next German attack. That attack started around 0400 hours.[40]

At 0415 hours, someone at the E Company command post reported, "E Company surrounded but can handle situation." Fortunately, Greer's temporary command post went live at almost the same time. Its new location was at the northern edge of the Djebel Berda hill mass, near Hill 477, and was much closer to the action. Fighting continued throughout much of the morning.

Thirty minutes after six, the German attack intensified. Enemy artillery plastered Djebel Berda, and five minutes later, machine-gun fire from MG 34s, located to the northeast, peppered the exposed ridgeline, signaling the onset of another German assault. Captain Jack B. Street, a company commander in the 1st Ranger Battalion, wrote, "German infantry in company strength attacked up the slopes at 0640 hours, firing machine gun pistols. The restricted area of the hill, the mixed personnel of the two companies, and the lack of shelter combined to cause serious confusion at the outset of the attack."[41]

By 0700 hours, 2nd Battalion reported heavy machine-gun fire on their positions. By 0930 hours, both companies reported that they were facing more than 300 German infantry. The Rangers requested artillery to disrupt the German attackers. For D Company, 1st Ranger Battalion, and E Company, 2nd Battalion, 18th Infantry, the battle had taken a turn for the worse.

The Rangers improvised. Darby sent one platoon from his C Company, under the command of Lt. Charles Shunstrom, to get around the German flank "to attempt the Ranger ruse that had worked so effectively in the past," as the Ranger colonel explained. Shortly afterward, the platoon was in place and requested a fire mission from the regimental cannon company. "Each of the six guns plowed six rounds into the Germans," wrote Darby. Shunstrom claimed that the barrage "really blew hell out of the Germans."[42]

Despite the successful strike, the pressure was just too strong. At 1040 hours, the regiment received permission to withdraw its battalions after nightfall. The Rangers would go last after 2nd Battalion.

When asked if they could cover the withdrawal for the other two battalions, Ranger Darby told Greer they could do it. "Our small force held off the Germans from the north slopes of Djebel Berda while the two battered battalions pulled back through the Rangers some two or more miles," remembered the Ranger commander. "The situation was still tight. Nevertheless, we stayed out on the right flank, practically cut off for three days but not giving an inch."[43]

On Hill 772, D Company acted as the rear guard for E Company, 2nd Battalion, and pinned down the attacking panzergrenadiers while E Company fell back to the northwest mid-morning. Afterward, the Germans attempted to envelope the lone Ranger company, but its commander saw the enemy flanking movement and ordered his men to pull out. Street later wrote, "The withdrawal was successfully accomplished, the company moving rapidly down near-vertical cliffs and talus slides to a wadi at the southwestern base of the Djebel Berda. The company marched three miles northwest through this wadi and rejoined the battalion."[44]

At 1400 hours, Shunstrom's platoon, which had grown to all of C Company, 1st Ranger Battalion, came under attack. "The German thrust at this far right flank position grew in strength," wrote Darby. "C Company was withdrawn behind the Germans." This attack was the costliest point of the battle for the Rangers. Captain James Lyle, the company commander, recorded eight casualties, including three killed in action: Sgts. Leonard H. Sporman, John J. Ball, and PFC Nelson Trent. For the entire period of March 14 through March 27, 1943, the battalion losses were only three killed in action and eighteen wounded in action. Considering the damage the Rangers inflicted on the Axis, it was a small price to pay.[45]

0920 to 2350 Hours, Thursday, March 25, 1943
Near Hill 4777, Djebel Berda, Tunisia
Command Post, 18th Infantry Regiment
Back at the 18th Infantry's new command post, Greer was processing the incoming reports. At 0920 hours, Colonel Gibb called him on the telephone from division.

"Can you tell me the situation of your units? Are they around [Hill] 772 or not?" he asked.

Greer assured him, "They are. 2nd is on the right, Rangers are in the middle, and 1st on the left. Two companies of Rangers are covering the gap." He then added, "The enemy came in on a position that they previously held. We have no evidence of force this morning. They came in on G Company under the cover of artillery."

The answer satisfied Gibb, who then hung up the phone. At 0930 hours, 2nd Battalion reported to Greer that E Company and one Ranger company were under attack on Hill 772. To counter this, the beleaguered Ranger company requested artillery. In addition, the Ranger commander spotted an enemy formation at Grid Y6272, twenty kilometers northeast of his location and south of the Dj el Hatay Pass. He suggested that air reconnaissance investigate the area.[46]

Somehow, Gibb heard the message from 2nd Battalion and called the 16th Infantry Regiment. He claimed he spoke directly with Sternberg and Darby. He said, "Just had conversation with the Ranger Battalion and 2nd Battalion, 18th Infantry. A company of Rangers and E Company are on Hill 772. Large patrols are coming in on all sides of them. The rest of the unit is [away] from 772 [to the] north. Rangers reported a big tank park at grid Y6272 and we had air reconnaissance fly over it."[47]

Ten minutes after the request, Greer instructed his regimental cannon company to provide indirect fire support for the forces on Hill 772. The colonel sensed he needed everyone to fall back or else risk losing 2nd Battalion and possibly the Rangers to the German onslaught. At 1040 hours, he received permission from his division to withdraw from Djebel Berda. Colonel York's 1st Battalion would initiate the retrograde, followed by Sternberg's 2nd Battalion and then Darby's Rangers. The withdrawal would begin at nightfall, and the Rangers would serve as the rear guard.[48]

At 1212 hours, the 18th Infantry command post informed division headquarters over the phone that E Company and the Rangers were no longer on Hill 772. According to reports, they claimed that "attacks are almost continuous."[49]

However, by 1324 hours, the situation had stabilized. The 18th Infantry summarized the morning's events when the command post called Danger Forward to tell them the good news. "From 1120 to 1140 the Ranger Battalion CP was shelled," reported the 18th Infantry. "Since then the enemy has been held back due to our arty fire. Things are now quiet. Our own company from 2nd Battalion who was attacked this morning is intact and in a new position and has stopped the attack."[50]

Later that afternoon, Greer ordered 3rd Battalion to occupy a position along the division's southern flank. Brown's battalion had been in the rear for the past two days to recover and refit from the battle on March 23. At 1645 hours, the 18th Infantry's duty officer logged the following message. "Situation from all battalions at this time is reported as being quiet. No movement seen and arty fire at minimum from both sides."

When the regimental commander received the news, he initiated the relief-in-place. Thirty minutes after the all clear, advance parties left for El Guettar to establish bivouac areas for Greer's two battalions (Darby's Rangers would leave later). At 1730, Greer ordered York and Sternberg to commence their retirement. Five minutes before eight o'clock that night, Greer departed his command post and headed to the base of Djebel Berda to ensure that the operation went according to plan.

Four hours later, 1st and 2nd Battalions informed the regimental command post they had arrived at El Guettar to assume the role as the division reserve. Greer's headquarters followed suit the next day. The Rangers did not leave until the morning of March 26, when 2nd Battalion from the 39th Infantry Regiment, 9th Infantry Division, relieved them. Like York and Sternberg, Darby led his battalion back to El Guettar to recuperate.[51]

The period from March 21 to 26 had been a tumultuous six days for Colonel Greer. His command sustained more than 326 casualties during that time. Thirty-three enlisted and two officers had died. One hundred and seventy-one enlisted and seven officers were wounded. Missing in action were 113 men, most of whom ended up as prisoners of war, and the majority were from G and K Companies.

Despite the losses, the regiment mounted up and moved north of Djebel Orbata to resume operations east of Bou Hamran on March 27. The men of 18th Infantry had won a great defensive battle, but the conflict in North Africa would continue for another seven weeks.[52]

1634 Hours, Friday, March 26, 1943
Bletchley Park, Milton Keyes, Buckinghamshire, England
Hut 3, United Kingdom's Government Code and Cypher School (ULTRA)
Fifteen hundred miles north of El Guettar, the code breakers at Bletchley Park continued their work. Analysts pored over another message from the 10th Panzer Division, intercepted by the British at noon on March 25. Despite the beating it took, the 10th Panzer was on the road to recovery.

According to the division's operations officer, it had twenty-six Mk IIIs in operation, and he expected another nine more to come on-line over the next few days. This was a significant increase, considering the division had only seventeen on March 24. Even more troublesome was the recovery and repair of the more dangerous Mk IVs. On March 24, the division had nine serviceable Mk IVs. One day later, it had fifteen, and the operations officer expected that his mechanics would repair another nine over the next few days, bringing his total to twenty-four.

Although the panzer division was far from 100 percent, it was far from beaten. The 1st Infantry Division had not crushed it, thereby allowing the enemy maintenance crews to recover their wounded metal monsters and tow them off the field of battle so that they could fight and kill Americans for another day. The GIs had a lot to learn when it came to winning modern wars, but they were learning fast.[53]

EPILOGUE

*"For a commander the agony of war is not in its dangers, depriva-
tions, or the fear of defeat, but in the knowledge that with each new
day men's lives must be spent to pay the costs of that day's objectives."*
—MAJOR GENERAL OMAR N. BRADLEY[1]

THE 1ST INFANTRY DIVISION'S BREAK FROM COMBAT WAS SHORT LIVED.
On March 28, Greer's 18th Infantry Regiment attacked enemy forces
north of El Guettar, near the town of Sakket, Tunisia. They continued
to battle for the town until April 3, when the Axis withdrew. Afterward,
the 18th Infantry pushed east toward El Maizila Ridge with the rest of
the division. By April 7, El Maizila and El Ayacha were in American
hands, and the El Guettar campaign for the 1st Infantry Division was
officially over.[2]

The El Guettar/Gafsa operation was a learning experience for the
rest of II Corps. There had been some hard-fought lessons. South of 1st
Infantry Division, the 9th Infantry Division took over the sector around
Djebel Berda. On March 28, it attacked but did not get far in the mountainous terrain. Patton wrote, "The extremely difficult terrain provided
one of the most formidable obstacles of all. Mere climbing of the series
of jagged and barren volcanic peaks was a feat of considerable endurance.
The men literally wore shoes and clothing to shreds."

North of the Big Red One, 1st Armored Division continued its
glacial pace eastward after capturing Maknassy on March 22. Patton
grew impatient with Ward, its commander. "Old Blood and Guts" partly
blamed himself for not continuing the advance eastward into the hills
after capturing the town. "Here I failed by not personally backing the

attack on the heights," wrote the general on April 1. "Ward fooled around for three days and let the enemy build up and then he attacked with great personal courage but failed to take the ridge."

On March 31, Ward assaulted the territory northeast of Maknassy "to draw enemy away from 1st and 9th Infantry Divisions." Due to German resistance in the hills, Ward's operation became a sideshow while the 1st and 9th Infantry Divisions became the main effort for the corps. On April 2, Patton received a letter from General Alexander, asking Patton to relieve Ward from his command and replace him with General Harmon, Fredendall's savior of Kasserine. Patton granted the request.[3]

Two days later, Patton sent his deputy, Omar Bradley, to deliver the bad news to Ward. Patton wrote in his diary that he agreed with Alexander's decision. "I should have relieved him on the 22 or 23 [March] but did not do so as I hated to change leaders in battle," he shared in his diary. "But a new leader is better than one who is timid."

Bradley did not wholly agree with Patton's decision, but "the relationship between them [Patton and Ward] had become so demoralized by distrust that it was better severed than patched up," wrote the deputy commander. This would not be the last time Bradley would find himself relieving a division commander.[4]

The Axis powers were reeling. Although Operation Pugilist had failed to crack open the Mareth Line decisively, Operation Supercharge II, Montgomery's partially successful attempt to flank it by driving north through the Tebaga Gap, had convinced von Arnim that the Italian First Army was doomed if it remained in southern Tunisia. He ordered General Messe to withdraw to the Enfidaville Line in northern Tunisia.

On April 6, the British Eighth Army launched a massive attack along Wadi Akarit, a short distance from II Corps' southeast boundary. The Axis lines shuddered and then shattered. Alexander sent a liaison officer to Patton on the morning of April 7 with the following message: "General Alexander is convinced that the big moment has now arrived for us to give a maximum of aid to the efforts of the British 8th Army. That we must push our armor out into EL GUETTAR section and must be prepared to accept casualties. Everything must be done to push forward."

In response, Patton dispatched Benson Force, a combined arms task force under the command of Col. Clarence C. Benson, the commander of 13th Armored Regiment, 1st Armored Division. The task force had two medium tank battalions, two armored field artillery battalions, one motorized infantry battalion from the 9th Infantry Division, and a slew of other support units. Benson Force received a direct order from Patton at 0930 hours on April 7 "to take his whole force and push vigorously until he reached the Mediterranean or until he made contact with the Germans."

The corps commander had seen Benson the previous night. Patton wrote, "I stopped at Benson's C.P. and told him that he must succeed or else and that I was disgusted with his slowness yesterday. I ordered him to push on till he got into a big fight or hit the ocean."

Benson also recalled the order. "Upon my return to the other portion of my command, which was back in the valley, an order arrived from General Patton," wrote the colonel. "It was on a piece of paper torn out of a pocket notebook, about 2" wide and 4" long, written in longhand with a pencil, and this is the order that put half an armored division into action that day: 'Attack and destroy the enemy; act aggressively. G.S.P., Jr.' That was all there was to it. We moved half an armored division 35 miles on that order that day."[5]

The Axis forces were in headlong retreat. With nothing in front of them, the American tanks raced to the coast. They blazed across the Tunisian countryside for nearly twenty miles and linked up with the lead elements of the British Eighth Army at 1610 hours that same afternoon. During their sprint to the Mediterranean, the Americans captured more than 1,000 Axis prisoners. It was an unequivocal victory. For several more days, operations continued in II Corps' northern sector as 1st Armored Division finally cleared the Germans in the area east of Maknassy and around Faid Pass.[6]

During this same time period, in western Tunisia, Anderson's British army simultaneously attacked through the Pichon-Fondouk Pass in an attempt to cut off the Italian First Army's escape. He was unsuccessful, and both the Italian First Army and the Fifth Panzer Army linked up in northern Tunisia on April 11 to ensure that the campaign for

North Africa would continue for another month. The next day, Anderson's British First Army and Montgomery's Eighth Army converged at the port of Sousse. In doing so, they squeezed U.S. Army II Corps out of the front lines.[7]

For the men of the 10th Panzer Division, the time period between March 23 and April 13 was one firefight after another. When the British ruptured the lines around Wadi Akarit, the 10th Panzer Division was still battling II Corps at Maknassy and Djebel Berda. Facing encirclement from the rear, the 10th Panzer Division received orders to withdraw and consolidate near Mezzouna, which was northeast of Maknassy. *Oberleutnant* Udo Balser of *Panzer Artillerie-Regiment 90* recalled the order to pull out on the night of April 6. "At 2200 hours on 6 April 1943 everyone was ordered to the regimental command post for a meeting of commanders: Tommy [the British] had broken through the Akarit position and was advancing west into our rear. Immediate position change without formation of a march column! The division to assemble in the Mezzouna area. That meant striking out on our own. We looked at each other silently. We had never experienced this before. But every minute was valuable and so we set to work. I pulled out with my battery at about 2400 hours." Several hours after staging his vehicles for the journey north, his convoy ran into trouble. "There we came upon the first traffic jam. From all sides units were trying to reach the road. Vehicle behind vehicle, tanks, trucks, assault guns, automobiles, and motorcycles."

Initially, the darkness of night concealed the massive parking lot of vehicles from prying Allied eyes in the air. At daybreak, American artillery pounded the abandoned battery positions of *Panzer Artillerie-Regiment 90*. But the 10th Panzer now was north of its old position. The men began to think they would escape unscathed.

Then an American fighter spotted them. Within minutes, bombers arrived. The pass became a gauntlet. "The most difficult part of our retreat, however, lay beyond the pass," recalled Balser. He continued, "I believe that it was also the hardest point in my life to that point. We had to pass through the narrows between the Sebkhet en Noual, a large salt lake, and another mountain chain (the Djebel bou Hedma, Djebel bou Ghabita and Djebel en Nedjilet). This narrows lay under heavy artillery fire from the mountains and under continuous attack by 20 to 30 fighter-bombers, which came down low to attack. We could see this clearly before we drove into the narrows. 'Minimum interval 300 meters, spread out, full gas!' I shouted to the men. Then we headed into the enemy fire. Shells burst all around. We were on a serving tray for the enemy in his high positions. But the artillery fire was not the worst. Swarms of enemy aircraft attacked us, diving repeatedly. Many of our division's vehicles were already burning. The fighter-bombers fired on the wrecks, preventing the recovery of the dead and wounded. Ammunition exploded. We ran for our lives away from the car, threw ourselves down, got up and ran, then down again. It was an inferno."

Caught in this maelstrom was *Oberstleutnant* Count Claus von Stauffenberg, the future failed assassin of Adolf Hitler. He was the division's operations officer. *Generalmajor* von Broich remembered seeing him amidst the carnage. "Driving through the completely open terrain, we were very soon attacked by about 20 fighters," wrote von Broich. "We managed to get away from the vehicle and spread out in the open. Fortunately the machine gun rounds missed us. We drove on and soon came upon von Stauffenberg's riddled car. We knew what had happened and feared the worst. Though seriously wounded, he escaped with his life that time—fate had preserved him for later."[8]

From April 8 to April 12, most of the 10th Panzer Division rolled northward to Tunis, while several of its units fought a furious rearguard action to allow the rest of the Italian First Army to escape to the Enfidaville Line. The line started at the town of Enfidaville on the coast and then curved to the west-northwest until it turned due north as it neared the Kebir River. On April 12, the mangled division reached its assigned assembly area to prepare for the final battles of Tunisia. Although it had survived the harrowing journey northward, the division was a shadow of its former self. Army Group Africa had few serviceable panzers left, and von Arnim decided to consolidate them into one panzer reserve. The 7th Panzer Regiment had only ten Mk IVs and seven Mk IIIs to offer to this force. By April 22, the bulk of the division was laagered west of Tunis, where it assumed the role of a mobile reserve for Army Group Africa.[9]

―――

Although the campaign for Tunisia was not over, it was time to pause and acknowledge the hard work and unwavering courage of several units in the American army. One stood out above the rest.

Patton recognized Allen's division on April 8, when he wrote a memorandum, congratulating the Big Red One. "For twenty-two days of relentless battle, you have never faltered," wrote Patton to the GIs of the First Infantry Division. "Over country whose rugged difficulty beggars description and against a veteran enemy cunningly disposed, you have pressed on. Undeterred by cold, by lack of sleep, and by continued losses, you have conquered. Your valorous exploits have brought undying fame to the soldiers of the United States."

Not to be outdone, Allen added his own words. "You have met and defeated the toughest units in the German Army with great credit to yourselves, the Division, and to your country," he wrote. "I attribute your success to the loyalty and cooperation of every man of this Division, to your cheerful discipline under great hardships and to your determination to get the job done. The German Army has learned to fear the 1st Infantry Division, just as it did in the last war."[10]

The losses during the four-week period were high but not crippling for the 1st Infantry Division. It sustained more than 1,301 casualties: 126 killed in action, 1,016 wounded in action, and 159 missing. On March 23, the Big Red One suffered 203 casualties, and the majority of those were from 3rd Battalion, 18th Infantry Regiment. Overall, II Corps listed 5,893 casualties for this period.

Losses were higher for the Axis. Although it was impossible to calculate accurately the number of wounded and killed, II Corps collected and registered 4,680 prisoners. Most of them were Italians (4,200 prisoners of war). Lieutenant Colonel Akers from the Corps G-3 section discovered 800 German graves along the roads between Gafsa and Gabes, though it was likely the Germans lost even more.[11]

Without a sector, II Corps did not have an active combat front. This changed when Alexander ordered Patton to shift the corps to the north and occupy a sector on the left flank of the British First Army for the final push toward Tunis and Bizerte. On April 15, the corps had a new commander, Omar Bradley. Patton, his work done, returned to Morocco to plan the invasion of Sicily.

Bradley prepared his corps for the last phase of the campaign. He arrayed his divisions thusly: Occupying the northernmost sector was 9th Infantry Division, followed by the 34th Infantry Division. In the south was the 1st Armored Division, and between it and the 34th was Allen's Big Red One.[12]

Alexander selected the British First Army to be the main effort for the final operation. II Corps would be a shaping operation to tie down forces north of Anderson's First Army. Once II Corps penetrated German lines, it would advance east toward Bizerte while the British First Army destroyed the bulk of Fifth Panzer Army and seize Tunis. In the south, Eighth Army would also be a shaping operation, its mission to tie down and destroy the Italian First Army along the Enfidaville Line. April 23 was D-Day.[13]

The 1st Infantry Division's mission was perhaps the most challenging. It had to penetrate enemy defenses on a ridge that ran along the north bank of the Tine River. Opposite the 1st Infantry Division was the crack *Fallschirmjäger* Regiment (Barenthin) from the Manteuffel Division.

Bradley recalled the moments leading up to the final offensive. He took stock of his division commanders and made his own assessments. As a corps commander, he credited Allen's leadership as one of the reasons for the 1st Infantry Division's successes on the battlefield. Yet he did not appreciate Allen's "maverick" temperament. "I found it difficult to persuade Terry to put his pressure where I thought it should go," wrote the new corps commander. "He would halfway agree on a plan, but somehow once the battle started this agreement seemed to be forgotten."

Bradley found Allen to be "stubborn and independent. Skillful, adept, and aggressive, he frequently ignored orders and fought his own way." Though his men loved him for it, Allen's scrappy and independent disposition lead to trouble in the coming months.[14]

On April 23, II Corps kicked off its attack. Initially, progress was sluggish. German units atop the dominating key terrain of Hill 609 blocked the 1st Infantry Division along an avenue of approach that became known as the Mousetrap. From there, German artillery forward observers rained steel on Allen's men, leaving them proverbial fish in a barrel.

Bradley called on the 34th Infantry Division to take the hill so that the Big Red One could advance. On April 29, a combined armor and infantry task force from the 34th overwhelmed the German defenders. They popped the cork out of the bottle and allowed the Big Red One to push northeast around the German flank while the 1st Armored Division exploited the seam to take Mateur on May 3.

On May 6, the doughboys of the Big Red One tangled with the survivors of Hill 609 on the heights around Chouigui. Unlike many of the Axis units collapsing throughout Tunisia that first week of May, the Barenthin Regiment fought hard and gave Allen a bloody nose. Bradley was less than thrilled. He wrote of Allen's attack, "The gesture was a foolish one and undertaken without authorization." Bradley felt Allen's assault, had it been successful, would have led nowhere except into more restrictive terrain. "A commander attacks, I reminded him, to take objectives, not to waste his strength in occupying useless ground."[15]

On the same day, British First Army launched Operation Vulcan. For Anderson, it was the final lunge. The remaining Axis forces were disintegrating or in headlong retreat to the coast. However, Kesselring had no plans for a German version of Dunkirk. The choice for the German or Italian foot soldier was death or surrender. On May 7, the U.S. 9th Infantry Division entered Bizerte while, to the south, Tunis fell to units of the British First Army.[16]

During this same period, the 10th Panzer Division continued to distinguish itself. For several weeks, starting on April 23, it fought battle after battle near Lake Sebkhet el Kourzia. During the fighting on April 25, *Oberst* Rudolf Gerhardt, the commander of the 7th Panzer Regiment, was wounded. Army doctors evacuated him to Germany. During that battle, twenty-six panzers of the 10th Panzer Division defeated an overwhelming British force from the British V Corps by using a reverse slope defense. The cost for the defenders was eleven priceless, irreplaceable panzers.

The battle for Tunisia already was lost, but the men continued to fight hard. *Oberst* Walter Straub, who served with the 7th Panzer Regiment, wrote, "The German tank crews sensed all too clearly that the end was approaching. The fighting units could only be supplied at night, for during the day enemy fighter-bombers buzzed like hornets, strafing and bombing anything that moved in and behind the German front."[17]

With each passing day, Allied air attacks, artillery barrages, and armored thrusts ground the 10th Panzer Division into dust. During the first week of May, the Allies split the Axis bridgehead in two. North of the penetration was the Fifth Panzer Army and south of it were the First Italian Army and the remnants of the *Deutschse Afrikakorps*. The bulk of the 10th Panzer Division was trapped with the First Italian Army and the *Deutschse Afrikakorps* outside of Tunis. To shorten the Axis lines, the 10th Panzer Division withdrew east toward Grombalia, southeast of Tunis. Some of the units, like the Panzer Regiment 7, dug in at the base of the Cap Bon Peninsula. The peninsula jutted out into the Mediterranean and formed the southern boundary of the Gulf of Tunis. Other elements, such as Major Drewe's *Kradschützen Battalion* 10, fought near the town of Hammam Lif on the coast to block the British from cutting the Italian First Army into two.

An artillery barrage injured Major Drewes during the fighting on May 8, and *Oberleutnant* Reile replaced him. After the British flanked the *Kradschützen Battalion* 10 at Hammam Lif, its battered dregs withdrew toward an assembly area south of Grombalia, where the rest of the division was holed up. "What was left of *Kradschützen Battalion* 10 assembled with the trains that had been sent back the previous day," recalled Reile. "There were about 200 men from the previous 850, a thrown-together lot from every company, mostly drivers, radio operators, armored car people, armed only with pistols. The most powerful weapon was an infantry gun with little ammunition."[18]

On May 10, the division ordered Reile "to burn all unnecessary vehicles and equipment. We were only to keep field kitchens and the trucks needed

191

to transport the remaining men now and when they became prisoners of war. Our main objective was to avoid taking any further casualties."

The same process was occurring in other units. *Oberfeldwebel* (S/Sgt.) Brümmer was a panzergrenadier in the Panzergrenadier Regiment 69. He wrote, "One machine gun squad after another pulled back from the firing line, disassembled its machinegun and scattered the parts. The same thing happened to the other weapons. . . . When the last machine-gun had been taken from the firing line and destroyed, a large white piece of cloth was raised on a pole near the battalion command post. From the enemy, who was still about 150 meters away, came loud shouts of joy. We stood up from our shelters and stood waiting for the cautiously advancing soldiers of a Canadian unit. This was a dangerous moment, for a rash act by someone could still have resulted in a bloodbath. But, thank God, it passed peacefully, to the visible relief of both sides." Elsewhere, the fighting flickered and then blew out. On May 12, *Generalmajor* von Broich surrendered to emissaries of the British Eighth Army. Von Arnim's command capitulated the same day. General Messe followed suit later that evening. The last unit of the 10th Panzer Division to surrender was the 7th Panzer Regiment. It waved the white flag on the morning of May 13.[19]

Field Marshall Kesselring, safe in Italy, recalled the final days. To him, the end came when the Allies broke through between May 5 and May 8. Still, he was not disappointed with his men. "Every soldier who fought in this campaign can hold up his head proudly," he wrote after the war.[20]

Dickson's staff tabulated the Axis losses of the last three weeks in the battles against II Corps. It was sobering. From April 21 to May 12, the Axis powers sustained 41,810 casualties. Another 1,130 were recovering in Allied hospitals. Germany bore the bulk of those loses against II Corps. In twenty-two days, the Wehrmacht had 1,230 killed in action, 1,245 wounded in action, and 36,720 captured. Italy had fifty killed in action, 120 wounded in action, and 5,090 captured. Overall, the total number of Axis soldiers who surrendered to the 18th Army Group was more than 275,000 men. This number exceeded the 91,000 at Stalingrad. It was a stunning victory for the Allies.

Germany could ill afford such defeats. In the span of five months, more than 400,000 Axis soldiers had become prisoners of war. Unlike the Russians, who could weather such losses, Germany could not. It was obvious to everyone except Hitler that the tide had turned in Russia and in the Mediterranean.

It was worse for Mussolini. *Il Duce*'s dream of a resurrected Roman *Mare Nostrum* in the twentieth century had become a nightmare. The war had grown increasingly unpopular at home, and with the Allies in firm control of the Mediterranean shipping lanes, Italy was ripe for the taking.[21]

On May 13, while Dickson was counting the prisoners for II Corps, General Alexander cabled his prime minister, Winston Churchill. "Sir," he began. "It is my duty to report that the Tunisian campaign is over. All enemy resistance has ceased. We are masters of the North African shores."[22]

During a Tunisia postmortem, Bradley reviewed the successes and failures of the American contribution to the Allied victory. He listed the strengths and flaws of each of his division commanders. Of Allen, he wrote, "Among the division commanders in Tunisia, none excelled the unpredictable Terry Allen in the leadership of troops. He had made himself the champion of the 1st Division GI and they in turn championed him." Still, Terrible Terry was not without his faults. "But in looking out for his own division, Allen tended to belittle the roles of the others and demand for his Big Red One prerogatives we could not fairly accord it," added Bradley.[23]

On July 10, 1943, Bradley's II Corps and Allen's 1st Infantry Division were back in action as the Allies commenced Operation Husky, the invasion of Sicily. Once again, the 1st Infantry Division led the way, beating back a major German counterattack at Gela right at the onset of the landings. If not for the hard-fighting doughboys of the Big Red One, the German soldiers of the Herman Goering Division might have thrown the Americans back into the sea.

Fortunately, the Allies achieved operational surprise since the Germans were convinced their enemies were preparing to land at either Sardinia or Greece. The Wehrmacht had shifted forces to meet those potential threats. As a result, one Italian army, which had several divisions of dubious quality, and two German divisions were the only units present when the Allies landed in southeastern Sicily.

Initially, the landings were a success. However, the terrain in Sicily favored the defender. With its mountainous terrain and narrow roads, a few regiments could tie up a corps if the ground was right. For several weeks, the 1st Infantry Division snaked around valleys and hiked over the hills and crags of Sicily until it reached Troina, a town sandwiched between Mount Etna to the east and the Nebrodi Mountains to the north. There, on August 1, it faced one of its toughest tests of the war as it battled the 15th Panzergrenadier Division. On August 6, the town finally fell to the 1st Infantry Division and the 39th Infantry Regiment from the 9th Infantry Division, but the cost to the Big Red One had been high.

"Sergeants were commanding platoons for the lack of officer replacements," wrote Bradley. The division had been fighting nonstop since the landings on July 10. It was burned out.

The same day the Big Red One captured Troina, General Bradley relieved Allen and Roosevelt of their command of the 1st Infantry Division.[24] Allen was told that his relief "was in compliance with the War Department policy for the rotation of commanders of combat experience." When Allen returned to the United States, he began to think otherwise. He wrote to a friend, "I distinctly received the impression that my relief had been initiated because of the need for rest and recuperation on my part. I base this on having received constant inquiries regarding my health. In fact, it was persistently rumored that I had suffered a physical breakdown."

Allen was incensed. He continued, "All of this was utterly ridiculous, [underlined by Allen] since I have always been completely 'fit' and in good physical condition."[25]

Bradley did not mention in his autobiography what he told Allen or Roosevelt in person. He did mention in his postwar account his personal reasons for the relief. "By now Allen had become too much of an individualist to submerge himself without the friction in the group undertakings of war," explained the II Corps commander. "The 1st Division, under Allen's command, had become too full of self-pity and pride. To save Allen both from himself and from his brilliant record and to save the division from the heady effects of too much success, I decided to separate them."

If Allen had to go, then so did Roosevelt. "Allen, I realized, would feel deeply hurt if he were to leave the division and Roosevelt were to remain," argued Bradley. "He might have considered himself a failure instead of the victim of too much success."

Allen's boss had other reasons, adding, "Any successor of Allen's would find himself in an untenable spot unless I allowed him to pick his own assistant commander. Roosevelt had to go with Allen for he, too, had sinned by loving the division too much."

For Bradley, a division was a "tool." It was a harsh realization but an understandable one during a time of total war when the nation's survival was at stake. He believed that "the only value that can be affixed to any unit is the tactical value of that unit winning the war. Even if the lives of those men assigned to it become nothing more than tools to be used in the accomplishment of that mission." In Bradley's eyes, both Roosevelt and Allen loved their men too much—too much to accomplish the mission as part of a greater mission underneath a corps command.

"For a commander the agony of war is not in its dangers, deprivations, or the fear of defeat," wrote Bradley, "but in the knowledge that with each new day men's lives must be spent to pay the costs of that day's objectives."[26]

Despite sacking the leaders of the Big Red One, the future commander of the 12th Army Group held both Allen and Roosevelt in high esteem. Unlike Fredendall, who never again led men into combat, the two relieved commanders returned to the battlefield a year later. Allen assumed command of the 104th Infantry Division and led it with distinction through several campaigns in northwest Europe until the end of the war. Roosevelt joined the 4th Infantry Division, where he resumed his role as an assistant division commander.

Serving in this role, Theodore Roosevelt Jr. made his greatest contribution to the war effort, landing with the division at Utah Beach on June 6, 1944. As the highest-ranking officer on the beach that morning, he realized that the landing craft carrying the 4th Infantry soldiers had landed at the wrong place. Instead of trying to adhere to a plan that was no longer viable, he decided to continue the landings at the current location because German resistance on Utah was negligible. His decision saved countless lives. Thanks to his quick thinking, Utah Beach was a cakewalk compared to Omaha. Eisenhower had decided to make him the new commander of the 90th Infantry Division in recognition of his achievements the following month.

Sadly, Theodore Roosevelt Jr. would never know. He died suddenly of a heart attack on the morning of July 12, 1944, shortly after seeing his son Quentin, who was also in Normandy with the 1st Infantry Division. He was laid to rest on July 14 in Ste. Mère-Eglise, France.[27]

His distant relative President Roosevelt awarded him the Medal of Honor on September 28, 1944, in recognition of his contribution on June 6. His citation read,

> *The President of the United States of America, in the name of Congress, takes pride in presenting the Medal of Honor (Posthumously) to Brigadier General Theodore Roosevelt, Jr. . . . United States Army, for gallantry and intrepidity at the risk of his life and beyond the call of duty on 6 June 1944, while serving as a commander in the 4th Infantry Division in France. After two verbal requests to accompany the leading assault elements in the Normandy invasion had been denied, Brigadier General Roosevelt's written request for this mission was approved and he landed with the first wave of the forces assaulting the enemy-held beaches. He repeatedly led groups from the beach, over the seawall and established them inland. His valor, courage, and presence in the very front of the attack and his complete unconcern at being under heavy fire inspired the troops to heights of enthusiasm and self-sacrifice. Although the enemy had the beach under constant direct fire, Brigadier General Roosevelt moved from one locality to another, rallying men around him, directed and personally led them against the enemy. Under his seasoned, precise, calm and unfaltering leadership, assault troops reduced beach strong points and rapidly moved inland with minimum casualties. He thus contributed substantially to the successful establishment of the beachhead in France.[28]*

His counterpart and former boss, Terry Allen, survived the war. He retired from the army in early 1946 after presiding over the deactivation of the 104th Infantry Division and moved with his family to El Paso, Texas, where he worked as a representative for an insurance company. There, Allen lived out the rest of his years until his death on September 12, 1969. He was buried at Fort Bliss National Cemetery, next to his son, Terry Jr., who died on October 17, 1967, leading a battalion in the steamy jungles of Vietnam.[29]

Terry Allen took care of the officers he liked. As evidence, he lobbied for Col. Frank Greer's promotion. Thanks to Allen's efforts, Greer was promoted to brigadier general. He left the regiment on May 23, 1943, to become the assistant division commander of the 79th Infantry Division. He held that post until January 1945. During that time, his division fought in Normandy and northern France. Afterward, he served in the War Department's Bureau of Public Relations. He retired shortly after the end of the war on August 31, 1946, at the rank of brigadier general. He died suddenly on May 17, 1949, in Gainesville, Florida, at the age of fifty-three.[30]

Lieutenant Colonel Robert H. York enjoyed a successful career after his stint as a battalion commander in the 18th Infantry. Impressed with his performance in North Africa and Italy, the army promoted him to colonel, and he assumed command of the 331st Infantry Regiment, 83rd Infantry Division, on July 7, 1944. He led the regiment for the rest of the war. Eventually after a decade of various staff jobs, now–Major General York took command of the 82nd Airborne Division on February 24, 1964, and deployed the division to the Dominican Republic in 1965. Two years later, Lieutenant General York took command of the XVIII Airborne Corps on August 1, 1967. He retired exactly one year later on August 1, 1968. He eventually moved to San Diego, where he died on April 15, 1988. His family buried him at West Point Cemetery.[31]

York's counterpart and friend, Lt. Col. Ben Sternberg, also did well in the army. For his service during the El Guettar campaign, the army awarded him the Distinguished Service Cross. After World War II, he bounced around, serving in various staff jobs. He did not command again until he took over the 5th Infantry Regiment on its return from the Korean War in 1954. In March 1966, he assumed command of the 101st Airborne Division and served in that capacity for fifteen months. Between commands, he was the senior personnel officer for the U.S. Eighth Army in Korea and for Military Assistance Command–Vietnam. He retired from the army after serving as an officer for thirty-three years and moved to Honolulu, Hawaii. He passed away on January 2, 2004.[32]

Colonel Courtney Brown's career was a moderate success compared to his two contemporaries. Like Sternberg, he was awarded the Distinguished Service Cross for his actions at El Guettar on March 23, 1943. He led the battalion throughout the rest of the Tunisian campaign. On July 15, 1943, five days after he landed at Gela, Sicily, Brown received a summons to see the new regimental commander, Col. George A. Smith Jr. The new commander of the 18th Infantry informed him that the army was rotating him back to the United States so that he could command another battalion. The army wanted to ensure that the new divisions would have seasoned, combat-tested officers in the ranks and selected him for that purpose.

Brown returned to the United States and assumed command of 3rd Battalion, 119th Infantry Regiment, 30th Infantry Division. He took the battalion to Normandy and led it through Operation Cobra and the seizure of the city of Aachen, Germany, in the fall of 1944. His postwar career was unremarkable, and he retired from the army on December 1, 1964, at the rank of colonel. He died forty years later on April 2, 2004, and his family buried him in Nyack, New York.[33]

The G-3, Lt. Col. Frederick W. Gibb, found success after serving as the operations officer for the 1st Infantry Division. In mid-July 1944, he replaced Colonel Taylor as the commander of the 16th Infantry Regiment. He led the regiment through several campaigns to include Aachen, Hürtgen Forest, the Bulge, and the final conquest of Germany. After the war, he served in various staff positions to include chief, Army War Plans Branch, and director of organization and training, Office of the Deputy Chief of Staff for Military Operations. After earning a promotion to major general in 1959, Gibb took over the 2nd Infantry Division and commanded it until June 1961, when he retired. He died on September 6, 1968, and his family buried him in Arlington National Cemetery.[34]

Lieutenant Colonel Herschel D. Baker, the commander of the 601st Tank Destroyer Battalion, remained in command for less than a month after El Guettar when the army ordered him to return to the United States. On April 26, Lt. Col. Walter Earle Tardy took over the 601st. Baker was awarded two Silver Stars for his service in North Africa. The army promoted him to colonel on October 29, 1944, and he retired at that rank on July 31, 1948. He passed away nearly fifteen years later on March 9, 1963.[35]

For many of the enlisted men, El Guettar was only the beginning. The Bowles twins from 2nd Battalion, 18th Infantry, saw action at Troina and then hit the beaches at Normandy on June 6, 1944. They were in the second wave and did not see much action that day. On D-Day plus one, Thomas learned that his brother Henry was wounded while leading a patrol. For several months, Henry was laid up in the hospital. He returned to the 18th Infantry in November 1944 and was wounded a second time in December, when the Germans kicked off their Ardennes offensive. Thomas fought through the hedgerows of Normandy, the streets of Aachen, and the snowdrifts of Belgium, but he never was seriously wounded. Both brothers miraculously survived the war. After the army discharged them in June 1945, they returned to Alabama. Henry married Norma Jean, and Thomas married Joyce Delano. As befitting twins, both became electricians. Henry passed away on December 8, 2006, and Thomas followed his brother on April 23, 2009.[36]

Like the Bowles twins, Walter David Ehlers, the mortar section leader from K Company, 3rd Battalion, 18th Infantry Regiment, lived a charmed life. He survived the rest of the Tunisian campaign and Sicily landings. Several weeks before D-Day, Ehlers's company commander petitioned for his transfer to L Company because K Company was in the second wave and the company commander did not want Walter and his brother, Roland, coming ashore at the same time because he expected a high number of casualties. The battalion command approved the request. Walter Ehlers was promoted to staff sergeant, and he became a squad leader in L Company.

On June 6, an incoming mortar round detonated on Roland's landing craft as he was exiting the ramp, killing him instantly. Several hundred meters farther down Omaha Beach, Walter's craft reached its debarka-tion point intact, and he led his squad ashore while bullets pelted the choppy water around him. He did not know of his brother's death until July. He was surviving and keeping his men alive. Despite the blizzard of raining shells and incoming machine-gun fire, his cool head somehow saved every man in his twelve-man squad throughout the hell that was D-Day. Ehlers boasted, "I got all of my men off the beach without a casualty, which was the best thing I ever did in my life." His heroics did not end there.[37]

Three days after the landings, Sergeant Ehlers was leading a patrol near Goville, France. Several German soldiers had the misfortune of Ehlers finding them. His Medal of Honor citation reads like an unbe-lievable Hollywood action movie:

> *Without waiting for an order, Staff Sergeant Ehlers, far ahead of his men, led his squad against a strongly defended enemy strong point, personally killing four of an enemy patrol who attacked him en route [sic]. Then crawling forward under withering machinegun fire, he pounced upon the gun crew and put it out of action. Turning his attention to two mortars protected by the crossfire of two machine-guns, Staff Sergeant Ehlers led his men through this hail of bullets to kill or put to flight the enemy of the mortar section, killing three men himself. After mopping up the mortar positions, he again advanced on a machinegun, his progress effectively covered by his squad. When he was almost on top of the gun he leaped to his feet and, although greatly outnumbered, he knocked out the position single-handed.[38]*

Ehlers remembered the incident decades later. "It was kill or be killed, that's what combat is all about. You delay, you flinch, and you're the one who is dead," said the staff sergeant.

When he discovered the mortar pit, he clicked his bayonet onto the muzzle of his rifle and charged. "When the Germans saw me, my God, their eyes got big, and they started to take off," said Ehlers. "Of course, I was as scared as they were. I didn't know there were eight or ten of them back there at the time. The bayonet really made the Germans, well, they didn't want any part of it. A man is more afraid of being stabbed to death than shot. They ran and I shot as many as I could."[39]

Ehlers continued his one-man show the next day when the Germans pinned down his platoon after it had ventured too far ahead of friendly lines. His platoon wanted to fall back, but he knew the Germans would slaughter them if they tried to escape. Instead, he told his squad to open fire on the Germans so that his platoon could withdraw. After the platoon safely had pulled out, Ehlers grabbed a Browning Automatic Rifle from a wounded comrade and laid down a curtain of suppressive fire so that his squad could extricate itself from the situation. During his one-man firestorm, a German sniper shot Ehlers, but he kept on fighting. After his men had retreated to safety, a now-wounded Ehlers carried the last wounded man over his shoulders to a covered and concealed position for treatment. Courting death, the fearless squad leader scurried back to his position to retrieve the rifle that he had left behind to carry the soldier.[40]

As a Medal of Honor recipient, the army authorized Ehlers to return home to see his family in December 1944 in Manhattan, Kansas. In recognition of his leadership skills, his command granted him a battle-field commission to second lieutenant. In early 1945, Lieutenant Ehlers departed the United States to rejoin the 18th Infantry Regiment and served out his tour, earning the Purple Heart three more times. After the war, he moved to Buena Park, California, and worked in the Veterans Administration. His wife, Dorothy, bore him a son and two daughters. His son, Walter Jr., followed his father's example. He earned a commission in the U.S. Army and retired as a lieutenant colonel. He even served in the Big Red One.[41]

Ehlers told an interviewer that Roland's death troubled him for the rest of his life. "I still have dreams about my brother. We're together, and suddenly he's gone. I am looking for him and can't find him. Fifty years. I'll probably dream about him tonight." Walter Sr. was reunited with his brother on February 20, 2014, at the age of ninety-two.[42]

For the officers and men of the 10th Panzer Division, El Guettar was close to the end, though they did not know it at the time. As stated previously, the 10th Panzer continued to fight for victory, even when it was a forlorn hope. Friedrich von Broich, the commander, received a meaningless promotion to *Generalleutnant* on May 1, 1943, as if Hitler thought a promotion would make him and his men fight harder. He surrendered the remnants of his division on May 12 and entered into captivity. The British authorities released him in October 1947, and he faded into obscurity. He died almost three decades later on September 24, 1974, in Leoni-by-Starnberg, Germany.[43]

Other officers and men were more fortunate. *Oberst* Rudolf Gerhardt's injury on April 23, 1943, resulted in his evacuation to Europe. Therefore, he was not present when the division surrendered in May. After a period of convalescence, he worked for Field Marshal Kesselring in Italy before he took command of the Panzer Lehr Regiment of the Panzer Lehr Division in November 1943. The Panzer Lehr Division was one of the German army's newest and premier divisions. It had the best equipment, and its officers and noncommissioned officers had been instructors before joining the unit. The Panzer Lehr Division entered the fighting in Normandy shortly after June 6, 1944, but by the following August, after two months of unrelenting combat against the American and British forces, it was a division in name only.

For a short time, Gerhardt commanded the Panzer Lehr Division as it staggered and stumbled across the German frontier to reach the Western Wall and safety. In January 1945, the Wehrmacht transferred Gerhardt to attend a general officer's course. On March 26, 1945, he became the acting commander of the 26th Panzer Division, and he continued in that capacity until the American army captured him on May 6, 1945. He died peacefully on November 10, 1964, in Münster, Germany.[44]

After the Axis surrender in Tunisia, the Wehrmacht reconstituted several of the divisions that had participated in the campaign. The 15th Panzer Division became the 15th Panzergrenadier Division and went on to fight in Sicily, Italy, France, and Belgium. The 21st Panzer Division also lived on and played a key role during the fighting in Normandy. However, the German high command decided not to rebuild the 10th Panzer. It died in May 1943. Although its history was short, it participated in many of the major German campaigns of World War II and added its own story to the Blitzkrieg legend.

Its adversary at El Guettar, the 1st Infantry Division, was only at the beginning of its journey. After El Guettar and Sicily, the Big Red One played a crucial role on June 6, 1944, when it landed on Omaha Beach. It clawed its way through the Normandy hedgerows and eventually reached the Siegfried Line that September. From there, it wrestled with the German army to take the city of Aachen, Germany, the first major German city to surrender to the western Allies. Afterward, the soldiers of the 1st Infantry Division fought in the battle of the Bulge and crossed the Rhine in 1945 and eventually ended up in Czechoslovakia that May, when the war in Europe ended. Many of the GIs who had fought and bled in the sands of North Africa were either dead or lying in a military hospital somewhere, recovering from their wounds, when the final shots were fired. Their contributions had been vital in the final Allied victory in the spring of 1945.

When it came to the impact of El Guettar, America's first major victory against the Germany army, A. J. Liebling probably said it best in his book *The Road Back to Paris*. He wrote, "If one American division could beat one German division, I thought then, a hundred American divisions could beat a hundred German divisions. Only the time was already past when Germany had a hundred divisions to spare from the Russian front, plus God knows how many more to fight the British, plus garrison troops for all the occupied countries. I knew deep down inside me after that the road back to Paris was clear."

Although the war was far from over in Europe, thanks to the Big Red One and other units, such as the 601st Tank Destroyer Battalion, the American soldier was learning how to defeat the German blitzkrieg. After El Guettar, it was no longer a question of *if* but *when*.[45]

ACKNOWLEDGMENTS

I COULD NOT HAVE WRITTEN THIS BOOK WITHOUT HELP. LIKE MY PAST endeavors, I had a great team behind me. First, I would like to thank Leanne Brennan from Breakthrough Entertainment and Samuel K. Dolan from Flight 33 Productions. Both provided original veterans' interview transcripts from the *Greatest Tank Battles* and *Patton 360* series, respectively. The unedited interviews provided incredible context for the book.

Next, I would like to thank Robert Haldeman, the creator and curator of the website www.tankdestroyer.net. Frankly, without him, this book would have never happened. Robert's website is a treasure trove of primary sources. His collection of documents pertaining to the 601st and 899th Tank Destroyer Battalions made this book possible. In addition, I would be remiss if I did not mention the contribution of the L. L. Gill Tank Destroyer Association, which donated many of the documents to Robert's website. When I discovered the website and read the material on the 601st, I realized how important the 601st was in the battle for El Guettar. Furthermore, thanks to Robert, I linked up with Victor Fail-mezger, who wrote a wonderful book on the 601st. Victor provided me with excerpts from the unpublished memoirs of Sgt. John Nowak. Robert also introduced me to Paul Stevens. Paul supplied me with several memorable photos of the men of the 601st for this book.

Thanks to the Internet, research has become a lot less laborious. When I wrote my first book with Don Cygan, *No Silent Night*, all of the primary source material came directly from several archives that I either visited or paid a researcher to visit. As I researched this book, I discovered a huge amount of source material online, which made my project a lot less time consuming. One institution that stands out is Colonel Robert R. McCormick Research Center, which is part of the First Division

Museum at Cantigny, in Wheaton, Illinois. There, one can find thousands of documents relating to the 1st Infantry Division in World War II. Paul Herbert is the executive director at the museum, and he put me in contact with Andrew Wood, who is one of the researchers at the center. Andrew went above and beyond the call of duty in providing me with valuable research material. Thank you Andrew.

Despite the growing number of primary source material one can find online, I still need someone to delve into the various archives for primary source material. For the National Archives at College Park, Maryland, I had Susan Strange, who was invaluable in finding thousands of unit records. For the Library of Congress, I had Vonnie Zullo, who scanned page after page of Patton's diary and Theodore Roosevelt Jr.'s letters to his family while he was the assistant division commander of the 1st Infantry Division. At the U.S. Army Heritage and Education Center in Carlisle, Pennsylvania, I had Thomas E. Buffenbarger, who sent me various documents relating to postwar veterans' interviews. Finally, I need to send a special thanks to Claudia Rivers, who works on the Special Collections Staff at the University of Texas El Paso Library. The library is home to the Terry de la Mesa Allen Collection. It is a great source of personal letters and so on from the commander of the Big Red One, whose family donated the collection after the general's death.

Families and friends also played an important role in this task. First, I would like to thank Timothy L. Bowles and the Bowles family for providing numerous photos and recorded interviews of the Bowles twins. The videos were replete with stirring vignettes about the battle of El Guettar. Timothy also runs a great website, dedicated to his father and uncle: http://bowlesusa.org. You can find many of the same items that I used for the book on the website.

Next, I would like to thank Dave and Eric at wartimepress.com for providing me with several editions of *Infantry Journal*. The journals had some great articles, written several months after the battles in North Africa. In addition, a special thanks to Bob Baumer, author of *American Iliad: The History of the 18th Infantry Regiment in World War II*. Bob provided me with information on Col. Robert York.

For photos of the battlefield today, I would like to thank Richard Scavetta. He was a public affairs staff member for U.S. Army Africa Command, and he was a participant in an El Guettar Staff Ride from 2012. He gave permission to use some of his photos.

Once again, for translations, I relied on my old warhorse, Dieter Stenger. Dieter's translations are top-notch. I used him before for several articles and most notably for *No Silent Night* and *Patton at the Battle of the Bulge*. I am sure I will use his services again! Thank you Dieter.

Of course, I need to mention, Matthew Davenport, author of *First Over There: The Attack on Cantigny, America's First Battle of World War*. He helped me by providing contacts at the First Division Museum and other general advice. His book on the Big Red One in World War I is an excellent source of history on the 1st Infantry Division. I would highly recommend it.

I cannot forget the hard work of my agent, Doug Grad, and the Doug Grad Literary Agency. Doug, thank you for your frank advice and keeping me on the right path. Also, many thanks to David Reisch, my editor at Stackpole Books.

Last but not least, I need to thank my wife, Caulyne, now Dr. Barron. She is my support and an amazing editor, and she only twitches slightly in these departures from academic writing ::grin::. Without her, none of these works would ever see the light of day. I love you, honey. Thank you!

NOTE ON SOURCES

LIKE MY PREVIOUS WORKS, I BASED THIS BOOK ALMOST ENTIRELY ON primary sources. The only time I relied on secondary sources was for biographical data or material that was necessary but mostly tangential to the overall story. For conversations that came directly from the radio logs of the headquarters of the 1st Infantry Division, the original recorder in March 1943 used shorthand and tended to delete indefinite and definite articles and the verb "to be" when he entered messages into the log. Instead of adding the [is] or [the], I added it without the brackets because it would have overwhelmed the reader and would have made the sentences hard to read. Hence, that is why I am writing the note here, so that the reader knows that I used some artistic license with those conversations, but it was minor. The colorful words present in the heated conversations were transposed verbatim from the headquarters' radio log.

ENDNOTES

Preface: Purple Heart Boxes versus Panzers

1. Carter 1947–1948, 18; a great introduction on the war in North Africa is George F. Howe's book *United States Army in World War II Mediterranean Theater of Operations. Northwest Africa: Seizing the Initiative in the West*. See pages 543 to 563 for El Guettar.
2. Jentz 2001, 19–20.
3. Zaloga, *M3 Infantry Half-Track 1940–1973* 2002, 4, 10–11, 28.
4. Harper, interview with Bill R. Harper for History Channel Show, *Patton 360*, 2008.
5. Sundstrom, "Use of Antitank Weapons and Individual Company Tactics" 1980s, 2.
6. Harper, interview with Bill R. Harper for History Channel Show, *Patton 360*, 2008.
7. Josowitz 1945, 3.
8. Baker, "Tank Destroyer Combat in Tunisia" 1944, 19–21; Baker, "Battle Operations Report" 1943, 3; Paulick March 1943, 1.
9. Schick 2013, 499.
10. Butler 1949–1950, 11; see Map D.
11. Kannicht 2012.
12. Gause 1946, 6.
13. Gause 1946, 6.
14. Headquarters 1943, Serial #1130; T. E. Morrison, Thomas E. Morrison Collection, AFC/2001/001/00869, Veterans History Project, American Folklife Center, Library of Congress 2001; T. E. Morrison, *Army Service Experience Questionnaire* 1999, 1, 20.
15. Critz, Lieutenant General Harry H. Critz, Senior Officers Oral History Program, Project 81-2, U.S. Army Military History Institute 1981, 35.
16. Carter 1947–1948, 18; see also Howe 1957, 543–63.

Introduction: The Opponents

1. Liebling, "Profiles: Find'em, Fix'em, and Fight'em Part I" 1943, 24; Allen, *1st Infantry Division Report on Combat* May 1943, 21–22.
2. For officer ranks, I use ranks they held during the battle of El Guettar in March 1943; National WW2 Museum 2016.
3. This number does not include the Philippine Division, which was destroyed when Japan conquered the archipelago in 1942; U.S. Government Printing Office 1948.
4. Wheeler 2007, 13.
5. Wheeler 2007, 62.
6. Wheeler 2007, 81–90.

7. Wheeler 2007, 95–98.
8. Wheeler 2007, 99–126.
9. Wheeler 2007, 128–29.
10. Wheeler 2007, 130–40.
11. Terry the Terror or Terry the Terrible was a name he earned while attending West Point; Astor 2003, 12–13, 92.
12. Liebling, "Profiles: Find'em, Fix'em, and Fight'em Part I" 1943, 22.
13. Astor 2003, 14–20.
14. Astor 2003, 31–54.
15. Liebling, "Profiles: Find'em, Fix'em, and Fight'em Part I" 1943, 24; Allen, *1st Infantry Division Report on Combat* May 1943, 21–22.
16. In 1928, he married Mary Frances at El Paso's Saint Patrick's Cathedral. He was a devout Catholic; Wheeler 2007, 69–90; Liebling, "Profiles: Find'em, Fix'em, and Fight'em Part I" 1943, 25.
17. Wheeler 2007, 77.
18. Marshall, Letter to "Frank R. McCoy" 1940; Liebling, "Profiles: Find'em, Fix'em, and Fight'em Part I" 1943, 26.
19. Marshall, "3-213, Letter to Brigadier General Terry de la Mesa Allen" 1942.
20. Bradley 1999, 110.
21. Mason, "Reminiscences and Anecdotes of World War II" 1988, 130.
22. Mason, "Reminiscences and Anecdotes of World War II" 1988, 134.
23. Jacobson 2001.
24. Ehrhardt 2005.
25. Jeffers 2002, 104–18; War Department 2016.
26. Jeffers 2002, 179–93.
27. Marshall, "3-026 Letter to Brigadier General Theodore Roosevelt Jr." 1941.
28. Marshall, "3-213 Letter to Brigadier General Terry de la Mesa Allen" 1942.
29. Bradley 1999, 110.
30. West Point Association 1968; Department of the Army 1944, 340.
31. John J. Sayen 2006, 16.
32. John J. Sayen 2006, 22.
33. John J. Sayen 2006, 9.
34. War Department July 11, 1942, 83.
35. Department of the Army 2004; Baumer, *American Iliad: The History of the 18th Infantry Regiment in World War II* 2004, 1.
36. Baumer, *American Iliad: The History of the 18th Infantry Regiment in World War II* 2004, 14.
37. Baumer, *American Iliad: The History of the 18th Infantry Regiment in World War II* 2004, 14; Command and General Staff School 1934, 4; Department of the Army 1944.
38. Department of the Army 1944, 1032.
39. Roncalio 1983, 2–3.
40. Mason, "Letter to Colonel Lloyd, concerning Robert York" Unknown, 1.

41. Department of the Army 1944, 883; West Point Association of Graduates 2004; Department of the Army 1950, 543.
42. Lt. Colonel Courtney P. Brown 2007; War Department 1943.
43. Department of the Army 2009.
44. Department of the Army 1944, 923.
45. Schick 2013, 1–3.
46. 9th (2nd Pomeranian) Uhlans served on the Western Front in World War I until November 1914, when it transferred to the Russian front, where it served until 1918. It finished the war on the Western Front; Andreas Altenburger 2016.
47. Lang, June 8, 1947, 14.
48. Andreas Altenburger 2016.
49. Niehorster, "Panzer-Division (Afrika), 23 October 1942."
50. Niehorster, "German Army: Tank Arrivals in North Africa 1941–1943," 2013.
51. Lefévre 1999, 78.
52. Andreas Altenburger 2016; Schick 2013, 482, 490.

Chapter 1: Prelude

1. George S. Patton, "Patton's Diary" 1943, March 6; Bradley 1999, 43.
2. Alexander 2015, 51–52.
3. Eisenhower 1997, 126.
4. Eisenhower 1997, 141.
5. Arnim, *Order for the Operation Frühlingwind (Part of Center for U.S. Army Military History Kasserine Pass Collection Volume I Part 1)* February 8, 1943, 1; Anderson 2015, 145; Alexander 2015, 57; Hains March 11, 1943.
6. Rommel, *Report to Commando Supremo (Part of Center for U.S. Army Military History Kasserine Pass Collection Volume I Part 2)* February 18, 1943.
7. Operations, Fifth Panzer Army 1943, 1.
8. Rommel, *Order for German Africa Corps, 19 February 1943 (Part of Center for U.S. Army Military History Kasserine Pass Collection Volume I Part 2)* 1943, 1–2.
9. German-Italian Panzer Army Command Post February 20, 1943, 1–2; 1st Battalion, 26th Infantry, suffered more than 160 casualties. Disturbingly, 74 percent of the casualties were missing in action, which meant they most likely became prisoners of war; Kelly 1943; Schick 2013, 474–75.
10. Schick 2013, 475–79; Zaloga, *Kasserine Pass 1943 Rommel's Last Victory* 2005, 56–57; Robinett March 1, 1943, 1–3.
11. Headquarters, Fifth Panzer Army 1943, 133–36; Ries 1943, 8–11.
12. D'Este 2002, 396–97.
13. Harmon also told Patton a great deal of information, concerning his son-in-law's fate. He learned that Fredendall could not rescue Waters's trapped battalion, and he advised Waters to surrender. Patton scribbled, "This was a mistake but I hope John [son-in-law] complied"; George S. Patton, "Patton's Diary" 1943, March 2.
14. Bradley 1999, 41–42.
15. D'Este 2002, 396–97.

16. George S. Patton, "Patton's Diary" 1943, February 23.
17. George S. Patton, "Patton's Diary" 1943, March 4–5; George S. Patton, *War as I Knew It* 1995, 376.
18. Eisenhower 1997, 150.
19. George S. Patton, "Patton's Diary" 1943, March 5; George S. Patton, *War as I Knew It* 1995, 376–77.
20. George S. Patton, "Patton's Diary" 1943, March 6; Bradley 1999, 43.
21. George S. Patton, "Patton's Diary" 1943, March 8, 10.
22. Bradley 1999, 44; George S. Patton, "Patton's Diary" 1943, March 6.
23. Goff 1994, 63.
24. Towne 2000, 44.
25. Roosevelt 1943, March 6.
26. Bradley 1999, 46–47; Koch 1999, 31.
27. Roosevelt 1943, March 6.
28. Ries 1943, Appendix B and C.
29. Bradley 1999, 51–52; Blumenson 1986, 260–61.
30. Akers March 4, 1943, 1.
31. K. C. Lambert, *Outline Plan Operation "WOP" 9 March 1943, II Corps Order* 1943, 1–3.
32. K. C. Lambert, *Field Order #3, Headquarters, II Corps, March 11* 1943.
33. Gibb, *Field Order #16, Headquarters, 1st Infantry Division, March 11* 1943, 1–2.
34. Ford 2012, 50–58; Dickson, *G-2 Summary #5, II Corps Headquarters, G-2 Section, Box 2646* March 17, 1943, 1–3.
35. George S. Patton, "Patton's Diary" 1943, March 12–13; Headquarters 1943, Msg 977, 980.
36. Colaccico, *Field Order #14, Headquarters, 18th Infantry Regiment, March 13* 1943, 1.
37. Brown March 13, 1943, 1–2; Middleworth 1943, 1–2.
38. Alexander 2015, 68; George S. Patton, "Patton's Diary" 1943, March 13.
39. Headquarters, 1st Infantry Division 1943, Msg 2–3; George S. Patton, *Report on Operation Conducted by II Corps, United States Army, Tunisia, 15 March–10 April 1943, Box 2606* 1943, 2–3.
40. Dickson, *G-2 Periodic Report No. 70, II Corps, from 0001 15 March to 2400 15 March, Box 2616* 1943, 1; Porter, *German Order of Battle in Tunisia, Box 5103* March 10, 1943, 7; Nafziger 1997.
41. George S. Patton, "Patton's Diary" 1943, March 15.
42. Headquarters, II Corps March 1943, March 15, Msg 42, 46; Headquarters 1943, Msg 987.
43. Gibb, *Field Order #18, Headquarters, 1st Infantry Division, March 15* 1943, 1–2.
44. George S. Patton, "Patton's Diary" 1943, March 16.
45. Allen, *Headquarters, 1st Infantry Division, Memorandum to Colonel Fechet, Colonel Greer, Lieutenant Colonel Baker, Lieutenant Colonel Howland* 1943.
46. Headquarters 1943, Msg 997; Headquarters, 1st Engineer Battalion 1943, 5; Bennett 1943, 24.

47. Headquarters 1943, Msg 998–1004.
48. Roosevelt 1943, March 20.
49. Headquarters 1943, Msg 1003–1011; Headquarters, 1st Infantry Division 1943, Msg 4.
50. Headquarters 1943, Msg 1017.
51. Roosevelt 1943, March 20.
52. Headquarters 1943, Msg 1021,1025–1027; Headquarters, 1st Infantry Division 1943, Msg 20.
53. George S. Patton, "Patton's Diary" 1943, March 17.
54. Allen, *Memorandum to Lieutenant Colonel Darby, 17 March, Headquarters, 1st Infantry Division, Box 5118* 1943.
55. Darby 2007, Loc 1194 of 3423; Headquarters 1943, Msg 1022, 1028, 1033; Headquarters, 1st Infantry Division 1943, Msg 14; Karbel April 9, 1943, 1.
56. Headquarters 1943, Msg 1036; Carter 1947–1948, 5–6.
57. Headquarters 1943, Msg 1037; Colaccico, Field Order #15, Headquarters, 18th Infantry Regiment, March 18, 1943.
58. Headquarters, II Corps March 1943, March 18, Msg 11, 48; Dickson, *G-2 Periodic Report No. 73, II Corps, from 0001 18 March to 2400 18 March, Box 2616* 1943; Temperino 2009, 113–14.
59. Dickson, *G-2 Periodic Report No. 74, II Corps, from 0001 19 March to 2400 19 March, Box 2616* 1943, 1–2; Dickson, *G-2 Summary #6, II Corps Headquarters, G-2 Section, Box 2646* April 2, 1943, 5; Headquarters, II Corps March 1943, 18 March, Msg 48; Francin March 21, 1943.
60. Headquarters, 1st Infantry Division 1943, March 19, Msg 7, 40; Walker 2012.
61. The analyst's picture of the 580th was not accurate. It had an armored car company, but it also had a company of 251 half-tracks with 18 × LMGs, 2 × HMGs, and 4 × 75mm infantry guns. Its support company had 3 × 75mm SP guns for antitank missions. It did have a flak battery with 4 × 88mm guns and 2 × LMGs; Porter, *German Order of Battle in Tunisia, Box 5103* March 10, 1943, 6–7; Nafziger 1997; Dickson, *G-2 Periodic Report No. 73, II Corps, from 0001 18 March to 2400 18 March, Box 2616* 1943.
62. George S. Patton, *Report on Operation Conducted by II Corps, United States Army, Tunisia, 15 March–10 April 1943, Box 2606* 1943, 3–4.
63. Carter 1947–1948, 7–8.
64. Carter 1947–1948, 9; Dickson, *G-2 Periodic Report No. 75, II Corps, from 0001 20 March to 2400 20 March, Box 2616* 1943.

Chapter 2: Night Attack
1. George S. Patton, "Patton's Diary" 1943, March 20; Gause 1946, 3.
2. Headquarters, 1st Infantry Division 1943, Msg 28; Allen, *Summary of the El Guettar Offensive (20 March to 6 April 1943) during the North African Campaign of World War II* 1943, 4; George S. Patton, *Report on Operation Conducted by II Corps, United States Army, Tunisia, 15 March–10 April 1943, Box 2606* 1943, 4.

3. Allen, *Summary of the El Guettar Offensive (20 March to 6 April 1943) during the North African Campaign of World War II* 1943, 4–5.

4. George S. Patton, "Patton's Diary" 1943, March 20; Gause 1946, 3.

5. Carter 1947–1948, 8–9.

6. Critz, *Gafsa-El Guettar Operation, March 10 to April 8* April 20, 1943, 1; Silva, "'B' Battery Catches It" 1994, 71–72.

7. Welply 2003, 5–7.

8. Ingersoll 1943, 122.

9. Street 1947–1948, 12.

10. M. J. King 1985, 10–12.

11. Department of the Army 1944, 798; Kays 2010, 53, 80–81; Street 1947–1948, 12.

12. Darby 2007, Chapter 5.

13. Ingersoll 1943, 142; Street 1947–1948, 13.

14. Ingersoll 1943, 142.

15. Since he wrote the account shortly after the operation, Ingersoll could not use real names. In his book, Pope was "Henry," and Darby was "Chittenden," I changed it back; Ingersoll 1943, 144–45.

16. Darby 2007, Chapter 5.

17. Headquarters, 1st Infantry Division 1943, Msg 5, 6.

18. Darby 2007.

19. In his account, Street wrote the attack started at 0500. He was off by one hour, according to the radio logs written at the time of the operation; Street 1947–1948, 13.

20. Ingersoll 1943, 147–48, 150–51.

21. Both Darby and Ingersoll claim it was a German 88. GIs tended to call all Axis guns in the Europe Theater 88s, so I do not know if this was an actual German antiaircraft gun; Ingersoll 1943, 152–53; Darby 2007, Loc 1259 of 3423.

22. Darby 2007, Loc 1259 of 3423.

23. Street 1947–1948, 13.

24. Darby 2007, Loc 1266 of 3423; Ingersoll 1943, 155–56.

25. Ingersoll 1943, 156–57; Darby 2007, Loc 1273 of 3423.

26. Ingersoll 1943, 160–63; Darby 2007, Loc 1273 of 3423; Street 1947–1948, 13; Karbel April 9, 1943, 1–2.

27. Headquarters 1943, Msg 1038, 1040.

28. Carter 1947–1948, 10–11.

29. Carter 1947–1948, 11–12.

30. Headquarters 1943, Msg 1085, 1042.

31. Headquarters 1943, Msg 1043; Headquarters, 1st Infantry Division 1943, Msg 2, 3.

32. Carter 1947–1948, 12–13; Baumer, *American Iliad: The History of the 18th Infantry Regiment in World War II* 2004, 88–89; Department of the Army 1949, 478.

33. Headquarters 1943, Msg 1044–1048.

34. The log listed the prisoners of war from the 131st Centauro Regiment, which I believe was a clerical error since the Centauro Division is actually the 131st Armored Division (Centauro); Headquarters 1943, Msg 1054, 1103; Carter 1947–1948, 12–13.

35. Roosevelt 1943.

36. Headquarters, 1st Infantry Division 1943, Msg 53; George S. Patton, "Patton's Diary" 1943, 22–23.
37. The last 1208 message said Hill 462, which did not make sense. I believe it was a typo, and it was Hill 482, which was where the other two battalions ended up that afternoon; Headquarters, 1st Infantry Division 1943, Msg 54, 58, 63, and 64.
38. Carter 1947–1948, 13; George S. Patton, "Patton's Diary" 1943, 22–23.
39. Headquarters 1943, Msg 1084, 1089.
40. Headquarters, 1st Infantry Division 1943, Msg 64; Headquarters 1943, Msg 1088, 1090, 1092, 1093.
41. Goff 1994, 66.
42. Headquarters 1943, Msg 1094; Headquarters, 32nd Field Artillery Battalion 1943, Msg 7; Headquarters, 1st Infantry Division 1943, 21 March, Msg 65–66.
43. Luftwaffe 1942, 7–12; Junkers Flugzeug und Motorwerke 1940, 0III-0IV.
44. Silva, "When Our Guns Get Overrun" 1994, 77.
45. Goff 1994, 66; U.S. Army and Army Air Force Casualty List 2013; Headquarters 1943, Msg 1105, 1096; Critz, *Gafsa-El Guettar Operation, March 10 to April 8* April 20, 1943, 2.
46. Marcus 2008.
47. Harper, *Greatest Tank Battles: The Battle of Tunisia* 2011.
48. T. E. Morrison, *Army Service Experience Questionnaire* 1999, 9.
49. Harper, *Greatest Tank Battles: The Battle of Tunisia* 2011.
50. We can only assume that the two who died were the other two men in the half-track. Morrison mentioned that "radio operator" was also killed in the track. Marcus did not mention in his interview who the others were; Marcus 2008; American Battle Monuments Commission 2013.
51. Marcus 2008; Miner March 26, 1943.
52. T. E. Morrison, Thomas E. Morrison Collection (AFC/2001/001/00869), Veterans History Project, American Folklife Center, Library of Congress 2001.
53. Greer's 2nd Battalion also reported tanks at 1845 hours in front of its position. That report did not reach the division according to the logs. We do not know what 2nd Battalion saw; Headquarters, 1st Infantry Division 1943, Msg 75–94, 106, 101, 110; Headquarters 1943, 1107; Dickson, *G-2 Periodic Report No. 76, II Corps, from 0001 21 March to 2400 21 March, Box 2616* 1943, 1; Carter 1947–1948, 14.
54. Kesselring, *Final Commentaries on the Campaign in North Africa 1941–1943 MS # C-075, Volume 3* December 1949, 12.
55. Kesselring, *Kesselring's View of the African War, MS # T-3 P1 Part II* 1954, 43; Howe 1957, 530–33; Ford 2012, 61.
56. Kesselring, *Final Commentaries on the Campaign in North Africa 1941–1943 MS # C-075, Volume 3* December 1949, 14.
57. Vaerst 1947, 2, 10; Arnim, *Erinnerungen an Tunesien MS # C-098* n.d., 84–85; the field marshal believed that the concept of the counterattack was sound, but he argued that von Arnim botched its execution because the army group commander did not allocate enough combat power for the envelopment. On another note, Kesselring kept on mistaking his months, but otherwise the dates checked out; Kesselring, *Final Com-*

mentaries on the Campaign in North Africa 1941–1943 MS # C-075, Volume 3 December 1949, 14–15; Schick 2013, 498–99; for more about "Hans Cramer," see Andreas Altenburger 2016.

58. Lang June 8, 1947, Part 2: 6, 11.
59. Schick 2013, 499.
60. George S. Patton, *Report on Operation Conducted by II Corps, United States Army, Tunisia, 15 March–10 April 1943, Box 2606* 1943, 4–5; Dickson, *G-2 Periodic Report No. 77, II Corps, from 0001 22 March to 2400 22 March, Box 2616* 1943, 1.
61. George S. Patton, "Patton's Diary" 1943, 24.
62. George S. Patton, *Report on Operation Conducted by II Corps, United States Army, Tunisia, 15 March–10 April 1943, Box 2606* 1943, 1); Dickson had predicted that the Germans would tap into their theater reserve back on March 17, but on the night of March 22, they had no indication that this had occurred; Headquarters, II Corps 1943, Msg 85; Howe 1957, 553; Dickson, *G-2 Periodic Report No. 77, II Corps, from 0001 22 March to 2400 22 March, Box 2616* 1943.
63. Headquarters, 1st Infantry Division 1943, Msg 17, 23.
64. Headquarters 1943, Msg 1119, 1121.
65. Carter 1947–1948, 15–16.
66. Headquarters, 1st Infantry Division 1943, Msg 36.
67. Carter 1947–1948, 15.
68. Carter 1947–1948, 15–16.
69. Headquarters 1943, Msg 1127; Carter 1947–1948, 16–17.
70. Headquarters 1943, Msg 1128.
71. Headquarters, 1st Infantry Division 1943, Msg 53.
72. Headquarters, 1st Infantry Division 1943, Msg 62; Headquarters, II Corps 1943, Msg 98.
73. Headquarters, 1st Infantry Division 1943, Msg 61.
74. G-3 Section, Headquarters, 1st Infantry Division 1943, 1–2; Headquarters, 32nd Field Artillery Battalion 1943.
75. Headquarters, 1st Infantry Division 1943, Msg 69.
76. Sound and flash was a technique for conducting counter battery on enemy artillery. The defenders would shoot an azimuth in the direction of the boom or flash from the artillery. Another person would shoot an azimuth at the same flash or boom from another location. Both would then shoot a resection. Where their lines intersect on a map is the location of the enemy artillery; Headquarters, 1st Infantry Division 1943, Msg 70. The operations overlay for March 22 was wrong. It placed 2nd Battalion, 18th Infantry, with 3rd Battalion on Dj El Mcheltat, which was no longer the case. It should have been south with 1st Battalion on Djebel Berda; Headquarters, 1st Infantry Division 1943.
77. I had to leave out parts of the quotes because the shorthand did not make sense; Headquarters, 1st Infantry Division 1943, Msg 73, 76.
78. Baker, "Battle Operations Report" 1943, 1–2.
79. Baker, "Tank Destroyer Combat in Tunisia" 1944, 20–21.

80. Headquarters, 1st Infantry Division 1943, Msg 2; Carter 1947–1948, 17–18; Headquarters, 1st Infantry Division March 1943, March 23, Msg 3, 5–7, 9, 10.

Chapter 3: Morning Attack

1. Viney 1994, 72; Frank A. Viney 2008.
2. Paulick March 1943, 1; Gioia March 23, 1943; Lehman 1943, 8.
3. Luthi 22 March, 1943.
4. Ritso March 1943.
5. Luthi March 22, 1943.
6. Mitchell March 27, 1943; Baker, "Tank Destroyer Combat in Tunisia" 1944, 22; F. X. Lambert March 1943; Lehman 1943, 8.
7. Ritchie March 1943.
8. Horne March 1943.
9. F. X. Lambert March 1943; Ritchie March 1943.
10. This time is based Colonel Greer's report that the 601st TD had withdrawn through his lines; Headquarters, 1st Infantry Division 1943, MSG 18.
11. Yowell March 27, 1943, 1; A. I. Raymond March 1943; Stima March 1943.
12. Raymond claimed it was a Tiger I. However, no record exists on the German side that indicates that Tiger Is were in the attack that morning. More than likely it was a Mk IV; A. I. Raymond March 1943; Hamel March 1943.
13. Yowell March 27, 1943, 1.
14. Lehman 1943, 9; Hamel March 1943.
15. Hamel March 1943.
16. Yowell March 27, 1943, 1; Hamel March 1943; Stima March 1943, 1–2.
17. Hamel March 1943; Nowak 1999, 2–3.
18. Cook March 27, 1943; War Department June 10, 1943, 3.
19. Cook March 27, 1943.
20. Yowell March 27, 1943, 2.
21. Nowak 1999, 3.
22. This is based on the report from 18th Infantry's radio log that first tank attack withdrew at approximately 0650 hours; Headquarters, 1st Infantry Division 1943, MSG 1140.
23. Sundstrom, "Story of the 601st Tank Destroyer Battalion" 1980s, 2–3.
24. Sundstrom, "Use of Antitank Weapons and Individual Company Tactics" 1980s, 1.
25. Sundstrom, *Statement of Captain Herbert E. Sundstrom, C Company, 601st Tank Destroyer Battalion* March 27, 1943, 1.
26. Sundstrom, *Statement of Captain Herbert E. Sundstrom, C Company, 601st Tank Destroyer Battalion* March 27, 1943, 1; Lester D. Matter March 27, 1943, 1; Migliaccio March 27, 1943.
27. McElroy March 27, 1943.
28. Harper, *Greatest Tank Battles: The Battle of Tunisia* 2011.
29. Munn March 27, 1943, 1; Sundstrom, *Statement of Captain Herbert E. Sundstrom, C Company, 601st Tank Destroyer Battalion* March 27, 1943, 1.

30. According to the radio logs, the Germans resumed their attack around 0700, when they attempted to flank the 601st from the south. Hence, the attack lasted until approximately 0750. On the other hand, the soldiers in their account reported that the next attack happened around 0800 to 0830. This does not correspond with the radio logs, so I decided to follow the logs since the participants were not entirely sure of the time hacks. The 899th passed the division artillery around 0947, and Lieutenant Richardson was there to greet them at the minefield; Headquarters 1943, MSG 1148.

31. Richardson March 27, 1943.

32. Bednarz March 27, 1943.

33. Manning was mistaken. German records did not indicate the presence of Mk VIs in the 10th Panzer Division that morning; Manning March 27, 1943.

34. Futuluychuk March 27, 1943.

35. Perry March 27, 1943; Futuluychuk March 27, 1943.

36. Richardson March 27, 1943.

37. Bednarz March 27, 1943.

38. Manning March 27, 1943.

39. Futuluychuk March 27, 1943.

40. Richardson March 27, 1943; Headquarters, 1st Infantry Division March 1943, Msg 38.

41. Headquarters, 1st Infantry Division 1943.

42. In his "Battle Operations Report", written several days after the battle, Colonel Baker acknowledged that platoon leaders Luthi and Lambert did the right thing when they withdrew their respective platoons. He admitted that when he first heard the news that he was not pleased with their decisions. Captain Mitchell, the B Company commander, also added that he did not authorize their withdrawal; Baker, "Battle Operations Report" 1943, 3; Stark March 1943.

43. Dragon March 27, 1943.

44. Mitchell March 27, 1943.

45. F. X. Lambert March 1943, 1; Ritso March 1943.

46. Ritso March 1943.

47. Ritso March 1943.

48. Mitchell March 27, 1943, 2.

49. Sundstrom, *Statement of Captain Herbert E. Sundstrom, C Company, 601st Tank Destroyer Battalion* March 27, 1943, 1.

50. Munn March 27, 1943, 1.

51. Perry March 27, 1943, 1.

52. Munn March 27, 1943, 1.

53. Perry March 27, 1943, 1.

54. Sundstrom, *Statement of Captain Herbert E. Sundstrom, C Company, 601st Tank Destroyer Battalion* March 27, 1943, 1.

55. Munn March 27, 1943, 1–2.

56. T. E. Morrison, *Army Service Experience Questionnaire* 1999, 42–43; T. E. Morrison, "The 601st Tank Destroyer Battalion at El Guettar 3-23-43" 1980s, 2–3.

57. Miner March 26, 1943.

58. Karolewksi March 26, 1943.
59. Conway March 26, 1943.
60. T. E. Morrison, Thomas E. Morrison Collection (AFC/2001/001/00869), Veterans History Project, American Folklife Center, Library of Congress 2001.
61. Miner March 26, 1943; E. A. Raymond 1944, 16–18. (T. E. Morrison, *Army Service Experience Questionnaire* 1999, 12 (42).
62. T. E. Morrison, "Letter about El Guettar" 1980s, 2–3.
63. Miner March 26, 1943.
64. Conway March 26, 1943.
65. Baker, "Battle Operations Report" 1943, 4.
66. T. E. Morrison, *Army Service Experience Questionnaire* 1999, 9.
67. Headquarters 1943, Msg 1130, 1131.
68. H. A. Smith 1948–1949, 10–11.
69. Headquarters 1943, Msg 1132–34.
70. H. A. Smith 1948–1949, 13; Schick 2013, 499. By the Military Table of Organization and Equipment (MTOE), the *Panzerjäger-Abteilung* 90 had nine Marder IIIs, mounting a captured Russian 76.2mm antitank gun; Niehorster, "Panzer-Division (Afrika) 23 October 1942" 1942. A German staff officer confirms this in a document from January 29, 1943, that stated that the 90th had nine Marders; Burklin January 29, 1943, Frame 390.
71. Schick 2013, 499–500; H. A. Smith 1948–1949, 13–15.
72. H. A. Smith 1948–1949, 13–15. The 69th Panzer Grenadier Regiment had an overabundance of light machine guns in late January 1943—more than allowed by MTOE. Likely, they still had the allocated amount by March; Burklin January 29, 1943, Folio 390.
73. Burklin January 29, 1943, Folio 390; Andreas Altenburger 2016; H. A. Smith 1948–1949, 14.
74. H. A. Smith 1948–1949, 14.
75. Lehman 1943, 9.
76. Kuehn 2016.
77. Lehman 1943, 9.
78. H. A. Smith 1948–1949, 14.
79. Headquarters 1943, Msg 1137, 1138, 1142.
80. According to Breitenberger, his platoon had six MG 34s, while Burkin listed that the 2/69th PzGdr had anywhere from eighteen to twenty-five MG 34s in each of the three line companies. They also had four MG 34s on tripods for each company. An American prisoner of war claimed that his company had only the M1919 air-cooled .30-caliber Browning machine guns, which matched the standard MTOE at the time; Burklin January 29, 1943, Folio 390; Kennedy 2000–2010; Breitenberger 1994, 83–84; *Interrogation Report of Private Frank T. Roll* March 24, 1943, Folio 1141.
81. Schick 2013, 499–500; Breitenberger 1994, 83–84.
82. Headquarters 1943, Msg 1143, 1144, 1146, 1159–1160; Roosevelt 1943.
83. Lindo 1994, 69–70.
84. Schick 2013, 500. The symbols indicate a self-propelled, 75mm gun. However, it is an infantry gun symbol, not an antitank one, which means it was probably an earlier

variant of a StuG III, which had a stubby 75mm gun designed for suppression of enemy weapon emplacements—not the destruction of enemy tanks; Burklin January 29, 1943; Jellinek March 25, 1943.

85. Lindo 1994, 70.

86. Ault, "Southern Tunisia" 1943, 308–10; News and Media 2001.

87. Goff 1994, 66–67; Headquarters, 1st Infantry Division 1943, Msg 10.

88. Porter, G-2 Periodic Report, 0001A March 24 to 2400A March 24, Headquarters, 1st Infantry Division, Box 5222 1943; Silva, "When Our Guns Get Overrun" 1994, 77; Couch, "Bitter Lessons" December 1944, 40.

89. Silva, "When Our Guns Get Overrun" 1994, 77.

90. Viney 1994, 72; Frank A. Viney 2008.

91. Zaloga, *US Anti-Tank Artillery 1941–45* 2005, 43; Couch, "Local Security of a Battalion Position" September 1943. Although it is not explicitly stated, I made the assumption that Smith's platoon was near C Battery since it was on the flanks, and it did not make sense to position it near A Battery, which was farthest from the Gabes road; W. Smith 1994, 78–79.

92. Kociuba 1994; Headquarters 1943, Msg 1151. We know that by 1050 hours, some of the crews had withdrawn from the gun line. In fact, one battery from the 5th Field Artillery was "cut off." According to the division artillery, they had lost communication with some of the units in the 32nd. Even worse, they were running out of ammunition, and it would be a while before they could restock the gun line. Kociuba also mentions the 18th Infantry. I'm wondering if he meant 3rd Battalion, 16th Infantry, which was behind the artillery gun line; Headquarters, 1st Infantry Division 1943, Msg 45.

93. Clarke 1994; Headquarters, 1st Infantry Division 1943.

94. Headquarters, 1st Infantry Division March 1943, Msg 8, 10, 11. Ironically, II Corps G-2 sent out a report at 0410 hours the morning of March 23. It mentioned that the 10th Panzer Division was moving south. However, whoever sent the report sent it only to the 34th and 9th Infantry Divisions and the 1st Armored Division—not to the Big Red One (who knows why the oversight?); Headquarters, II Corps March 1943, Msg 8.

95. Headquarters, 1st Infantry Division 1943, Msg 7, 10, 12, 13; Headquarters, 16th Infantry Regiment March 23, 1943, Msg 2.

96. Headquarters, 1st Infantry Division March 1943, Msg 22; Headquarters, 1st Infantry Division 1943, Msg 14.

97. Zaloga, *US Field Artillery of World War II* 2007, 21–22, 24; Rance December 1943, 886.

98. United States Army Air Force 1942, 31; Williams April 9, 1943, 8, 10–11. The 81st arrived in North Africa shortly after the invasion in December 1942; Office of Air Force History 1983, 146; Headquarters, 1st Infantry Division 1943, Msg 15.

99. Headquarters, 1st Infantry Division March 1943, Msg 21; Headquarters, 1st Infantry Division 1943, Msg 18.

100. Headquarters, 1st Infantry Division 1943, Msg 21–25; Headquarters, 1st Infantry Division March 1943, Msg 35.

101. This is a great story and a great quote. Who knows if it was true? Liebling was at the battle, but he was not inside the command post when Allen reputedly made this

remark. However, we have no reason to doubt it. Therefore, I included it in this story; Liebling, "Profiles: Find'em, Fix'em, and Fight'em Part II" 1943, 28.

102. Allen, *Summary of the El Guettar Offensive (20 March to 6 April 1943) during the North African Campaign of World War II* 1943, 5.

103. See note 101 above.

104. Headquarters, 1st Infantry Division 1943, Msg 21–25; Headquarters, 1st Infantry Division March 1943, Msg 35.

105. Headquarters, 1st Infantry Division 1943, Msg 33.

106. Headquarters, 1st Infantry Division 1943, 45; Gibb, *Inclosure No. 6, to the 1st U.S. Infantry Division Report, G-3 Report, 15 January 1943 to 8 April 1943, Ousseltia Valley Operation, Kasserine Operation, Operation "WOP," El Guettar Operation* 1943, 10–11.

107. Mason, "Reminiscences and Anecdotes of World War II" 1988, 134–35.

108. Headquarters, 1st Infantry Division 1943, Msg 46.

109. Headquarters, 1st Infantry Division 1943, Msg 44.

110. Zaloga, *M10 and M36 Tank Destroyers 1942–53* 2002, 19.

111. Battalion Adjutant, 899th Tank Destroyer Battalion January 1 to December 1943, 12.

112. Department of the Army 1948, 1826.

113. Marshall, "Letter to Major General Andrew D. Bruce, #3-488" 1943.

114. Battalion Adjutant, 899th Tank Destroyer Battalion January 1 to December 1943, 13–14.

115. Baker, "Battle Operations Report" 1943, 4.

116. J. W. Morrison April 15, 1943, 1; Headquarters, 1st Infantry Division March 1943, Msg 38; *Our Battalion, 899th Tank Destroyer Battalion History* 1945, 20.

117. Viney 1994, 72–73.

118. Harper, *Greatest Tank Battles: The Battle of Tunisia* 2011.

119. Baker, "Battle Operations Report" 1943, 4.

120. *Our Battalion, 899th Tank Destroyer Battalion History* 1945, 8; Battalion Adjutant, 899th Tank Destroyer Battalion January 1 to December 1943, 2–3, 16; Kean June 27, 1943, 6–10. Although observers report that up to seven tank destroyers were hit, the 899th repair logs only list four M10s damaged or destroyed on March 23, and all were from B Company; Miller August 10, 1945; Yeide 2007, 65–66.

121. Towne 2000, 47–48.

122. Battalion Adjutant, 899th Tank Destroyer Battalion January 1 to December 1943, 16.

123. Liebling, *Liebling World War II Writings: The Road Back to Paris, Mollie and Other War Pieces, Uncollected War Journalism, Normandy Revisited* 2008, 304–5.

124. Headquarters, II Corps March 1943, Msg 9, 12, 13, 22.

125. Dickson, *G-2 Periodic Report No. 77, II Corps, from 0001 22 March to 2400 22 March, Box 2616* 1943.

126. George S. Patton, "Patton's Diary" 1943, 24–25.

127. Headquarters, II Corps March 1943, Msg 19, 28, 31, 42, 43, 45, 47; George S. Patton, "Patton's Diary" 1943, 24–25.

128. Dickson, *G-2 Periodic Report No. 78, II Corps, from 0001 23 March to 2400 23 March, Box 2616* 1943; Headquarters, II Corps March 1943, Msg 40.

Chapter 4: Afternoon Attack

1. Liebling, "Profiles: Find'em, Fix'em, and Fight'em Part II" 1943, 28.
2. Towne 2000, 48–49.
3. Bleichfield April 15, 1943, 2.
4. Towne 2000, 48–49.
5. I believe Morrison is referring to the rest of the battalion. His platoon still had all their trucks in the fight; T. E. Morrison, "Letter about El Guettar" 1980s, 1.
6. T. E. Morrison, "Letter about El Guettar" 1980s, 4–6.
7. Roosevelt's report on the prisoners is mistaken. The division cage had no one from the 7th German Infantry. He probably meant the 7th Panzer Regiment, which was active in the battle; Headquarters, 1st Infantry Division 1943, Msg 68.
8. Headquarters, 16th Infantry Regiment March 23, 1943, Msg 4; Headquarters, F Company, 16th Infantry 1945, 4; Heil 1949–50, 8–9; Headquarters 1943, Msg 1162.
9. Headquarters, 1st Infantry Division 1943, Msg 58, 59; Bennett 1943, 25–26.
10. Headquarters, 1st Infantry Division 1943, Msg 61.
11. Headquarters, 1st Infantry Division 1943, Msg 69.
12. George S. Patton, *Report on Operation Conducted by II Corps, United States Army, Tunisia, 15 March–10 April 1943, Box 2606* 1943, 4–5; Headquarters, 1st Infantry Division 1943, Msg 65.
13. Liebling, "Profiles: Find'em, Fix'em, and Fight'em Part II" 1943, 28.
14. Headquarters, II Corps March 1943, Msg 58; Headquarters, 1st Infantry Division March 1943, Msg 103.
15. Headquarters, 1st Infantry Division 1943, Msg 86.
16. Headquarters 1943, Msg 1185.
17. The recorded conversation does not mention Tyson. His name is not mentioned elsewhere in the journal. It is possible the recorder just did not know his name since he had been in command for only several months; Headquarters, 1st Infantry Division 1943, Msg 89.
18. Robinson Jr. 1943, 1–2.
19. Allen's tongue-in-cheek message could have been a disaster. It revealed to the Germans that we were listening to their radio transmissions; Headquarters 1943, Msg 1188; Allen, *Summary of the El Guettar Offensive (20 March to 6 April 1943) during the North African Campaign of World War II* 1943, 6–7.
20. Headquarters, 1st Infantry Division 1943, Msg 90, 93; Headquarters, 1st Infantry Division March 1943, Msg 125.
21. Headquarters, 1st Infantry Division 1943, Msg 77.
22. War Department October 11, 1943, 48–52; John J. Sayen 2006, 28. On his own initiative, Lieutenant Colonel Rowland created a "D" Company while in North Africa; Kays 2010, 55–56.
23. Department of the Army 2011.

24. Department of the Army 1944, 798; Kays 2010, 53.

25. Lehman 1943, 8.

26. Paradoxically, the unit journal mentioned that A Company received word of the attack at 1615 hours—fifteen minutes after the original time for the German assault; Headquarters, 1st Engineer Battalion 1943, 6.

27. Kays 2010, 82–83.

28. Gibb, *Inclosure No. 6, to the 1st U.S. Infantry Division Report, G-3 Report, 15 January 1943 to 8 April 1943, Ousseltia Valley Operation, Kasserine Operation, Operation "WOP," El Guettar Operation* 1943, 11.

29. Kays 2010, 83; Rowland April 20, 1943, 2.

30. Baker's report totally corroborates what Perry and Munn mentioned in their respective versions. To Baker, the men were more important. It was easy for the U.S. Army to replace vehicles. Crews were another story; Baker, "Battle Operations Report" 1943, 5.

31. Baker, "Tank Destroyer Combat in Tunisia" 1944, 28.

32. Darby 2007, Loc 1301 of 3423.

33. Also see note #22 on page 28; Baker, "Tank Destroyer Combat in Tunisia" 1944, 28–29.

34. Darby 2007, Loc 1304–1305 of 3423.

35. This is based on the report from 18th Infantry's radio log that first tank attack withdrew at approximately 0650 hours; Headquarters, 1st Infantry Division 1943, MSG 1140.

36. Martin 1943.

37. Harper, *Greatest Tank Battles: The Battle of Tunisia* 2011.

38. Munn March 27, 1943, 2.

39. Martin 1943; World War II Army Enlistment Records 2013.

40. Silva, "When Our Guns Get Overrun" 1994, 77.

41. Headquarters, 32nd Field Artillery Battalion 1943, Msg 6.

42. Silva, "When Our Guns Get Overrun" 1994, 77–78.

43. Andrus April 18, 1943, 2, 5.

44. Lehman 1943, 9.

45. Headquarters 1943, Msg 1190–1199, 1216.

46. Lehman 1943, 9.

47. Lehman 1943, 9.

48. H. A. Smith 1948–1949, 17–18.

49. G-3 Section, Headquarters, 1st Infantry Division 1943.

50. H. King April 14, 1943, 1; Headquarters, 1st Infantry Division 1943, Msg 95–97.

51. G-3 Section, Headquarters, 1st Infantry Division 1943.

52. Headquarters, 1st Infantry Division 1943.

53. G-3 Section, Headquarters, 1st Infantry Division 1943.

54. Headquarters, 1st Infantry Division 1943, Msg 97–102, 121; Headquarters, 26th Infantry Regiment 1943, March 23, 1745, 1810; Headquarters, 26th Infantry Regiment 1943, 49–50.

55. Lehman 1943, 9.

56. "Francis H. Tripp" 2016; Baumer, *American Iliad: The History of the 18th Infantry Regiment in World War II* 2004, 99; Roland G. Inman—Prisoner of War Record 2016; World War II Army Enlistment Records 2016.
57. *Interrogation Report of Private Frank T. Roll* March 24, 1943.
58. Ehlers n.d.
59. Kuehn 2016.
60. I am not entirely sure Raymer is the author of the citation, though it would make sense that he was. For awards like the DSC, a commissioned officer, usually the company commander or the platoon leader would have written the citation. Evidence for this is the use of the pronoun "our" and "we" throughout the citation; War Department June, 43–44.
61. Wyatt 1944; Cantor 2012; K Company Headquarters May 3, 1941.
62. Ehlers maintained that the friendly fire killed scores of soldiers. According to Ehlers, the forward observer accidentally called for fire on his own position, and, being a mortarman himself, Ehlers's assessment might be the closest we will get to the truth; Wyatt 1944.
63. Although Ehlers claimed the friendly fire barrage caused many of the casualties atop the hill, it is hard to estimate if that was the major culprit behind K Company's losses. We do know that many of the casualties were prisoners of war since we have obtained interrogation reports from the battle on the German side; Ehlers n.d.; Thompson April 16, 1943, 1.
64. Headquarters 1943, Msg 1214; Lehman 1943, 9.
65. War Department 1944; Moore 1996, 86–87; War Department June, 42–44; *Interrogation Report of Private Frank T. Roll* March 24, 1943; "Francis H. Tripp Jr.—Prisoner of War" 2016; "Rifle Regiment 18" 2016.
66. Lehman 1943, 9; Kuehn 2016.
67. Breitenberger 1994, 84; Schick 2013, 500.
68. Headquarters, 1st Infantry Division 1943, Msg 103, 104; Headquarters, 1st Infantry Division 1943.
69. Hansen n.d., 4/19 to 4/20; Kaufman 2012.
70. Andrus April 18, 1943, 5.
71. Dickson, *G-2 Summary #6, II Corps Headquarters, G-2 Section, Box 2646* April 2, 1943, 4–5.

Chapter 5: Spoiling Attack
1. A. L. Winters, *Reporter Interviews Arthur* 2007.
2. Lewin 2008, 120.
3. Although we do not know for sure if it was a woman who translated this particular document, because of the preponderance of females, a woman likely was the translator; Operations Section, 10th Panzer Division March 24, 1943, 1–3.
4. Headquarters 1943, Msg 1208; Carter 1947–1948, 23.
5. Headquarters, 1st Infantry Division 1943, Msg 22.
6. H. Bowles, *Henry-Silver Star* 2006; H. Bowles, *Shootout! The Big Red One* 2006; Gavalas February 9, 1944.

7. "A Tale of Twins" 1994.
8. Headquarters, 1st Infantry Division 1943; Ault, "Two Days in Foxholes Cost Unit 50 Men; Company G Takes Ridge Near El Guettar, Then Loses It to Encircling Germans" 1943.
9. T. Bowles, *Tom on the Hill* 2006.
10. Ault, "Southern Tunisia" 1943, 310.
11. T. Bowles, *Tom on the Hill* 2006.
12. Carter 1947–1948, Map B, 18.
13. American Battle Monuments Commission 2013; Daws 1948.
14. A. L. Winters, *Arthur L. Winters Talks about Dees* 2007.
15. Fogel, "The Sabre and Sash of 1941" 1941, 28.
16. Ault, "Southern Tunisia" 1943, 310; Social Security Death Index 2013.
17. Ault, "Two Days in Foxholes Cost Unit 50 Men; Company G Takes Ridge Near El Guettar, Then Loses It to Encircling Germans" 1943.
18. T. Bowles, *Tom Talks about El Guettar* 2006; T. Bowles 2005.
19. Headquarters, 1st Infantry Division 1943, Msg 25–27; Headquarters, 1st Infantry Division 1943, Msg 22; Headquarters 1943, Msg 1208, 1209; Gibb, *Inclosure No. 6, to the 1st U.S. Infantry Division Report, G-3 Report, 15 January 1943 to 8 April 1943, Ousseltia Valley Operation, Kasserine Operation, Operation "WOP," El Guettar Operation* 1943, 11; Street 1947–1948, 16–17.
20. George S. Patton, "Patton's Diary" 1943, 26–27.
21. Headquarters, 1st Infantry Division 1943, Msg 42; Heil 1949–50, 9; Gibb, *Inclosure No. 6, to the 1st U.S. Infantry Division Report, G-3 Report, 15 January to 8 April 1943, Ousseltia Valley Operation, Kasserine Operation, Operation "WOP," El Guettar Operation* 1943, 11; Gibb, *Headquarters, 1st Infantry Division Overlay Showing Tentative Defense Plan 25 March* 1943; Street 1947–1948, 16–17.
22. Schick 2013, 500; Jellinek March 25, 1943.
23. T. Bowles, *Tom on the Hill* 2006.
24. Ault, "Southern Tunisia" 1943, 310.
25. A. L. Winters, *Reporter Interviews Arthur* 2007.
26. T. Bowles 2005; Headquarters, 1st Infantry Division 1943.
27. Ault, "Southern Tunisia" 1943, 310–11.
28. A. L. Winters, *Reporter Interviews Arthur* 2007.
29. Ault, "Southern Tunisia" 1943, 312.
30. T. Bowles 2005.
31. Other accounts contradicted Bowles's number. Ault's versions were 133 to 153 survivors. In his *Times* article, he mentioned 133 survivors, while in his chapter titled "Southern Tunisia," he mentioned 153. Ault was there the morning after and spoke with the men of Company G; T. Bowles, *Tom on the Hill* 2006; T. Bowles, *Tom Talks about El Guettar* 2006.
32. T. B. Winters 2007.
33. A. L. Winters, *Reporter Interviews Arthur* 2007.
34. Headquarters 1943, Msg 1226, 1231.
35. H. Bowles, *Shootout! The Big Red One* 2006.

36. T. Bowles, *Tom on the Hill* 2006.
37. T. Bowles 2005.
38. Headquarters, 1st Infantry Division 1943, Msg 80, 81, 82, 88; Karbel April 9, 1943, 1.
39. Headquarters, 1st Infantry Division 1943, Msg 5, 6.
40. Headquarters 1943, Msg 1229, 1232, 1230, 1236; Street 1947–1948, 17–18.
41. Street 1947–1948, 18.
42. Darby 2007, Loc 1317 of 3423.
43. Darby 2007, Loc 1321–1325 of 3423; Headquarters 1943, Msg 1246, 1249.
44. Headquarters 1943, Msg 1230, 1236, 1233, 1237; Street 1947–1948, 18–19.
45. Darby 2007, Loc 1317–1321 of 3423; Karbel April 9, 1943, 1–2.
46. Headquarters 1943, Msg 1237.
47. When Greer said, "No evidence of any force that morning," I had a hard time trying to figure what he meant. The 2nd Battalion was under considerable stress at the time. Maybe it was a garbled notation on the part of the recorder. The next message from Gibb is more puzzling. According to Message 44, he has a better picture of 2nd Battalion's plight, but we have no record that he spoke directly with Colonel Sternberg or Colonel Darby; Headquarters 1943, Msg 41, 44.
48. Headquarters 1943, Msg 1240, 1246, 1249; Street 1947–1948, 19; Karbel April 9, 1943, 1.
49. Headquarters, 1st Infantry Division 1943, Msg 57.
50. Headquarters, 1st Infantry Division 1943, Msg 65.
51. Headquarters 1943, Msg 1258–1267; Street 1947–1948, 19.
52. Headquarters 1943, 1273.
53. Operations Section March 25, 1943.

Epilogue

1. Bradley 1999, 154–55.
2. Gibb, *Inclosure No. 6, to the 1st U.S. Infantry Division Report, G-3 Report, 15 January 1943 to 8 April 1943, Ousseltia Valley Operation, Kasserine Operation, Operation "WOP," El Guettar Operation* 1943, 15–16.
3. George S. Patton, *Report on Operation Conducted by II Corps, United States Army, Tunisia, 15 March–10 April 1943, Box 2606* 1943, 6–7; George S. Patton, "Patton's Diary" 1943, April 1–2.
4. George S. Patton, "Patton's Diary" 1943, April 4; Bradley 1999, 64–65.
5. George S. Patton, *Report on Operation Conducted by II Corps, United States Army, Tunisia, 15 March–10 April 1943, Box 2606* 1943, 11–12; Alexander 2015, 74–75; George S. Patton, "Patton's Diary" 1943, April 7; Benson 1944, 4.
6. George S. Patton, *Report on Operation Conducted by II Corps, United States Army, Tunisia, 15 March–10 April 1943, Box 2606* 1943, 12–13.
7. Ford 2012, 87–92.
8. Schick 2013, 510–12.
9. Schick 2013, 515–17; Vaerst 1947, Skizze 2.
10. George S. Patton and Terry de la Mesa Allen 1943.

11. George S. Patton, *Report on Operation Conducted by II Corps, United States Army, Tunisia, 15 March–10 April 1943, Box 2606* 1943, 13–14.
12. George S. Patton, *Report on Operation Conducted by II Corps, United States Army, Tunisia, 15 March–10 April 1943, Box 2606* 1943, 12; Bradley 1999, 69–71, 76; Eisenhower 1997, 154.
13. Vaerst 1947, 16; Alexander 2015, 75–76; Zaloga, *Kasserine Pass 1943 Rommel's Last Victory* 2005, 80–89.
14. Bradley 1999, 81.
15. Bradley 1999, 90–93.
16. Anderson 2015, 154–55.
17. Schick 2013, 527.
18. Schick 2013, 537–41.
19. Schick 2013, 542–47.
20. Kesselring, *Kesselring's View of the African War, MS # T-3 P1 Part II* 1954, 55.
21. Dickson, *Enemy Equipment Destroyed and Captured 2000A 11 May to 2000A 12 May, Headquarters, II Corps, Box 5103 Folder 214* May 13, 1943; Howe 1957, 666.
22. Alexander 2015, 88.
23. Bradley 1999, 100.
24. Bradley 1999, 154–57; Albert N. Garland, Howard McGaw Smyth, and assisted by Martin Blumenson 1993, 324–47.
25. Allen, "Letter to Mr. E. C. Heid" 1943, 2.
26. Bradley 1999, 154–55.
27. Jeffers 2002, 260–64.
28. War Department 2016.
29. Astor 2003, 329, 348–52, 358.
30. Department of the Army 1948, 2217; Baumer, *American Iliad: The History of the 18th Infantry Regiment in World War II* 2004, Loc 3227–3232; U.S. Army Center of Military History 1945; Sarantakes 2004, 146; Raum 2009.
31. Ben Sternberg and Jack M. Strauss 1988.
32. West Point Association of Graduates 2004.
33. Headquarters, U.S. Army-North African Theater of Operations 1943; Baumer, *American Iliad: The History of the 18th Infantry Regiment in World War II* 2004, Loc 3588 of 9266; Carafano 2008, 134–35; Baumer, *Aachen: The U.S. Army's Battle for Charlemagne's City in World War II* 2015, 11–12, 125–26, 166, 176–77, 180, 235, 321–22, 337; "Colonel Courtney P. Brown" 2007; Department of the Army 1967, 133.
34. West Point Association 1968.
35. Josowitz 1945, 14; Department of the Army 1949, 613; International Wargraves 2009; War Department 2016.
36. "A Tale of Twins" 1994; Bello 2009; Lair 2007.
37. Gary Warner 2014.
38. War Department 1944.
39. Gary Warner 2014.
40. War Department 1944.

41. Goldstein 2014.
42. Gary Warner 2014.
43. Andreas Altenburger 2016.
44. Many historians, like Wolfgang Benz, have criticized Franz Kurowski's works for being too pro-Nazi. That said, I decided to include this citation since I was only seeking biographical information on certain officers, which Kurowski's work provided. I do not condone his viewpoints, nor do I support them; Kurowski 2011, 221–22.
45. Liebling, *Liebling World War II Writings: The Road Back to Paris, Mollie and Other War Pieces, Uncollected War Journalism, Normandy Revisited 2008*, 307–8.

Bibliography

"A Tale of Twins." June 6, 1994. www.bowlesusa.org/twins.html (accessed April 30, 2016).

Akers, Russell F. *Outline Plan, Operation "WOP," Headquarters II Corps.* Warning Order. Wheaton, IL: Department of the Army, March 4, 1943.

Alexander, Harold. "Field Marshal Viscount Alexander of Tunis' Despatch on the African Campaign from El Alamein to Tunis, 10 August 1942 to 13 May 1943." In *Despatches from the Front: The Commanding Officers' Reports from the Field and at Sea North Africa and the Middle East 1942–1944, El Alamein, Tunisia, Algeria, and Operation Torch*, by John Grehan and Martin Mace, 1–95. South Yorkshire: Pen & Sword Military, 2015.

Allen, Terry de la Mesa. *1st Infantry Division Report on Combat.* After Action Report. University of Texas, El Paso, Special Collections Department. El Paso, TX: Department of the Army, May 1943.

———. *Headquarters, 1st Infantry Division, Memorandum to Colonel Fechet, Colonel Greer, Lieutenant Colonel Baker, Lieutenant Colonel Howland.* Memorandum. Wheaton, IL: Department of the Army, 1943.

———. "Letter to Mr. E.C. Heid." Special Collections, University of Texas, El Paso, Library, December 13, 1943.

———. *Memorandum to Lieutenant Colonel Darby, 17 March, Headquarters, 1st Infantry Division, Box 5118.* Memorandum. College Park, MD: Department of the Army, 1943.

———. *Summary of the El Guettar Offensive (20 March to 6 April 1943) during the North African Campaign of World War II.* After Action Report, University of Texas, El Paso, Special Collections Department, El Paso, TX: Department of the Army, 1943.

American Battle Monuments Commission. "Nels J. De Jarlais." September 30, 2013. https://www.fold3.com/page/529882094_nels_j%20de%20jarlais/details (accessed May 1, 2016).

American Battle Monuments Commission. "Henry H. Hunt, Jr." September 30, 2013. https://www.fold3.com/page/529883023_henry_h_hunt_jr/details (accessed July 4, 2016).

———. "Kenneth Lynch." September 30, 2013. https://www.fold3.com/page/529883 667_kenneth_lynch/about (accessed July 4, 2016).

Anderson, Kenneth. "Lieutenant General K.A.N. Anderson's Despatch on Operations in North West Africa, 8 November 1942 to 13 May 1943." In *Despatches from the Front: The Commanding Officers' Reports from the Field and at Sea North Africa and the Middle East 1942–1944, El Alamein, Tunisia, Algeria, and Operation Torch*, by John Grehan and Martin Mace, 129–61. South Yorkshire: Pen & Sword Military, 2015.

Andreas Altenburger. "Freiherr von Broich, Friedrich Kurt Hans." *L*2016. www .lexikon-der-wehrmacht.de/Gliederungen/Panzerdivisionen/Gliederung.htm (accessed March 27, 2016).

———. "Hans Cramer." 2016. www.lexikon-der-wehrmacht.de/Personenregister/ C/CramerHans-R.htm (accessed July 22, 2016).

———. "Panzer-Artillerie-Regiment 90." 2016. www.lexikon-der-wehrmacht.de/Glie derungen/PanzerArtReg/PAR90-R.htm (accessed February 15, 2016).

———. "Panzergrenadier-Regiment 86." 2016. www.lexikon-der-wehrmacht.de/Glie derungen/Panzergrenadierregimenter/PGR86-R.htm (accessed March 30, 2016).

———. "Panzer-Regiment 7." 2016. www.lexikon-der-wehrmacht.de/Gliederungen/ Panzerdivisionen/Gliederung.htm (accessed March 30, 2016).

———. "Schützen-Regiment 69." 2016. www.lexikon-der-wehrmacht.de/Gliederungen/ Schutzenregimenter/SR69-R.htm (accessed March 30, 2016).

———. "Schützen-Regiment 86." 2016. www.lexikon-der-wehrmacht.de/Gliederungen/ Schutzenregimenter/SR86-R.htm (accessed March 30, 2016).

Andrus, Clift. *Unit Report of Operations from 4 March, 1943 to 8 April, 1943. Headquarters, First U.S. Infantry Division Artillery.* Unit Operations Report. Wheaton, IL: Department of the Army, April 18, 1943.

Arnim, Hans-Jürgen von. *Erinnerungen an Tunesien MS # C-098.* After Action Report. College Park, MD: Foreign Military Studies, n.d.

———. *Order for the Operation Frühlingwind (Part of Center for U.S. Army Military History Kasserine Pass Collection Volume I Part 1).* Operations Order. College Park, MD: Department of the Army, February 8, 1943.

Astor, Gerald. *Terrible Terry Allen: Combat General of World War II—The Life of an American Soldier.* New York: Ballantine Books, 2003.

Ault, Phil. "Southern Tunisia." In *Springboard to Berlin*, by Ned Russell, Leo Disher, Phil Ault, and John A. Parris, 283–316. New York: Thomas Y. Crowell Company, 1943.

———. "Two Days in Foxholes Cost Unit 50 Men; Company G Takes Ridge Near El Guettar, Then Loses It to Encircling Germans." *New York Times*, March 28, 1943.

Baker, Herschel D. "Battle Operations Report." March 28, 1943. tankdestroyer.net/ images/stories/ArticlePDFs/601st_Battle_Operations_Report_El_Guettar_ Mar._23_1943—10_pages.pdf (accessed March 18, 2015).

———. "Tank Destroyer Combat in Tunisia." January 1944. http://tankdestroyer.net/ images/stories/ArticlePDFs/TD_Combat_in_Tunisia_Jan_1944.pdf (accessed March 18, 2015).

Battalion Adjutant, 899th Tank Destroyer Battalion. *Unit History, 899th Tank Destroyer Battalion, Box 18748.* Unit History. College Park, MD: Department of the Army, January 1–December 1943.

Baumer, Robert W. *Aachen: The U.S. Army's Battle for Charlemagne's City in World War II.* Mechanicsburg, PA: Stackpole Books, 2015.

———. *American Iliad: The History of the 18th Infantry Regiment in World War II.* Bedford, PA: Aberjona Press, 2004.

Bednarz, Louis J. *Statement of Sergeant Louis J. Bednarz, C Company, 601st Tank Destroyer Battalion.* After Action Report. Dwight D. Eisenhower Presidential Library. Abilene, KS: Department of the Army, March 27, 1943.

Bello, Gloria. "Thomas E. Bowles." April 27, 2009. www.findagrave.com/cgi-bin/fg.cgi ?page=gr&GRid=36424618 (accessed August 23, 2016).

Bennett, Thomas E. *Gafsa-El Guettar Operation Box 5253.* After Action Report. College Park, MD: Department of the Army, 1943.

Benson, Clarence C. "Some Tunisian Details." *Field Artillery Journal,* January 1944, 2–7.

Bleichfield, Samuel. *Report After Action against Enemy. Headquarters, First Medical Battalion, First Infantry Division.* After Action Report. Wheaton, IL: Department of the Army, April 15, 1943.

Blumenson, Martin. *America's First Battles, 1776–1965.* Lawrence: University Press of Kansas, 1986.

Bowles, Henry. Interview by Timothy Bowles. *Henry-Silver Star,* May 5, 2006.

Bowles, Thomas. Interview by Timothy Bowles. *Tom on the Hill,* May 5, 2006.

———. Interview by Timothy Bowles. *Tom Talks about El Guettar,* May 5, 2006.

Bowles, Timothy. "North Africa—The Last Stand of Company G." May 23, 2005. http://bowlesusa.org/ww2/index2.php?option=com_content&task=view&id= 18&Itemid=43&pop=1&page=0# (accessed May 4, 2016).

Bradley, Omar N. *A Soldier's Story.* New York: Modern Library, 1999.

Breitenberger, Ernst. "A Grenadier on the Other Side." In *Proud Americans: Men of the 32nd Field Artillery Battalion in Action, World War II, as Part of the 18th Regimental Combat Team,* 83–84. Malcolm Marshall, 1994.

Brown, M. M. *G-2 Estimate No. 1: Operation "WOP," Headquarters, 1st Armored Division.* G-2 Intelligence Estimate. Wheaton, IL: Department of the Army, March 13, 1943.

Burklin, Wilhelm. *Military Table of Organization and Equipment for 10 Panzer Division.* Military Table of Organization and Equipment, Captured German Records. Alexandria, VA: 10. Panzer Division, January 29, 1943.

Butler, Allen S. *The Operations of the First Infantry Division at El Guettar, 20–30 March 1943, Tunisian Campaign.* Battle Analysis Paper. Fort Benning, GA: Department of the Army, Advanced Infantry Officers Course, 1949–1950.

Cantor, Eddie. "Eddie Cantor Pays Tribute to Hero, Tupper Man Blinded at El Guettar." *Tupper Lake Free Press,* October 17, 2012, 7.

Carafano, James Jay. *After D-Day: Operation Cobra and the Normandy Breakout.* Mechanicsburg, PA: Stackpole Books, 2008.

Carter, Sam. *The Operations of the 1st Battalion, 18th Infantry (1st Division) at El Guettar, Tunisia, 17–25 March, 1943 (Tunisian Campaign) (Personal Experience of a Heavy-Weapons Company Commander).* Battle Analysis Paper. Fort Benning, GA: Department of the Army, Advanced Infantry Officers Course, 1947–1948.

Clarke, Gerard. "Where Men Have Bled." In *Proud Americans: Men of the 32nd Field Artillery Battalion in Action, World War II, as Part of the 18th Regimental Combat Team*, by Malcolm Marshall, 73. Malcolm Marshall, 1994.

Colaccico, Frank. *Field Order #14, Headquarters, 18th Infantry Regiment, March 13*. Field Order. Wheaton, IL: Department of the Army, 1943.

———. *Field Order #15, Headquarters, 18th Infantry Regiment, March 18*. Field Order. Wheaton, IL: Department of the Army, 1943.

"Colonel Courtney P. Brown." March 4, 2007. www.findagrave.com/cgi-bin/fg.cgi?page =gr&GRid=19214007 (accessed March 26, 2016).

Command and General Staff School. "Annual Report of the Command and General Staff School, Fort Leavenworth, Kansas." 1934. http://usacac.army.mil/sites/ default/files/documents/cace/CARL/Reports/rep1934.pdf (accessed March 20, 2016).

Conway, John J. *Statement of Sergeant John J. Conway, A Company, 601st Tank Destroyer Battalion*. After Action Report. Dwight D. Eisenhower Presidential Library. Abilene, KS: Department of the Army, March 26, 1943.

Cook, Leo G. *Statement of Leo G. Cook, C Company, 601st Tank Destroyer Battalion*. After Action Report. Dwight D. Eisenhower Presidential Library, Abilene, KS: Department of the Army, March 27, 1943.

Couch, Joseph R. "Bitter Lessons." *Field Artillery Journal*, December 1944, 40–41.

———. "Local Security of a Battalion Position." *Field Artillery Journal*, September 1943, 647.

Critz, Harry Herndon. *Gafsa-El Guettar Operation, March 10 to April 8*. After Action Report. Wheaton, IL: Department of the Army, April 20, 1943.

———. Interview by Jerry Gid Bryan. Lieutenant General Harry H. Critz, Senior Officers Oral History Program, Project 81-2, U.S. Army Military History Institute, Carlisle, PA, 1981.

Darby, William O., with William H. Baumer. *Darby's Rangers: We Led the Way*. New York: Ballantine Books, 2007.

Daws, Alex. "Application for Headstone or Marker for Bobby Dees." June 11, 1948. https://www.fold3.com/image/317525867 (accessed May 1, 2016).

Department of the Army. "18th Infantry." January 14, 2004. www.history.army.mil/html/ forcestruc/lineages/branches/inf/0018in.htm (accessed March 24, 2016).

———. "1st Engineer Battalion." April 16, 2011. www.history.army.mil/html/forcestruc/ lineages/branches/eng/0001enbn.htm (accessed April 3, 2016).

———. "2nd Battalion, 32nd Field Artillery Regiment." February 6, 2009. www.history .army.mil/html/forcestruc/lineages/branches/fa/0032fa02bn.htm (accessed March 26, 2016).

———. "Army Register, 1944." 1944. https://fold3.com/image/312803603/?terms=frank %20greer (accessed March 2016, 20).

———. "Army Registers, 1948 Volume 2." 1948. https://www.fold3.com/image/3121 26414/?terms=maxwell%20tincher (accessed February 21, 2016).

———. "Army Registers, 1949." 1949. https://www.fold3.com/image/312910672/?terms =Herbert%20Scott-Smith (accessed June 10, 2016).

———. "Army Registers, 1950." 1950. https://www.fold3.com/image/312143854/?terms =Ben%20Sternberg (accessed August 19, 2016).

———. "Army Registers, 1967, Volumes 2 and 3." 1967. https://www.fold3.com/image/ 312773771/?terms=courtney%20brown (accessed August 20, 2016).

D'Este, Carlos. *Eisenhower: A Soldier's Life*. New York: Henry Holt and Company, 2002.

Dickson, Benjamin A. *Enemy Equipment Destroyed and Captured 2000A 11 May to 2000A 12 May, Headquarters, II Corps, Box 5103 Folder 214*. Enemy Casualty List. College Park, MD: Department of the Army, May 13, 1943.

———. *G-2 Periodic Report No. 70, II Corps, From 0001 15 March to 2400 15 March, Box 2616*. G-2 Periodic Report. College Park, MD: Department of the Army, 1943.

———. *G-2 Periodic Report No. 73, II Corps, From 0001 18 March to 2400 18 March, Box 2616*. G-2 Periodic Report. College Park, MD: Department of the Army, 1943.

———. *G-2 Periodic Report No. 74, II Corps, From 0001 19 March to 2400 19 March, Box 2616*. G-2 Periodic Report. College Park, MD: Department of the Army, 1943.

———. *G-2 Periodic Report No. 75, II Corps, From 0001 20 March to 2400 20 March, Box 2616*. G-2 Periodic Report. College Park, MD: Department of the Army, 1943.

———. *G-2 Periodic Report No. 76, II Corps, From 0001 21 March to 2400 21 March, Box 2616*. G-2 Periodic Report. College Park, MD: Department of the Army, 1943.

———. *G-2 Periodic Report No. 77, II Corps, From 0001 22 March to 2400 22 March, Box 2616*. G-2 Periodic Report. College Park, MD: Department of the Army, 1943.

———. *G-2 Periodic Report No. 78, II Corps, From 0001 23 March to 2400 23 March, Box 2616*. G-2 Periodic Report. College Park, MD: Department of the Army, 1943.

———. *G-2 Summary #5, II Corps Headquarters, G-2 Section, Box 2646*. Periodic Report. College Park, MD: Department of the Army, March 17, 1943.

———. *G-2 Summary #6, II Corps Headquarters, G-2 Section, Box 2646*. Periodic Report. College Park, MD: Department of the Army, April 2, 1943.

Dragon, Michael H. *Statement of Sergeant Michael H. Dragon, B Company, 601st Tank Destroyer Battalion*. After Action Report. Dwight D. Eisenhower Presidential Library. Abilene, KS: Department of the Army, March 27, 1943.

Ehlers, Walter David. Interview by Mike Farrar. Walter David Ehlers Collection (AFC/2001/001/80593) Veterans History Project, American Folklife Center, Library of Congress, Washington, DC, n.d.

Ehrhardt, Roy S. Interview by Jesse Diaz. Roy S. Ehrhardt Collection (AFC/2001/001/38175), Veterans History Project, American Folklife Center, Library of Congress, Washington, DC, November 22, 2005.

Eisenhower, Dwight D. *Crusade in Europe*. Baltimore: Johns Hopkins University Press, 1997.

Fogel, Maurice D., ed. "The Sabre and Sash of 1941." 1941. http://digitalwolfgram .widener.edu (accessed May 2, 2016).

Ford, Ken. *The Mareth Line 1943*. Oxford: Osprey Publishing, 2012.

Francin, M. E. *Result of the Prisoners of War Interrogation, 32nd Field Artillery, Box 5222*. Prisoner of War Interrogation Report. College Park, MD: Department of the Army, March 21, 1943.

"Francis H. Tripp." 2016. https://www.fold3.com/page/85162456_francis_h_tripp/ details (accessed April 8, 2016).

"Francis H. Tripp Jr.—Prisoner of War." 2016. http://wwii-pows.mooseroots.com/l/ 114507/Francis-H-Tripp-Jr (accessed April 12, 2016).

"Frank A. Viney." November 27, 2008. https://www.fold3.com/search/#s_given_name= Frank&s_surname=Viney&ocr=1&preview=1&offset=1&t=848,831 (accessed February 28, 2016).

Futuluychuk, Steve. *Statement of Sergeant Steve Futuluychuk, C Company, 601st Tank Destroyer Battalion*. After Action Report. Dwight D. Eisenhower Presidential Library. Abilene, KS: Department of the Army, March 27, 1943.

G-3 Section, Headquarters, 1st Infantry Division. *Addendum to Unit Journal, 1st Infantry Division for March 23, 1943, Box 5118*. Unit Journal Addendum. College Park, MD: Department of the Army, 1943.

———. *22 March 1943 Fragmentary Order, Box 5118*. Fragmentary Order. College Park, MD: Department of the Army, 1943.

Garland, Albert N., and Howard McGaw Smyth, assisted by Martin Blumenson. *Sicily and the Surrender of Italy*. Washington, DC: Center of Military History, U.S. Army, 1993.

Gause, Alfred. *German-Italian Army Group Africa (8 November 1942–13 May 1943), Manuscript D-385*. Foreign Military Studies, September 19, 1946.

Gavalas, Leonidas. *Award of Silver Star to Technician Grade 5 Henry D. Bowles, Headquarters and Headquarters Company, Second Battalion, 18th Infantry*. Award Citation. Department of the Army, February 9, 1944.

German-Italian Panzer Army Command Post. *Intelligence Evening Report. Radio Message to O.K.H. Army G.S. Section Fremde Heere West III (Part of Center for U.S. Army Military History Kasserine Pass Collection Volume I Part 2)*. Intelligence Evening Report. College Park, MD: Department of the Army, February 20, 1943.

Gibb, Frederick W. *Field Order #16, Headquarters, 1st Infantry Division, March 11*. Field Order. Wheaton, IL: Department of the Army, 1943.

———. *Field Order #18, Headquarters, 1st Infantry Division, March 15*. Field Order. Wheaton, IL: Department of the Army, 1943.

———. *Headquarters, 1st Infantry Division Overlay Showing Tentative Defense Plan 25 March*. 16th Infantry Overlays. Wheaton, IL: Department of the Army, 1943.

———. *Inclosure No. 6, to the 1st U.S. Infantry Division Report, G-3 Report, 15 January 1943 to 8 April 1943, Ousseltia Valley Operation, Kasserine Operation, Operation "WOP," El Guettar Operation*. After Action Report. Wheaton, IL: Department of the Army, 1943.

Gioia, Joseph A. *Battle Operation Report, First Platoon, Reconnaissance Company, 601st Tank Destroyer Battalion*. After Action Report. Abilene, KS: Department of the Army, March 23, 1943.

Goff, Allston S. "From Wagon Mound to the Fire at El Guettar." In *Proud Americans: Men of the 32nd Field Artillery Battalion in Action, World War II, as Part of the 18th Regimental Combat Team*, 62–67. Malcolm Marshall, 1994.

Goldstein, Richard. "Walter Ehlers, Last of Medal of Honor Recipients in D-Day Attack, Dies at 92." *New York Times*, February 21, 2014.

Hains, Peter C. *Report of Lessouda Force, Headquarters 1st Armored Regiment (Part of Center for U.S. Army Military History Kasserine Pass Collection Volume I Part 1)*. After Action Report. College Park, MD: Department of the Army, March 11, 1943.

Hamel, Victor T. *Statement of Corporal Victor T. Hamel, B Company. 601st Tank Destroyer Battalion*. After Action Report. Dwight D. Eisenhower Presidential Library. Abilene, KS: Department of the Army, March 1943.

Hansen, Chester B. "Notes for a Soldier's Life." Carlisle, PA, n.d.

Harper, Bill R. Interview by Breakthrough Entertainment. *Greatest Tank Battles: The Battle of Tunisia*, March 14, 2011.

———. Interview by Flight 33 Productions. *Interview with Bill R. Harper for History Channel Show, Patton 360*, July 3, 2008.

Headquarters, 18th Infantry Regiment. *Journal, 18th Infantry February and March*. Journal. Wheaton, IL: Department of the Army, 1943.

Headquarters, F Company, 16th Infantry. *History of Company "F," 16th Infantry, from 1 July 1942 to 10 May 1945*. Company History. Wheaton, IL: Department of the Army, 1945.

Headquarters, Fifth Panzer Army. *Fifth Panzer Army, War Diary (Extract), 18–23 February 1943 (Part of Center for U.S. Army Military History Kasserine Pass Collection Volume I Part 2)*. War Diary. College Park, MD: Department of the Army, 1943.

Headquarters, 1st Engineer Battalion. *Inclosure No. 15, Unit Journal, 1st Engineer Battalion, January 29 to April 14, 1943, Box 5204*. Unit Journal. College Park, MD: Department of the Army, 1943.

Headquarters, 1st Infantry Division. "Bobby Dees, General Order No. 25." *Military Times Hall of Valor*. 1943. http://valor.militarytimes.com/recipient.php?recipientid =70288 (accessed May 16, 2016).

———. *G-2 Journal, Box 5034*. G-2 Journal. College Park, MD: Department of the Army, 1943.

———. *G-2 Journal, Box 5035*. G-2 Journal. College Park, MD: Department of the Army, March 1943.

———. *G-3 Journal, March 14, 1943 Box 5118*. G-3 Journal. College Park, MD: Department of the Army, 1943.

———. *G-3 Journal, March 17, 1943 Box 5118*. G-3 Journal. College Park, MD: Department of the Army, 1943.

———. *G-3 Journal, March 18, 1943 Box 5118*. G-3 Journal. College Park, MD: Department of the Army, 1943.

———. *G-3 Journal, March 20, 1943 Box 5118*. G-3 Journal. College Park, MD: Department of the Army, 1943.

———. *G-3 Journal, March 21, 1943 Box 5118*. G-3 Journal. College Park, MD: Department of the Army, 1943.

———. *G-3 Journal, March 22, 1943 Box 5118*. G-3 Journal. College Park, MD: Department of the Army, 1943.

———. *G-3 Journal, March 23, 1943 Box 5118.* G-3 Journal. College Park, MD: Department of the Army, 1943, Box 5118.

———. *G-3 Journal, March 24, 1943 Box 5118.* Unit Journal. College Park, MD: Department of the Army, 1943.

———. *G-3 Journal, March 25, 1943 Box 5118.* G-3 Journal. College Park, MD: Department of the Army, 1943.

———. "Gerard T. Clarke, General Orders No. 65." 1943. http://valor.militarytimes .com/recipient.php?recipientid=69986 (accessed April 16, 2016).

———. *Overlay #10 to Accompany G-3 Periodic Report 240001 March 1943.* Operations Overlay. Wheaton, IL: Department of the Army, 1943.

———. *Overlay #9 to Accompany G-3 Periodic Report 2400 22 March 1943.* Operations Overlay, Wheaton, Illinois: Department of the Army, 1943.

———. "Salvatore DeSantis, General Orders No, 28." 1943. http://valor.military.times .com/recipient.php?recipientid=70263 (accessed May 4, 2016).

Headquarters, 16th Infantry Regiment. *16th Infantry Journal.* Operations Journal. First Division Museum. Wheaton, IL: Department of the Army, March 23, 1943.

Headquarters, 26th Infantry Regiment. *History of the 26th Infantry in the Present Struggle, El Guettar.* Unit History. Wheaton, IL: Department of the Army, 1943.

———. *26th Infantry Regiment Journal.* Unit Journal. Wheaton, IL: Department of the Army, 1943.

Headquarters, 32nd Field Artillery Battalion. *Unit Journal, March 21, 1943, Box 5222.* Unit Journal. College Park, MD: Department of the Army, 1943.

Headquarters, II Corps. *G-2 Journal, Box 2624.* G-2 Journal. College Park, MD: Department of the Army, March 1943.

———. *G-3 Journal, 22 March 1943, Box 2659.* G-3 Journal. College Park, MD: Department of the Army, 1943.

Headquarters, U.S. Army–North African Theater of Operations. "Courtney P. Brown, General Order No. 48." 1943. http://valor.militarytimes.com/recipient.php?recipient id=6532 (accessed August 20, 2016).

Heil, George J. *The Operation of Company F, 16th Infantry (1st Infantry Division) at El Guettar, Tunisia, 29 March 1943 (Tunisian Campaign) (Personal Experience of a Company Commander).* Staff Paper. Fort Benning, GA: Advanced Infantry Officers Course, 1949–1950.

Horne, James G. *Statement of Sergeant James G. Horne, B Company, 601st Tank Destroyer Battalion.* After Action Report. Dwight D. Eisenhower Presidential Library. Abilene, KS: Department of the Army, March 1943.

Howe, George F. *United States Army in World War II Mediterranean Theater of Operations. Northwest Africa: Seizing the Initiative in the West.* Washington, DC: Office of the Chief of Military History, Department of the Army, 1957.

Ingersoll, Ralph. *The Battle Is the Pay-Off.* New York: Harcourt, Brace and Company, 1943.

International Wargraves. "Colonel Herschel David Baker." March 4, 2009. www.find agrave.com/cgi-bin/fg.cgi?page=gr&GSvcid=663329&GRid=24461506& (accessed August 23, 2016).

Interrogation Report of Private Frank T. Roll. Interrogation Report. Captured German Records. Alexandria, VA: 10. Panzer Division, March 24, 1943.

Jacobson, Andrew Jake. Interview by Jennifer Touhey and Shaun Ridley. Andrew Jake Jacobson Collection (AFC/2001/001/56228) Veterans History Project, American Folklife Center, Library of Congress, Washington, DC, 2001.

Jeffers, H. Paul. *Theodore Roosevelt Jr.: The Life of a War Hero.* Novato, CA: Presidio Press, 2002.

Jellinek, W. *Preliminary Interrogation Report on Franz Strohmeier, G-2, 1st Infantry Division, Box 5035.* Interrogation Report. College Park, MD: Department of the Army, March 25, 1943.

Jentz, Hilary Doyle, and Tom Jentz. *Panzerkampfwagen IV Ausf. G, H and J.* Oxford: Osprey Publishing, 2001.

Josowitz, Edward L. "An Informal History of the 601st Tank Destroyer Battalion." *Tank Destroyer.* 1945. www.tankdestroyer.net/ArticlePDFs2/601st_Tank_Destroyer_ History_Part_1.pdf (accessed March 18, 2015).

Junkers Flugzeug und Motorwerke. "Ju 87 B-2 Betriebsanleitung." *Avialog.* June 1940. www.avialogs.com/index.php/en/aircraft/germany/junkers/ju87stuka/ ju-87-b-2-betriebsanleitung.html (accessed July 3, 2016).

K Company Headquarters. *Company "K," Eighteenth Infantry.* Company Roster. Wheaton, IL: Department of the Army, May 3, 1941.

Kannicht, Joachim. Interview by Breakthrough Entertainment Inc. *Interview with Joachim Kannicht, 21st Panzer Division,* January 25, 2012.

Karbel, Howard W. *After Action Report, 1st Ranger Battalion, Box 16911.* After Action Report. College Park, MD: Department of the Army, April 9, 1943.

Karolewksi, Chester. *Statement of Sergeant Chester Karolewski, A Company, 601st Tank Destroyer Battalion.* After Action Report. Dwight D. Eisenhower Presidential Library. Abilene, KS: Department of the Army, March 26, 1943.

Kaufman, Leslie. "Chester Hansen, a Rare Diarist of World War II, Dies at 95." *New York Times,* October 5, 2012, D8.

Kays, William M. *Letters from a Solder: A Memoir of World War II.* Wimke Press, 2010.

Kean, W. B. *General Orders 43, Section II, Awards of Silver Star, Box 18748.* General Orders. College Park, MD: Department of the Army, June 27, 1943.

Kelly, John C. *Combat 26 (-) Unit Report from: February 18, 1943 to February 24, 1943 (Part of Center for U.S. Army Military History Kasserine Pass Collection Volume I Part 1).* Unit Report. College Park, MD: Department of the Army, 1943.

Kennedy, Gary. "The United States Infantry Battalion, 1942 to mid 1943." 2000–2010. http://bayonetstrength.150m.com/UnitedStates/Infantry/united_states_infantry _battalion%201942%20to%20mid%201943.htm (accessed February 20, 2016).

Kesselring, Albert. *Final Commentaries on the Campaign in North Africa 1941–1943 MS # C-075, Volume 3.* Commentary. College Park, MD: Foreign Military Studies, December 1949.

———. *Kesselring's View of the African War, MS # T-3 P1 Part II.* After Action Report. College Park, MD: Foreign Military Studies, 1954.

King, Harrison. *Battalion Diary, 701st Tank Destroyer Battalion.* Battalion Diary. Dwight D. Eisenhower Presidential Library. Abilene, KS: Department of the Army, April 14, 1943.

King, Michael J. "Leavenworth Papers, No. 11. Rangers: Selected Combat Operations in World War II." June 1985. www.cgsc.edu/carl/download/csipubs/king.pdf (accessed June 14, 2016).

Koch, Oscar W. *G-2: Intelligence for Patton.* Atglen, PA: Schiffer Military History, 1999.

Kociuba, Raymond. "In Combat You Don't Know." In *Proud Americans: Men of the 32nd Field Artillery Battalion in Action, World War II, as Part of the 18th Regimental Combat Team*, 83. Malcolm Marshall, 1994.

Kuehn, Edward R. "Brief History of the 18th Infantry Regiment." 2016. 18infantry.org/ Brief_History_by_Edward.php (accessed February 20, 2016).

Kurowski, Franz. *Elite Panzer Strike Force: Germany's Panzer Lehr Division in World War II.* Mechanicsburg, PA: Stackpole Books, 2011.

Lair, Sandra. "Henry Dee Bowles." September 17, 2007. www.findagrave.com/cgi-bin/ fg.cgi?page=gr&GRid=21626770 (accessed August 23, 2016).

Lambert, Francis X. *Statement of First Lieutenant Francis X. Lambert, Company B, 601st Tank Destroyer Battalion.* After Action Report. Dwight D. Eisenhower Presidential Library. Abilene, KS: Department of the Army, March 1943.

Lambert, Kent C. *Field Order #3, Headquarters, II Corps, March 11.* Field Order. Wheaton, IL: Department of the Army, 1943.

———. *Outline Plan Operation "WOP" 9 March 1943, II Corps Order.* Warning Order. Wheaton, IL: Department of the Army, 1943.

Lang, Rudolf. *Battle of Kampfgruppe Lang in Tunisia (10th Panzer Division) December 1942 to 15 April 1943. MS# D173.* After Action Report. College Park, MD: Foreign Military Studies, June 8, 1947.

Lefévre, Eric. *Panzers in Normandy: Then and Now (Reprint).* London: After the Battle Magazine, 1999.

Lehman, Milton. "The History of One Day's Battle." *Stars and Stripes*, May 1, 1943, 8–9.

Lewin, Ronald. *Ultra Goes to War.* South Yorkshire: Pen & Sword, 2008.

Liebling, A. J. *Liebling World War II Writings: The Road Back to Paris, Mollie and Other War Pieces, Uncollected War Journalism, Normandy Revisited.* New York: Library of America, 2008.

———. "Profiles: Find'em, Fix'em, and Fight'em Part I." *New Yorker*, April 24, 1943, 22–26.

———. "Profiles: Find'em, Fix'em, and Fight'em Part II." *New Yorker*, May 1, 1943, 24–30.

Lindo, Richard. "Distinguished Service." In *Proud Americans: Men of the 32nd Field Artillery Battalion in Action, World War II, as Part of the 18th Regimental Combat Team*, by Malcolm Marshall, 69–70. Malcolm Marshall, 1994.

Luftwaffe. "L.DvT.2087 D-1/Wa Ju 87 D-1 Bedienungsvorschrift-Wa." January 1942. www.avialogs.com/index.php/en/aircraft/germany/junkers/ju87stuka/ldvt2087-d -1-wa-ju-87-d-1-bedienungsvorschrift-wa.html (accessed July 3, 2016).

Luthi, Robert A. *Statement from Robert A. Luthi, Company B, 601st Tank Destroyer Battalion.* After Action Report. Dwight D. Eisenhower Presidential Library. Abilene, KS: Department of the Army, March 22, 1943.

Manning, Henry G. *Statement of Sergeant Henry G. Manning, C Company, 601st Tank Destroyer Battalion.* After Action Report. Dwight D. Eisenhower Presidential Library. Abilene, KS: Department of the Army, March 27, 1943.

Marcus, Lawrence. Interview by Flight 33 Productions. *Interview with Lawrence Marcus, Battle 360,* July 1, 2008.

Marshall, George C. "3-026 Letter to Brigadier General Theodore Roosevelt, Jr." December 21, 1941. marshallfoundation.org/library/digital-archive/to -brigadier-general-theodore-roosevelt-jr (accessed March 24, 2016).

———. "3-213 Letter to Brigadier General Terry de la Mesa Allen." June 5, 1942. marshallfoundation.org/library/digital-archive/to-brigadier-general-terry-de -la-m-allen (accessed March 22, 2016).

———. "Letter to Frank R. McCoy." *Frank R. McCoy Papers.* Washington, DC: Library of Congress, September 25, 1940.

———. "Letter to Major General Andrew D. Bruce, #3-488." January 30, 1943. https:// www.google.com/url?sa=t&rct=j&q=&esrc=s&source=web&cd=3&ved=0ahUKE wiR6c2cwYrLAhVM5GMKHZeKD8IQFggpMAI&url=http%3A%2F%2Fmar shallfoundation.org%2Flibrary%2Fwp-content%2Fuploads%2Fsites%2F16%2F 2014%2F06%2F3-488.doc&usg=AFQjCNF0p7CD8CCTnQwod6aPbhl7r_GS (accessed February 21, 2016).

Martin, Ralph G. "The Halftrack Wolf-Packs." *Yank, The Army Weekly* 1, no. 45 (April 25, 1943).

Mason, Stanhope B. "Letter to Colonel Lloyd, concerning Robert York." *Robert Baumer Collection.* Birmingham, AL, n.d.

———. "Reminiscences and Anecdotes of World War II." Wheaton, IL, 1988.

Matter, Lester D., Jr. *Statement of First Lieutenant Lester D. Matter, Jr., C Company, 601st Tank Destroyer Battalion.* After Action Report. Dwight D. Eisenhower Presidential Library. Abilene, KS: Department of the Army, March 27, 1943.

McElroy, Robert C. *Statement of Sergeant Robert C. McElroy, C Company, 601st Tank Destroyer Battalion.* After Action Report. Dwight D. Eisenhower Presidential Library. Abilene, KS: Department of the Army, March 27, 1943.

Middleworth, Henry B. *Intelligence Annex to Field Order #14, Headquarters, 18th Infantry Regiment, March 13.* Intelligence Annex. Wheaton, IL: Department of the Army, 1943.

Migliaccio, Salvatore H. *Statement of Corporal Salvatore H. Migliaccio, C Company, 601st Tank Destroyer Battalion.* After Action Report. Dwight D. Eisenhower Presidential Library. Abilene, KS: Department of the Army, March 27, 1943.

Miller, Harley N. *Amendment to Report of Combat, This Headquarters (899th Tank Destroyer Battalion) for the Period of March 15 1943 to April 11 1943. Dated April 15, 1943. Box 18749.* Vehicle Status Report. College Park, MD: Department of the Army, August 10, 1945.

Miner, Frederick B. *Statement of First Lieutenant Frederick B. Miner, A Company, 601st Tank Destroyer Battalion.* After Action Report. Dwight D. Eisenhower Presidential Library. Abilene, KS: Department of the Army, March 26, 1943.

Mitchell, Henry E. *Battle Operation Report of Captain Henry E. Mitchell, Commanding Officer Company B.* After Action Report. Dwight D. Eisenhower Presidential Library. Abilene, KS: Department of the Army, March 27, 1943.

Moore, Anne Carroll. *The First: A Brief History of the 1st Infantry Division, World War II.* Wheaton, IL: Cantigny First Division Foundation, 1996.

Morrison, Joseph W. *Report of Combat, 899th Tank Destroyer Battalion, Period March 15, 1943 to April 11, 1943.* Operations Report. Dwight D. Eisenhower Presidential Library. Abilene, KS: Department of the Army, April 15, 1943.

Morrison, Thomas E. Interview by U.S. Army Military Institute. *Army Service Experience Questionnaire.* Carlisle Barracks, PA: Department of the Army, 1999.

————. "Letter about El Guettar." 1980s. tankdestroyer.net/images/stories/Article PDFs2/601st-Pers_Narr_T._Morr_El_Guettar_3.pdf (accessed July 11, 2016).

————. "The 601st Tank Destroyer Battalion at El Guettar 3-23-43." 1980s. tank destroyer.net/images/stories/ArticlePDFs2/601st-Pers_Narr_T._Morr_El_ Guettar.pdf (accessed July 11, 2016).

Morrison, Thomas E. Interview by Thomas Swope. Thomas E. Morrison Collection (AFC/2001/001/00869), Veterans History Project, American Folklife Center. Washington, DC: Library of Congress, July 29, 2001.

Munn, Charles M. *Statement of Second Lieutenant Charles M. Munn, C Company, 601st Tank Destroyer Battalion.* After Action Report. Dwight D. Eisenhower Presidential Library. Abilene, KS: Department of the Army, March 27, 1943.

Nafziger, G. F. "Organization of German 3rd, 33rd, 220th, and 580th Panzer (Motorized) Reconnaissance Battalions, North Africa, 29 September 1942." 1997. www .cgsc.edu/CARL/nafziger/942GIMC.pdf (accessed June 6, 2016).

National WW2 Museum. *By the Numbers: The US Military.* 2016. www.nationalww2 museum.org/learn/education/for-students/ww2-history/ww2-by-the-numbers/ us-military.html (accessed March 13, 2016).

News and Media. "Legendary Journalist Phil Ault '35 Remembered." July 31, 2001. www .depauw.edu/news-media/latest-news/details/11579 (accessed April 20, 2016).

Niehorster, Leo. "German Army: Tank Arrivals in North Africa 1941–1943." March 23, 2013. www.niehorster.org/011_germany/afv-strengths/North-Africa_arrivals.htm (accessed March 30, 2016).

————. "Panzer-Division (Afrika) 23 October 1942." October 23, 1942. niehorster.org/ 011_germany/42_organ/42-10-23/42_div_pz.html (accessed February 15, 2016).

Nowak, John. "Memoirs of John Nowak, 601st Tank Destroyer Battalion." Edited by Norma Nowak and Linda Nowak, August 1999.

Office of Air Force History. *Air Force Combat Units of World War II.* Edited by Maurer Maurer. Washington, DC: Department of the Air Force, 1983.

Operations, Fifth Panzer Army. *Conference on 19 February 1943—at 0945 Hours (Part of Center for U.S. Army Military History Kasserine Pass Collection Volume I Part 2).* Conference Notes. College Park, MD: Department of the Army, 1943.

Operations Section, 10th Panzer Division. *Mar 25; Situation Report from 10th Panzer Division for Mar 25; HW1/1520.* ULTRA Decrypt. Kew: National Archives, March 25, 1943.

———. *North Africa, 10th Panzer Division Strength and Forces Available Greatly Weakened by Allied Attacks with Superior Strength, March 24 HW1/1515.* ULTRA Decrypt. Kew: National Archives, March 24, 1943.

Our Battalion, 899th Tank Destroyer Battalion History. Munich: Knorr & Hirrh, 1945.

Patton, George S., Jr. "Patton's Diary." Washington, DC: Library of Congress, 1943.

———. *Report on Operation Conducted by II Corps, United States Army, Tunisia, 15 March–10 April 1943, Box 2606.* After Action Report. College Park, MD: Department of the Army, 1943.

———. *War as I Knew It.* Boston: Houghton Mifflin, 1995.

Patton, George S., and Terry de la Mesa Allen. *Commendation to the 1st Infantry Division, Headquarters II Corps, April 8.* Commendation, Wheaton, IL: Department of the Army, 1943.

Paulick, Michael. *Battle Operations Report, Reconnaissance Company, 601st Tank Destroyer Battalion.* After Action Report. Dwight D. Eisenhower Presidential Library. Abilene, KS: Department of the Army, March 1943.

Perry, John C. *Statement of First Lieutenant John C. Perry, C Company, 601st Tank Destroyer Battalion.* After Action Report. Dwight D. Eisenhower Presidential Library. Abilene, KS: Department of the Army, March 27, 1943.

Porter, Robert W. *G-2 Periodic Report, 0001A March 24 to 2400A March 24, Headquarters, 1st Infantry Division, Box 5222.* G-2 Periodic Report. College Park, MD: Department of the Army, 1943.

———. *German Order of Battle in Tunisia, Box 5103.* Order of Battle Report. College Park, MD: Department of the Army, March 10, 1943.

Rance, A. J. "Corps Artillery: How It Was Employed." *Field Artillery Journal*, December 1943, 886–88.

Raum, Andrea Hooe. "BG Francis Upton "Frank" Greer." May 10, 2009. www.findagrave.com/cgi-bin/fg.cgi?page=gr&GRid=36936820 (accessed August 17, 2016).

Raymond, Adolph I. *Statement of Sergeant Adolph I. Raymond, B Company, 601st Tank Destroyer Battalion.* After Action Report. Dwight D. Eisenhower Presidential Library. Abilene, KS: Department of the Army, March 1943.

Raymond, Edward A. "Slugging It Out." *Field Artillery Journal*, January 1944, 14–20.

Richardson, Samuel G. *Statement of Second Lieutenant Samuel G. Richardson, C Company, 601st Tank Destroyer Battalion.* After Action Report. Dwight D. Eisenhower Presidential Library. Abilene, KS: Department of the Army, March 27, 1943.

Ries, F. W. *Report on Operations, Headquarters II Corps, 2 May 1943 (Part of Center for U.S. Army Military History Kasserine Pass Collection Volume I Part 2).* After Action Report. College Park, MD: Department of the Army, 1943.

"Rifle Regiment 18." 2016. wwii-pows.mooseroots.com/d/f/Rifle/Regiment-0018 (accessed April 12, 2016).

Ritchie, Harry J. *Statement of Corporal Harry J. Ritchie, B Company, 601st Tank Destroyer Battalion.* After Action Report. Dwight D. Eisenhower Presidential Library. Abilene, KS: Department of the Army, March 1943.

Ritso, John C. *Statement of John C. Ritso, Company B, 601st Tank Destroyer Battalion.* After Action Report. Dwight D. Eisenhower Presidential Library. Abilene, KS: Department of the Army, March 1943.

Robinett, Paul M. *Operations Report, Bahiret Foussana Valley, 20 February 1943 to 25 February 1943 (Part of Center for U.S. Army Military History Kasserine Pass Collection Volume I Part 2).* Operations Report. College Park, MD: Department of the Army, March 1, 1943.

Robinson, L. G., Jr. *Report of Operations for Period 4 March 43 through 8 April 43, 5th Field Artillery Battalion.* Operations Report. Wheaton, IL: Department of the Army, 1943.

"Roland G. Inman—Prisoner of War Record." 2016. wwii-pows.mooseroots.com/l/49952/Roland-G-Inman (accessed April 12, 2016).

Rommel, Erwin. *Order for German Africa Corps, 19 February 1943 (Part of Center for U.S. Army Military History Kasserine Pass Collection Volume I Part 2).* Operations Order. College Park, MD: Department of the Army, 1943.

———. *Report to Commando Supremo (Part of Center for U.S. Army Military History Kasserine Pass Collection Volume I Part 2).* Request for Information. College Park, MD: Department of the Army, February 18, 1943.

Roncalio, Teno. "Letter to Herbert J. Lloyd concerning Robert H. York." *Robert Baumer Collection.* Cheyenne, WY, November 30, 1983.

Roosevelt, Theodore, Jr. "Letter to His Wife." *Theodore Roosevelt (1887–1944) Papers Box 9-10.* Washington, DC: Library of Congress, March 25, 1943.

Rowland, Henry C. *Report, after Action against Enemy as Required by AR 345-105. 1st Engineer Battalion, Box 5204.* After Action Report. College Park, MD: Department of the Army, April 20, 1943.

Sarantakes, Nicholas Evan. *Seven Stars: The Okinawa Battle Diaries of Simon Bolivar Buckner, Jr. and Joseph Stillwell.* College Station: Texas A&M University Press, 2004.

Sayen, John J., Jr. *U.S. Army Infantry Divisions, 1942–43.* Oxford: Osprey Publishing, 2006.

Schick, Albert. *Combat History of the 10. Panzer Division: 1939–1943.* Translated by Robert Edwards. Winnipeg: John Fedorowicz, 2013.

Shootout! The Big Red One. Directed by Douglas Cohen, performed by Henry Bowles, 2006.

Silva, Francis E. "'B' Battery Catches It." In *Proud Americans: Men of the 32nd Field Artillery Battalion in Action, World War II, as Part of the 18th Regimental Combat Team,* 71–72. Malcolm Marshall, 1994.

Silva, Francis E. "When Our Guns Get Overrun." In *Proud Americans: Men of the 32nd Field Artillery Battalion in Action, World War II, as Part of the 18th Regimental Combat Team,* 77–78. Malcolm Marshall, 1994.

Smith, Herbert A. "Operations of the 3rd Battalion, 18th Infantry (First Infantry Division) at El Guettar, 17–23 March 1943, (Tunisian Campaign), Personal Experience of Executive Officer, Heavy Weapons Company." 1948–1949. www.benning .army.mil/library/content/Virtual/Donovanpapers/wwii/STUP2/Smith,%20Her bert%20A%20Jr%20CPT.pdf (accessed February 14, 2016).

Smith, Walt. "The Ring of Steel." In *Proud Americans: Men of the 32nd Field Artillery Battalion in Action, World War II, as Part of the 18th Regimental Combat Team,* by Macolm Marshall, 78–79. Malcolm Marshall, 1994.

Social Security Death Index. "Frank W. Jakob." October 7, 2013. https://www.fold3 .com/page/15816929_frank_w jakob/stories (accessed May 2, 2016).

Stark, Kenneth B. *Statement of First Lieutenant Kenneth B. Stark, B Company, 601st Tank Destroyer Battalion.* After Action Report. Dwight D. Eisenhower Presidential Library. Abilene, KS: Department of the Army, March 1943.

Sternberg, Ben, and Jack M. Strauss. "Robert H. York." 1988. apps.westpointaog.org/ Memorials/Article/11323 (accessed August 17, 2016).

Stima, Michael W. *Statement on Battle of March 23, 1943, Company B, 601st Tank Destroyer Battalion.* After Action Report. Dwight D. Eisenhower Presidential Library. Abilene, KS: Department of the Army, March 1943.

Street, Jack B. *The Operations of the First Ranger Battalion, El Guettar, 21–26 March, 1943 (Tunisian Campaign) (Personal Experience of a Company Commander).* Advanced Infantry Officers Course Monograph. Fort Benning, GA: Academic Department, Infantry School, 1947–1948.

Sundstrom, Herbert E. *Statement of Captain Herbert E. Sundstrom, C Company, 601st Tank Destroyer Battalion.* After Action Report. Dwight D. Eisenhower Presidential Library. Abilene, KS: Department of the Army, March 27, 1943.

———. "Story of the 601st Tank Destroyer Battalion." 1980s. tankdestroyer.net/images/ stories/ArticlePDFs2/601st-Pers_Narr_H._E._Sundstrom-5_pg.pdf (accessed July 11, 2016).

———. "Use of Antitank Weapons and Individual Company Tactics." 1980s. tank destroyer.net/images/stories/ArticlePDFs2/601st-Pers_Narr_H._E._Sund strom.CO_C_C-3_pg.pdf (accessed July 11, 2016).

Temperino, Dario. *Reggimento Cavalleggeri Di Lodi (15) 1859–1995.* 2009.

Thompson, Percy W. *Battle of El Guettar Lessons Learned—Annex No. 2.* Lessons Learned. Wheaton, IL: Department of the Army, April 16, 1943.

Towne, Allen N. *Doctor Danger Forward: A World War II Memoir of a Combat Medical Aidman, First Infantry Division.* Jefferson, NC: McFarland, 2000.

U.S. Army Air Force. "Pilot's Flight Operating Instructions for Army Models P-39K-1 and P-39L-1 Airplanes T.O. No. 01-110FG-1." December 20, 1942. www.wwii aircraftperformance.org/P-39/P-39K-1_L1_Operating_Instructions.pdf (accessed March 5, 2016).

U.S. Army and Army Air Force Casualty List. "Wadislaw F. Wesgan." October 31, 2013. https://www.fold3.com/page/638668699_wadislaw_f%20wesgan/details (accessed July 3, 2016).

U.S. Army Center of Military History. "79th Infantry Division." December 1945. www .history.army.mil/documents/eto-ob/79id-eto.htm (accessed August 17, 2016).

U.S. Government Printing Office. *Combat Chronicles of U.S. Army Divisions in World War II.* October 1948. www.history.army.mil/html/forcestruc/cbtchron/cbtchron .html (accessed March 13, 2016).

Vaerst, Gustav von. *Operations of the Fifth Panzer Army in Tunisia MS # D-001.* After Action Report. College Park, MD: Foreign Military Studies, 1947.

Viney, Frank. "Under a Panzer Attack." In *Proud Americans: Men of the 32nd Field Artillery Battalion in Action, World War II, as Part of the 18th Regimental Combat Team,* 72–73. Malcolm Marshall, 1994.

Walker, Ian W. *Iron Hulls, Iron Hearts: Mussolini's Elite Armoured Divisions in North Africa.* Ramsbury: Crowood Press, 2012.

War Department. *Engineer Field Manual—Engineer Troops FM 5-5.* Washington, DC: War Department, October 11, 1943.

———. "Herschel D. Baker." 2016. http://valor.militarytimes.com/recipient.php?recipi entid=100024 (accessed August 23, 2016).

———. *Infantry Field Manual: Rifle Regiment FM 7-40 Change 1.* Washington, DC: War Department, July 11, 1942.

———. *Technical Manual 9-306, 75-MM Gun M1897A4 Mounted in Combat Vehicles.* Washington, DC: War Department, June 10, 1943.

———. "The Distinguished Service Cross Recipients World War II." 1943. www .homeofheroes.com/members/02_DSC/citatons/03_wwii-dsc/army_bj.html (accessed March 26, 2016).

———. "Theodore Roosevelt, Jr., General Orders No. 77." 2016. valor.militarytimes .com/recipient.php?recipientid=2922 (accessed March 24, 2016).

———. "Valor—First Infantry Division." *Infantry Journal,* June 1944, 42–44.

———. "Walter D. Ehlers, General Order 91." December 19, 1944. www.cmohs.org/ recipient-detail/2724/ehlers-walter-d.php (accessed August 20, 2016).

———. *War Department General Order No. 60, Company K, 18th Infantry, El Guettar, Tunisia, March 23, 1943.* General Order. Washington, DC: War Department, 1944.

Warner, Gary, Tom Berg, and Jebb Harris. "Walt Ehlers, World War II Medal of Honor Recipient, Dead at 92." *Orange County Register,* February 20, 2014.

Welply, Mir Bahmanyar, and Michael Welply. *Darby's Rangers 1942–45 (Warrior).* Oxford: Osprey Publishing, 2003.

West Point Association. "Frederick W. Gibb." September 6, 1968. apps.westpointaog .org/Memorials/Article/9852 (accessed June 5, 2016).

West Point Association of Graduates. "Ben Sternberg 1938." 2004. apps.westpointaog .org/Memorials/Article/11268 (accessed August 19, 2016).

Wheeler, James Scott. *The Big Red One: America's Legendary 1st Infantry Division from World War I to Desert Storm.* Lawrence: University Press of Kansas, 2007.

Williams, Paul L. *Report of Operations Conducted by XII Air Support Command, United States Army Air Force, Tunisia, 13 January 1943 to 9 April 1943, Box 2606.* Operations Report. College Park, MD: Department of Army, April 9, 1943.

Winters, Arthur L. Interview by Timothy Bowles. *Arthur L. Winters Talks about Dees,* May 8, 2007.

———. Interview by Timothy Bowles. *Reporter Interviews Arthur*, May 8, 2007.

Winters, Thomas Bowles, and Arthur Winters. Interview by Timothy Bowles. *Tom and Arthur Talk*, May 8, 2007.

World War II Army Enlistment Records. "James E. Markle." October 30, 2013. https://www.fold3.com/page/85488330_james_e%20markle/details (accessed July 10, 2016).

———. "Roland G Inman." 2016. www.fold3.com/page/83253728_roland_g inman/details (accessed April 12, 2016).

Wyatt, Ken. "Blinded Devens Hero Wins DSC for Tunisian Bravery." *Boston Traveller*, June 8, 1944.

Yeide, Harry. *The Tank Killers: A History of America's World War II Tank Destroyer Force.* Philadelphia: Casemate Publishers, 2007.

Yowell, John D. *Battle Operations of Lieutenant John D. Yowell, Platoon Commander, 1st Platoon, Company B, 601st Tank Destroyer Battalion, Battle of March 23, 1943.* After Action Report. Dwight D. Eisenhower Presidential Library. Abilene, KS: Department of the Army, March 27, 1943.

Zaloga, Steven J. *Kasserine Pass 1943 Rommel's Last Victory.* Oxford: Osprey Publishing, 2005.

———. *M3 Infantry Half-Track 1940–73.* Oxford: Osprey Publishing, 2002.

———. *M10 and M36 Tank Destroyers 1942–53.* Oxford: Osprey Publishing, 2002.

———. *US Anti-Tank Artillery 1941–45.* Oxford: Osprey Publishing, 2005.

———. *US Field Artillery of World War II.* Oxford: Osprey Publishing, 2007.

INDEX

Note: The day-to-day chronology for the El Guettar campaign (March 8 to April 7) is indexed under the "Battle of Guettar." Military units are indexed by nationality (British, German, Italian, U.S.) and are arranged by decreasing size from larger to smaller (Army, Corps, Division, Regiment, Battalion). Non-American individuals are identified by nationality (British, German, Italian). Abbreviation "TD" stands for Tank Destroyer.